The Legacy of the Crash

The Legacy of the Crash

How the Financial Crisis Changed America and Britain

Edited by
Terrence Casey

Associate Professor of Political Science and Head of Department,
Department of Humanities and Social Sciences, Rose-Hulman
Institute of Technology

First published 2011 by
PALGRAVE MACMILLAN

Palgrave Macmillan in the UK is an imprint of Macmillan Publishers Limited,
registered in England, company number 785998, of Houndmills, Basingstoke,
Hampshire RG21 6XS.

Palgrave Macmillan in the US is a division of St Martin's Press LLC,
175 Fifth Avenue, New York, NY 10010.

Palgrave Macmillan is the global academic imprint of the above companies
and has companies and representatives throughout the world.

Palgrave® and Macmillan® are registered trademarks in the United States,
the United Kingdom, Europe and other countries

ISBN-13:   978-0-230-30458-1   hardback
ISBN-13:   978-0-230-30459-8   paperback

This book is printed on paper suitable for recycling and made from fully
managed and sustained forest sources. Logging, pulping and manufacturing
processes are expected to conform to the environmental regulations of the
country of origin.

A catalogue record for this book is available from the British Library.

A catalog record for this book is available from the Library of Congress.

10 9 8 7 6 5 4 3 2 1
20 19 18 17 16 15 14 13 12 11

Printed and bound in Great Britain by
CPI Antony Rowe, Chippenham and Eastbourne

To my wife Allison and our greatest legacies – Maria, Jack, and Oliver

Contents

Part III: The Shifting Ground of Public Policy

List of Tables and Figures

Tables

Figures

Preface and Acknowledgments

This volume was born of a conference organized by the British Politics Group of the American Political Science Association in September 2010 entitled 'The UK and US in 2010: Transition and Transformation'. The worst financial crisis since the Great Depression slammed both the British and American economies full force in September 2008, obliterating the political and economic verities of the previous three decades. By 2010 the aftershocks still resonated. The moment was thus opportune for a collective assessment of how these events were transforming these polities – whether this represented a critical juncture in which political and economic relationships and institutions would be remade. That both states were then governed by relatively new administrations rendered these questions even more intriguing. The result was a lively one-day conference with 14 panels and over 90 participants. Given the size of the event it was not possible to include everyone in the volume that follows. Many a worthy paper had to be left by the wayside, hopefully to be picked up by other venues. My thanks go out to all who made it such a wonderful event.

No one can pull off something like this without the support and assistance of numerous colleagues. First and foremost I would like to thank Susan Sell of George Washington University. I pursued my graduate studies at GW and Susan was one of my professors and mentors. In her current role as Director of the Institute for Global and International Studies in the Elliott School of International Affairs, she offered to host the event. Without her willing support neither the conference nor this volume would have come to fruition. Special thanks also to her assistant, Mike Salamon, who saw to our every need leading up to and during the day of the event. Thanks also to the faculty in the GWU Department of Political Science, from which I earned my doctorate, and the Elliott School of International Affairs, for whom I worked as both a teaching assistant and visiting instructor. I want to extend my personal gratitude to Harvey Feigenbaum – who taught me how to be a great researcher – and Henry Nau – who taught me how to be a great teacher. To the extent that I do not live up to their standards, the fault is entirely my own.

This volume is not only a product of its contributors, but also of the larger British Politics Group. The BPG is full of many wonderful people who are also exceptional scholars, and my personal and professional life has been greatly enriched by being a member. I am particularly privileged that they have entrusted me with the role of Executive Director. Everyone in the BPG is thus deserving of thanks. I would like to single out Janet Laible, who served as the co-chair of the conference and beyond that has always been unselfish in giving her time to the group. Thanks are also warranted for Justin Fisher, our president at the time of the conference, who was not only a very able executive, but retains an uncanny ability to locate the best breakfast spot in any city on earth. Graham Wilson has proven a worthy successor, although he has yet to prove himself on the dining front. Thanks also go out to our APSA program chair, Florence Faucher-King; our newsletter editor, Tom Wolf; our webmaster (and emergency sommelier), Alistair Howard; and to all who serve or have served on the BPG executive

This is the second volume that I have edited for Palgrave Macmillan, an exceptionally supportive and professional organization. My special thanks to Amber Stone-Galilee, who marshaled the project from the conference through completion, and to Liz Blackmore for her tireless work in moving the book from manuscript through production – and especially for not giving me too much grief that my contributions were the last ones submitted!

A nod of appreciation also to my colleagues in the Department of Humanities and Social Science at the Rose-Hulman Institute of Technology. Teaching politics at a small engineering school in western Indiana where I am the sole political scientist was not perhaps my 'dream job' coming out of grad school. Yet I reside in a world of outstanding students and colleagues who are both incomparable teachers and first-rate scholars. I am lucky to be part of such a fine academic family. I am also doubly blessed at home. I could never have achieved as much as I have without the loving support of my wife Allison (who had the stamina and perseverance to get her nursing degree with three kids and a husband occupied by teaching and editing books) and our children Maria, Jack, and Oliver – excellent legacies indeed! Thanks for everything.

Terrence Casey
Terre Haute, Indiana, USA

Notes on Contributors

Edward Ashbee is an Associate Professor in the Department of Business and Politics, Copenhagen Business School (Denmark). His books include *The US Economy Today, The Bush Administration, Sex and the Moral Agenda* and *US Politics Today*, (Manchester University Press). He co-edited *The Politics, Economics, and Culture of Mexican-US Migration: Both Sides of the Border* (Palgrave Macmillan) and has had articles published in journals such as *Parliamentary Affairs*, *Politics*, the *Political Quarterly* and *Society*.

Tim Bale is a graduate of Cambridge, Northwestern and Sheffield Universities. He is now Professor of Politics at the University of Sussex. He is the author of *The Conservative Party from Thatcher to Cameron* (Polity, 2011) and *European Politics: A Comparative Introduction* (Palgrave Macmillan, 2008).

Michael J. Brogan is an Assistant Professor of Political Science at Rider University located in Lawrenceville, New Jersey. He has published articles in such journals as *Lex-Localis*, *Public Administration Quarterly*, and the *Journal of Psychoeducational Assessment*. He is currently working on a book project entitled *Precision Politics: Evaluating the Impact of Political Institutions, Elections, and Economic Conditions on State-Level Budget Forecasting Errors* (Lexington, 2013).

Terrence Casey is an Associate Professor of Political Science and Head of the Department of Humanities and Social Sciences at the Rose-Hulman Institute of Technology in Terre Haute, Indiana. He also serves as the Executive Director of the British Politics Group of the American Political Science Association. His previous books include *The Social Context of Economic Change in Britain* (Manchester University Press, 2002) and *The Blair Legacy* (Palgrave Macmillan, 2009).

David Coates holds the Worrell Chair in Anglo-American Studies at Wake Forest University. He has written extensively on US and UK political economy, labor movements and progressive politics. His recent writing on the financial crisis is in *Answering Back: Liberal Responses to Conservative Arguments* (Continuum, 2010) and *Making the Progressive Case* (Continuum, 2011).

Arthur I. Cyr is the Clausen Distinguished Professor and Director of the Clausen Center for World Business at Carthage College. He previously served as President of the Chicago World Trade Center and Vice President of the Chicago Council on Foreign Relations. His books include *Liberal Politics in Britain* (John Calder and Transaction Press, 1977, rev. edn 1988), *British Foreign Policy and the Atlantic Area: The Techniques of Accommodation* (Macmillan, 1979), and *After the Cold War: American Foreign Policy, Europe and Asia* (Macmillan, 1997, rev. edn 2000). His articles have appeared in numerous journals, including *Armed Forces and Society, Comparative Politics, International Affairs, Parliamentary Affairs, Policy Sciences, Political Science Quarterly, RUSI Journal,* and *Society.*

Kara Dickstein graduated summa cum laude from Wake Forest in May 2010 with a BA in economics. She headed the research team that helped produce David Coates' *Answering Back: Liberal Responses to Conservative Arguments* (Continuum, 2010). She is currently doing graduate work in International Political Economy at the London School of Economics.

Juan S. Gil is a graduate summa cum laude from Florida International University with a BA in philosophy and a BA in political science.

Wyn Grant is Professor of Politics at the University of Warwick and Vice-President of the International Political Science Association. He has written extensively on British politics, comparative public policy and research methods.

Robin Kolodny is Associate Professor of Political Science at Temple University, where she has taught since 1991. During Academic Year 2008–09, Kolodny was a Fulbright Distinguished Scholar to the United Kingdom, affiliated with the University of Sussex. She is the author of *Pursuing Majorities: Congressional Campaign Committees in American Politics* (University of Oklahoma Press, 1998) as well as numerous articles on political parties in Congress, in elections, and in comparative perspective. She is a member of the Academic Advisory Board of the Campaign Finance Institute in Washington, DC, and a Fellow at the Sussex European Institute (SEI) in the United Kingdom.

Richard J. Maiman is Professor of Political Science Emeritus at the University of Southern Maine. Since 2000 he has been a Visiting Fellow at the Human Rights Centre at the University of Essex. In 2011 he is a Fulbright Scholar at the Centre for Human Rights in the Faculty of Law at the University of Pretoria in the Republic of South Africa. His book, *Divorce Lawyers at Work: Varieties of Professionalism in Practice*, co-authored with Lynn Mather and Craig McEwen, won the APSA's C. Herman Pritchett Award for 'the best book on law and courts' in 2000.

John E. Owens is Professor of United States Government and Politics in the Centre for the Study of Democracy at the University of Westminster, Faculty Fellow in the Center for Congressional and Presidential Studies at the American University in Washington, DC, and Associate Fellow at the Institute for the Study of the Americas in the University of London's School of Advanced Study. He is the author of numerous articles in leading journals and book chapters on the US Congress, congressional-presidential relations, and comparative legislative politics. His most recent book coedited with Ricardo Pelizzo is *The 'War on Terror' and the Growth of Executive Power? A Comparative Perspective* (Routledge). Previous publications include *America's 'War on Terrorism': New Dimensions in United States Government and National Security* (with John W. Dumbrell), *Congress and the Presidency: Institutional Politics in a Separated System* (with Michael Foley), *Leadership in Context* (with Erwin C. Hargrove); and *The Republican Takeover of Congress* (with Dean McSweeney). He is a member of the editorial boards of the *Congress and the Presidency*, *Journal of Legislative Studies* and *Politics & Policy*.

Nicol C. Rae is Senior Associate Dean in the College of Arts and Sciences and Professor of Politics and International Relations at Florida International University. He is the author of *The Decline & Fall of the Liberal Republicans: From 1952 to the Present* (Oxford University Press, 1989), *Southern Democrats* (Oxford University Press, 1994), and *Conservative Reformers: The Republican Freshmen and the Lessons of the 104th Congress* (M.E. Sharpe, 1998), and co-author (with Colton C. Campbell) of *Impeaching Clinton: Partisan Strife on Capitol Hill* (University of Kansas Press, 2003).

Mark Shephard is Senior Lecturer at the University of Strathclyde. He is the author of numerous articles on different aspects of the British, Scottish, and European parliaments, as well as the US Congress. His work has appeared in leading journals, including *Political Studies*, the *Journal of Legislative Studies, British Journal of Politics and International Relations, British Politics, Public Administration*, and the *Journal of Elections, Public Opinion and Parties*. He is also a contributor to *Legislative Oversight and Budgeting: A World Perspective* (edited with Rick Stapenhurst, Riccardo

Pelizzo, David M. Olson and Lisa von Trapp, 2008). His current research interests include comparative youth parliaments, comparative committees, parliamentary questions and accountability, elite policy actions versus rhetoric, and social media discourse and its effects on attitudes towards constitutional issues.

Alex Waddan is a member of faculty at the University of Leicester in the UK. His publications include the books *The Politics of Social Welfare* (Edward Elgar, 1997), *Clinton's Legacy?* (Palgrave, 2002) and *The Politics of Social Policy* (forthcoming Georgetown University Press, co-authored with Professor Daniel Beland). He has also published various journal articles on US social policy, including pieces in *Political Science Quarterly*, *Political Studies* and the *Journal of Social Policy*.

Graham Wilson was born and educated in the United Kingdom and began his career teaching American politics at the University of Essex. He was a Professor of Political Science and Public Policy at the University of Wisconsin Madison from 1984 to 2007 where he taught and published in both the American and comparative politics fields. He moved to Boston University in 2007 and is currently the Chair of its Political Science Department. He contributed to and co-edited the *Oxford Handbook of Business and Government* which appeared in the spring of 2010 and has published on the British election of 2010.

1
Introduction: The Political Challenges of Hard Times

Terrence Casey

They called it the 'Great Moderation'. While this specifically referred to a trend of reduced macro-economic volatility among the major advanced economies since the late 1980s, it encapsulated a wider political and economic meaning. It marked the extended period of economic growth from the early 1990s into the 2000s, growth that was attributed to an encouraging combination of free market economic policies at home and globalization abroad. In this view, post-war economic history began with the 'Long Boom', 30 years of full employment and unparalleled economic growth. The period also coincided with the widespread adoption of Keynesian macro-economic policies, intended to smooth the business cycle, and the social welfare state, serving to protect vulnerable workers and allowing them to become stable mass consumers. Yet by the late 1960s the model was already showing its contradictions, particularly a 'spending ratchet' (Crouch, 2009). Keynes called for the state to spend when the economy was in recession, but democratically elected governments found it difficult to take away the goodies when the boom years returned, as Keynes also advised. This fed into rising spending and higher prices, hindering productivity and profitability. Add in the cost-push of oil prices and the result was the rampant inflation and stagnant growth ('stagflation') of the 1970s. Attempts to restore the balance through even more spending only fed the inflationary spiral. Keynesianism was tested and four ᴬ wanting, offering a political opening for leaders advocating a return to liberal economics; hence the label 'neoliberalism'.

Both Margaret Thatcher's Conservatives and Ronald Reagan's Republicans rejected the verities of the 'post-war consensus'. Rather than continuing state-centered economic governance, Reagan declared that

1

'government was the problem'. The solution was simple: get the state out of the way. Although varied in application across governments, the basic rationale was that by shifting resources out of the government's control – where political pressures led to economically inefficient decision-making – and into the private sector – where competition and market forces provided appropriate signals – these policies would remove the barriers to (private) investment, spur entrepreneurialism and innovation, and increase the trend growth rate of the economy. The initial shock therapy of extremely tight monetary policy and slashed budgets, intended to combat (as they saw it) the greater evil of inflation, produced sharp recessions in both economies. By the mid 1980s, however, prices were tamed and robust growth returned. Both leaders were rewarded for the economic turnaround with re-election, twice in Thatcher's case (Reagan, of course, being constitutionally limited to two terms). Boom turned to bust, however, as overheating markets required the reapplication of monetary brakes, producing another recession in the early 1990s. For critics of neoliberalism, this was evidence that the program was a failure, unable to deliver stable growth. Yet the critics were premature, for that very moment saw a confluence of positive trends: the end of the Cold War, which provided not only a fiscal 'peace dividend' but the opening up of vast new capitalist markets; the expansion of other major developing markets, especially China and India; the realization of full cost advantages of globalized production; and development of a new wave of information technology, both creating new markets (such as mobile phones) and greatly enhancing productivity in existing industries (such as retail). The result in the 1990s was a heady period of strong economic growth, improved fiscal balances, and relative international stability, for Britain and America at least. To be sure, there were economic crises during this period, most notably in East Asia in 1997 and Russia in 1998. Yet all were contained without major impacts on global growth. In the minds of policymakers these were thus isolated and manageable events in countries on the periphery of the global economy.[1] Problems hit home at the end of the decade when the overinflated expectations of new internet-based enterprises led to the 'dot com bust'. Yet rapid action by the Federal Reserve limited the damage to a relatively short recession. Even with 9/11 and the two wars that followed, both America and Britain continued with strong growth and low unemployment – economic records envied by many of their competitors – into the middle of the 2000s. The Anglophone economies had been buffeted by recession and war, but with flexible financial markets and adroit monetary authorities, the business cycle was tamed. The Great Moderation appeared to be here to stay.

It all came crashing down in 2008, punctuated by one dramatic weekend in mid-September. Economic conditions had started to slip by the end of 2007. The Fed had pursued an expansionary monetary policy for most of the decade which, along with other incentives, fed especially into a booming housing market in the United States. With credit flowing freely and inflationary pressures building up, the Fed began to raise rates. With that the housing bubble began to deflate. Those who had taken out minimum down payment mortgages with high variable interest rates (the so-called 'subprime mortgages') now found themselves with huge debt on declining value assets. The economic damage of this might have been contained in the most overheated regional American markets except that these mortgages had been bundled together, securitized, and sold off to other investors all over the world. A dramatic downturn in the US housing market would thus send seismic shocks throughout the global financial system. (The details are examined in Chapters 3 and 4.)

That major financial firms were in crisis was evident in late 2007. Northern Rock first sought emergency cash from the Bank of England in September 2007. Gordon Brown's government then spent the next four months seeking a private sector buyer for the bank until finally nationalizing Northern Rock in February 2008. In the same month the giant Swiss bank UBS announced $11.3 billion in losses for the fourth quarter, mainly from writing off US mortgages (James, 2009, p. 103). In March 2008 the Federal Reserve provided $29 billion in financing to allow JP Morgan to buy the struggling Bear Stearns, a deal quickly thrown together over a weekend of negotiations. The 'conservatorship' (effectively nationalization) of two major government-sponsored mortgage enterprises – Fannie Mae (short for the Federal National Mortgage Association) and Freddie Mac (Federal Home Loan Mortgage Corporation) followed in early September. Throughout the summer Lehman Brothers saw its profits and share value continue to slip. On 10 September they announced a $3.9 billion loss. By the evening of Friday 12 September Secretary of the Treasury Henry Paulson and Federal Reserve Bank of New York President Timothy Geithner called an emergency meeting of the leading financial figures on Wall Street to try and find a buyer for Lehman over that weekend, the same approach taken to deal with Bear Stearns. Both the Bank of America and Barclays emerged as potential buyers. Barclays took the lead, but British regulators raised objections and the British government was not willing to underwrite the sale unless matched by similar action from their US counterparts (James,

2009, p. 112). Whether by choice or by necessity – and this is still a point of controversy[2] – no US government money was forthcoming. Lehman Brothers filed for bankruptcy on 15 September 2008.

The news exploded on the markets on that Monday morning and investors, already skittish, went into full-fledged panic. The financial dominoes started to fall quickly. Bank of America bought Merrill Lynch that day. American International Group (AIG) received an $85 billion bailout the following day from the Treasury in exchange for a roughly 80 percent equity stake in the company. Uncertainty fed the contagion. The international financial system was flooded with derivatives and securities sold by these failing institutions, obscuring any estimate of their real value and vastly enhancing the risks of counterparty default. The logical response was to stop lending, producing a 'credit crunch' that would be devastating to the real economy if not resolved quickly. Bernanke and Paulson thus sought more comprehensive legal authority to bail out banks for fear that inaction would lead to complete financial collapse and economic depression. The result was a $700 billion proposal to Congress for a Troubled Asset Relief Program (TARP), albeit without any clear guidelines as to how the program would work,[3] submitted on 20 September. The government seemed to be flailing, throwing around hundreds of billions of dollars but offering no clear indication of who would or would not be protected (Taylor, 2009, p. 29). Members of Congress, mainly Republican members in the House of Representatives, balked, expressing concerns with the size of the program, the means of implementation, and fundamentally whether the government should be providing such a massive bailout of the banks, a point which rankled their free market principles and raised problems of moral hazard. Days of tense negotiations followed between Congressional leaders, the White House, and Treasury officials, descending to the tragic-comic incident of Secretary Paulson getting down on one knee and begging Speaker of the House Nancy Pelosi to keep her Democratic members in support of TARP. Faced with the legislation being blocked, President Bush is said to have declared in private, 'If money isn't loosened up, this sucker could go down' (*New York Times*, online edition, 26 September 2008). Despite the President's urging, TARP was initially defeated in the House 205–228, with 133 Republicans and 95 Democrats voting against it. The market response was forceful and negative, with the Dow Jones Industrial Average experiencing its largest single-day point drop ever. Fear of economic Armageddon focused Congress' attention. On 1 October the bill easily passed the Senate and was sent back to the House, where it passed on 3 October with a comfortable majority.[4] Armageddon may have been averted, but enormous damage was already done. The 'Great Moderation' had collapsed into the 'Great Recession'.

As would be expected, there has been plenty of finger-pointing in the aftermath of the disaster, and economic Cassandras such as Peter Schiff, Nassim Taleb, and Noriel Roubini now seeming amazingly prescient. Explanations for the crisis have largely broken down along ideological lines. On the one side are those who see this as a failure of markets or, more precisely, the decades of deregulation that allowed the financial system to develop unchecked and devolve into an inherently unstable sort of 'casino capitalism' (for example, see Cassidy, 2009; Posner, 2009; Stiglitz, 2010). Banks made increasingly risky bets on an asset bubble and governments stood by and let them do it. When it all went bust, taxpayers were left holding the bill – a system of privatized profits and socialized risk. In counterpoint are scholars who see the crisis manifesting from government policies and regulations that encouraged misguided economic decisions, such as excessively loose monetary policy encouraging subprime lending (see Taylor, 2009; Brooks, 2010; Wallison, 2009; Jablecki and Machaj, 2009; Freidman, 2009). Even the official report of US Financial Crisis Inquiry Commission was reduced to battling opinions from the Democratic and Republican appointed members (FCIC, 2011). Suffice it to say that those who want to boil the crisis down to either 'too little regulation' or 'too much government' will find the facts wanting. Or, more accurately, there is an element of truth in both arguments. It may provide moral or political comfort to identify a sole culprit, be it greedy bankers, economic theorists, short-sighted politicians, misguided regulators, or irresponsible homeowners. Reality though is closer to the plot of Agatha Christie's *Murder on the Orient Express*, where everyone was guilty.

The United States and Britain were the exemplars of the free market revolution that swept the globe at the end of the twenty-first century. The financial crisis was incubated within these economies before infecting global markets. The damage, moreover, was as bad (or worse) in the host economies than in many other states. *The Legacy of the Crash* explores how the financial crisis of 2008 changed the economics and politics of both the United States and Britain. First and foremost it is important to understand the causes and consequences of the economic crisis. Even to informed observers, the causes of the crash remain uncertain. How did this crisis happen? More precisely, how did a downturn in the US housing market mutate into a crisis that nearly brought down the global financial system? There is certainly no dearth of published narratives as to how this disaster befell us, although as indicated above there is very little consensus on the matter. This is hardly surprising; scholars still argue vehemently over the causes of the Great Depression after all. Terrence Casey (Chapter 3) and David Coates and Kara Dickstein (Chapter 4) offer explanations of the current crisis which, while overlapping in much of their analysis, place different emphases in terms of causation. For Coates and Dickstein, the crisis was more of a systemic problem of the Anglo-American economic model. The neoliberal era saw a marked decline in manufacturing and an increased reliance on financial services as a driver of growth. Yet that growth was founded on the accumulation of private debt, leaving the American and British economies dangerously exposed once the credit crunch hit. Casey's perspective is that the crisis stemmed from the interaction of economic policy, especially an expansionary monetary policy, and specific financial regulations, coupled with the incentives firms faced to create innovative and hence profitable investment opportunities in integrated and flexible financial markets. That is, a permissive policy and regulatory environment provided the economic space in which private actors then took excessive risks.

The contrast between these arguments highlights a fundamental question: did this crisis result from specific policy failures, or was this a systemic crisis of the neoliberal growth model? The issue is first taken up by Wyn Grant (Chapter 2), who explores the similarities and differences between the British and American political economies. For many scholars, particularly those writing in the 'varieties of capitalism' mode (Hall and Soskice, 2001), the US and UK were treated as undifferentiated archetypes of the Anglo-Saxon model. Grant makes clear that while there are many similarities between the two systems, there were always substantial differences, particularly in the prevalence of alternatives. International position, ideological predispositions, and the sclerotic nature of the US policy-making created a political barrier to the adoption of more interventionist economic policies. British policy-makers have long seen the more state-directed continental economies as alternatives to their market-oriented model, a position reinforced by their membership in the European Union. The potential to opt for industrial policies is what he dubs the 'dirigiste temptation'. Even if done grudgingly, choices made in the immediate aftermath of the crisis seemed to confirm that both Washington and London had given in to temptation. Banks were bailed out or nationalized, controlling stakes were purchased in automakers, and both governments passed substantial stimulus packages in an attempt to kick-start growth. Policies in the interim, however, suggest that this renewed burst of statism may be short-lived. Grant notes that the policies of the Cameron government represent a return to 'business as usual' and an implicit acceptance of the continued utility of neoliberal economic governance. That is hardly a surprise; that President Obama's approach is little different is rather unexpected. This is much by default as by design, as Casey observes in Chapter 3. A fully articulated alternative economic model that has the backing of electorally viable groups has yet to emerge in either country. Despite what for some was incontrovertible evidence that the neoliberal model was inherently flawed, it remains alive and well in both Britain and America.

Regardless of the causes, the depth of the crisis demanded a considerable response, reviewed in detail in Chapters 3–5. Following the triage of the bank bailouts, regulators in both the US and UK had to reconfigure the rules and regulations of the financial system to prevent a future crash. With no consensus on the causes of the crisis, the paths of regulatory reform were and are riddled with partisan barricades. Nevertheless, as epitomized by the Oscar award-winning documentary *Inside Job,* the image in the popular mind is of a finance industry dominated by greedy rogues who used the misguided analysis of free market academics to convince ideologically-blinded politicians in Washington, themselves backed Wall Street money, to cut the regulatory coils and let them run wild. In this atmosphere the major institutions took out enormous and increasingly risky bets that spectacularly went bust. Being 'too big to fail', however, the taxpayer was handed the bill. One would expect democratic politics to translate this perspective into serious financial market reforms. The details are discussed below, but given the intensity of the crisis, what is most surprising[5] is how modest those reforms have been. Both governments have implemented some limits on the type and scale of financial bets that firms can make, created more effective means to deal with troubled banks, and put in place systemic monitoring facilities. Yet financial institutions are even more concentrated than before the crash and the new regulations do not fundamentally prevent markets from developing new and risky financial instruments. The fact that Wall Street and the City of London offered only trifling resistance to these new regulations indicates their confidence that these rules will not hinder their profitability. Market trends seem to have proven them right so far; as Coates and Dickstein record, profitability has already returned to the banking sector as a whole.

The rest of the economy was another matter. Both governments sought to reinvigorate growth by implementing stimulus packages on a scale not seen since the 1970s. London and Washington took different approaches to fiscal stimulus, as Edward Ashbee explores in Chapter 5. The Obama administration passed a much larger package (as a percentage of gross domestic product, GDP) than that pushed by Brown in the UK. There was equally a difference in timing: the British stimulus was largely frontloaded to 2009, whereas the bulk of American spending would not kick in until 2010 or later. Fiscal policies have converged somewhat since then, with a budget-cutting Conservative-led Coalition government in the UK, and more fiscally conservative Republicans winning seats in the 2010 congressional elections. Nevertheless, Ashbee attributes the variations in fiscal response more to the institutional architecture of the two states rather than the ideological preferences of those in power. The more fluid and open nature of policy-making in the US allowed politically well-connected economic interests, particularly in high-tech sectors, to push for greater spending, a difficult strategy in the more cloistered world of Whitehall. The more important question is the impact of these policies. Debates continue to swirl among economists on this point.[6] Paul Krugman, for example, argues Obama has been too timid; the stimulus should be much greater and directed at public works projects. Others, especially Robert Barro question the evidence of the 'multiplier effect'[7] that underpins Krugman's support for Keynesian stimulus (Barro, 2009). Regardless of who has the better of the argument, the key political facts are that the recovery to date has been both modest and insecure while government balances have gone increasingly into the red. Whether or not fiscal policy is sufficient to the scale of the problem is now somewhat beside the point; the political winds are blowing in favor of fiscal retrenchment, not further stimulus. The great challenge for both economies through the rest of the decade is to master the delicate task of getting the books in order without squashing economic revival.[8]

Great challenges, of course, offer great opportunities. The crash followed decades of (in the view of many now discredited) neoliberal economic reforms championed forcefully by the parties of the right, Conservatives in Britain and Republicans in the US. Progressive leaders, having spent those decades railing against the dangers of unfettered capitalism and the retreat of the state, would be expected to be well placed to charge boldly into this political breech. To be sure, this prospect was going to be more difficult in the UK given that the Labour Party, the professed party of the left, had governed for ten years while embracing the market; they could hardly blame their problems on the Tories. The 2010 general election thus saw a strong swing to the Conservatives, albeit not quite enough to give them an outright majority. For a time, however, it looked as if the US was heading in more resolutely progressive direction as Barack Obama comfortably won election in the midst of the crisis. With increased Democratic majorities in Congress he was able to pass the stimulus package, health care reform, and financial market reforms. Yet public revulsion over the bank bailouts (even if initiated under George W. Bush) and the advancement of what was portrayed as 'socialized medicine' produced a backlash, manifest in the conservative Tea Party movement (see Chapter 8 by Arthur Cyr). The 'shellacking', as President Obama put it, of the Democrats in the midterm elections saw the ebb of the progressive tide. With unemployment stuck at 9 percent and an approval rating below 50 percent, the ability of Obama to reunite his electoral base from 2008 is hardly certain (although the dearth of competitive Republican challengers to date helps). In short, rather than an anti-capitalist sentiment sweeping away the political proponents of free markets, what we find instead in both the United States and Britain are volatile electorates who have been inclined toward candidates of the right as of late. Thus perhaps the most intriguing paradox of post-crash politics is why the left has done so poorly in an environment tailor-made for their message.

The answer to this puzzle is threefold, elaborated by Graham Wilson in Chapter 7. For one, rightly or wrongly, public opinion largely blames government and politicians rather than the executives of the financial industry for the catastrophe. More importantly, left-leaning governments are hindered by the constraints that markets place on political choice. Drawing on the analysis of Charles Lindbloom (1977), Wilson notes that the privileged position of finance in the US and UK forced political leaders to serve their needs. Barack Obama and Gordon Brown may have been loath to hand over enormous government checks to bankers who had proven themselves so irresponsible, but unless they were willing to see the collapse of the financial system, devastating ordinary citizens, they had no choice. To make matters worse, they then were blamed for the economic damaged caused by the bankers. Still, those center-left politicians were not just victims of circumstance in Wilson's view; they equally have been incapable of articulating an alternative vision. For Brown this would have required a reversal of both policy and rhetoric. The New Labour project was premised on increasing economic growth, especially by supporting the financial institutions of the City of London. Obama was better placed to aggressively pin the blame on financiers and their Republican protectors, but that would have gone against his ideal of being a 'post-partisan' president. The net result is that Labour and the Democrats offer little more than softer versions of the policies advocated by their opponents. Meanwhile progressive left organizations outside of the major political parties, particularly labor unions, have been relegated to rearguard actions to resist the austerity measures being imposed to deal with the fiscal calamity. Wilson speculates as to possible strategies for the revival of the left, but the path to electoral success remains unclear. In the rubble of the crash, the left continues to sift aimlessly, seemingly incapable of designing a substitute for the neoliberal edifice.

Politics being something of a zero-sum game, the downfall of the left has been a boon to the right. Since the crash the Conservatives are now in government, albeit in coalition with the Liberal Democrats, while the Republicans regained in the 2010 midterm elections many of seats they had lost in the *annus horribilus* of 2008. Tim Bale and Robin Kolodny chronicle these successes (Chapter 6) and the nature of the Conservative-Republican 'special relationship' going back to its zenith under Thatcher and Reagan. The comparable trajectories of the recent ascendance of the Tories and the Republicans are countered by some conspicuous ideological distinctions. David Cameron consciously and explicitly moved his party to the political center, with a strong emphasis on convincing voters that the National Health Service (NHS) was safe in Conservative hands. Republicans, conversely, found their voice in opposition to Obama's healthcare plan and rode the more extremist Tea Party movement to victory.[9] There has been something of a convergence since the 2010 elections as both parties have focused on the need for sharp reductions in spending to rebalance the books to address ballooning national debts. Conservatives and Republicans alike have staked a position that the voters, recognizing the urgency of the fiscal predicament, will reward them for being the ones willing to deliver needed frugality.[10] Whether voters will be so supportive when theoretical reductions turn into genuine cuts is another question.

Based on the evidence that Michael Brogan presents in Chapter 10 from the last elections the answer derives from the interaction of economic performance and voter partisanship. Voters were angry about the state of the economy and, excluding dedicated Labour or Democratic partisans, wanted to punish the incumbent parties. But the voting decision was a two-step process that Brogan labels 'aggrieved acquiescence'. Rejection of the incumbents for their economic management did not automatically translate into support for the Conservatives and Republicans. In line with this observation, Bale and Kolodny note that the crisis forced the Tories to shift their focus from 'sharing the proceeds of growth' to the need to cut the deficit, undercutting their image among the wider electorate as a safe alternative to Labour. This helps us to understand the inability of the Conservatives to win an outright majority in the House of Commons in 2010 – and may provide comfort to those supporting Obama's reelection in 2012. It equally highlights the challenge facing the Labour Party and

Republican nominees for the White House. Discontent may not be enough to win enough votes; an alternative strategy that appeals to the broad middle of voters is needed as well.

The 2010 British general election also produced the greatest surprise of post-crash politics: a Coalition government. It is the first since the Second World War and an ideologically 'unnatural' coalition of Conservatives and Liberal Democrats at that. As Arthur Cyr reviews in Chapter 8, for a brief moment during the campaign it looked as if the Lib Dems might fulfill the promise of their predecessor Social Democratic Party to 'break the mold of British politics' as their new and telegenic leader Nick Clegg scored a clear victory in the eyes of most pundits in the first pre-election premier debates, pushing up the party's poll numbers. The public love affair proved instead to be a brief flirtation, as their leaders' debate performance did not convert into extra votes for Lib Dem candidates. On election day they came up well short of their expectations, actually losing five of their previous 62 seats. With Cameron's Conservatives also falling short, Clegg was put in the position of kingmaker nonetheless. Despite the closer ideological affinity to Labour, Cyr contends the Lib Dems went into a coalition with the Tories because they were more likely to be able to deliver on their promises, including the potential to achieve the Liberal Democrat's Holy Grail: electoral reform. The coalition agreement included a promise to hold a referendum to replace the current first-past-the-post system for Westminster elections with an alternative vote system.[11] The Conservatives held to their promise, although in the end the measure was decisively rejected by over two-thirds of the voters in a referendum on 5 May 2011. Despite a good deal of acrimony between the coalition partners over the tenor of the Alternative Vote (AV) campaign, they seem to have weathered this rough patch and look capable of maintaining the political marriage as committed in the coalition agreement, through the end of this parliament in 2015.

On the American side, the economic crisis and the policy responses to it generated the Tea Party movement, their rise recounted by Cyr. A decentralized grassroots movement rather than a proper political party, the Tea Party is the latest incarnation of a longstanding strain of American populism going back to the Jacksonian era. The commonality of all American populist movements is the defense of 'the little guy' against the malignant influence of 'bigness', be they Big Government, Big Business, Big Oil, Big Banks, and so on. To the benefit of the Republican Party, Tea Partiers aimed their vitriol against 'Big Government' in the guise of the Obama administration rather than 'Big Business'. How much influence Tea Party activists will have on the 2012 Republican primaries remains to be seen, but as Cyr notes the historical tendency is for the ideas and interests of third parties to be enveloped into the platforms of the two major parties. This is at one with the broader tendencies identified by Nicol Rae and Juan Gil (Chapter 9) for US political parties to become more ideological and polarized over the last 50 years. For much of the post-war period scholars of American politics looked with envy to the more centralized, mass party British system, lamenting the disorganized, decentralized, state-dominated American parties. By Rae and Gil's appraisal social forces have pushed American parties into something of a de facto convergence on this model, as heightened social cleavages and party polarization serve to mimic the function if not the form of mass parties. At the same time Britain retains the mass party structure while both the Conservative and Labour parties have seen a sharp decline in membership as socio-economic class has receded as a defining political cleavage. This element of convergence aside, the UK system has also seen the rise of regional parties and, especially with the inclusion of the Liberal Democrats in government, the emergence of a meaningful multiparty system.

Beyond political trends, public policy issues loom large. Integral to the debates over fiscal retrenchment is the issue of health care, examined by Alex Wadden in Chapter 11. With rising costs and an aging population, health care is set to gobble up an increasing portion of government resources in both countries. Upon assuming office, President Obama aimed to succeed where Bill Clinton had failed: in passing a comprehensive health care reform. The debate over what would become the Affordable Care Act (ACA – derided as 'Obamacare' by its detractors) dominated the first 18 months of the current administration. The plan sought to both bring millions of uninsured Americans into coverage and reduce the overall costs of health care by 'bending the cost curve'. Its net impact remains to be seen, but as Wadden notes, the prospects look better for expanding coverage than containing costs. Either way, the program has not increased in popularity since its passage as Democratic supporters had hope. A Gallup poll taken in early 2011 showed that 46 percent of Americans favored its repeal. On the British side socialized medicine in the form of the NHS has such deep-seated and widespread support that the Conservatives specifically promised to protect it from spending cuts in their 2010 manifesto. Once in office, however, Secretary of State Andrew Lansley produced a White Paper calling for relatively radical reforms, pushing more spending decisions down to the General Practitioner (GP) level. At the time of this writing (summer 2011) the government is backtracking on many of these reforms and their exact plans for the NHS remain uncertain. Regardless, Wadden reminds us that, given its overall cost and the fact that it touches on basic societal values, health care will remain an intense political issue for years to come.

The primary focus of this volume is domestic rather than foreign policy, yet the financial crisis hit at a time of war, with both Britain and America engaged in battle in Iraq and Afghanistan. Chapters 12 and 13 explore how the executives in both states have managed this challenge, with emphasis on their relations with other institutions. George W. Bush and Tony Blair were, in different ways and at different times, accused of erroneously abusing executive power to prosecute these wars and the larger 'war on terror'. John Owen and Mark Shephard examine the extent to which this concentration of executive power and discretion has been continued or checked by the new administrations in power. Owens and Shephard found that while the Obama administration and Cameron government may have adopted a softer tone, the accretion of executive power in relation to the war on terror continued unabated, even increasing in some areas. The fear of terrorism remains high and both the White House and Downing Street are committed to taking decisive action to combat it when appropriate, a point illustrated by Obama's ordering of the mission to kill Osama bin Laden. Neither President Obama nor Prime Minister Cameron have shown any intention of ceding authorities already accrued by their predecessors.

Congress and Parliament may remain relatively supine in the face of their respective executives' claim to prosecute the war on terror without limits. In contrast Richard Maiman sketches how both nation's judiciaries have been increasingly assertive in challenging executive authority. Structurally the two judicial systems are quite different. The independent US Supreme Court has an established record of ruling on the constitutionality of the actions of the other branches of government. Historically the Appellate Committee of the House of Lords, otherwise known as the 'Law Lords', has not played this role in the British system. The transformation of the Law Lords into a separate Supreme Court has coincided with an increase in the prominence of judicial voices in debates regarding the proper limits to executive power. This increased sense of empowerment may not have quite transformed the British Supreme Court into the co-equal players that are their American counterparts. Both judiciaries nevertheless share a determination to erect legal limitations to claims of unfettered authority in regards to combatting terrorism – hardly surprising in the US, but highlighting the continued advance of a 'rights revolution' in the UK.

In the concluding chapter, Terrence Casey attempts to provide some coherence to the broader social, economic, and political trends evident in this 'age of austerity'. A rising material standard of living, to include home ownership, has long been central to the ideal of the 'American Dream' as well as Britain's identity as a 'property owning democracy'. The gnawing fear is that this most recent crisis was not just a cyclical downturn that can be countered by appropriate policies, but indicative of structural flaws in the basic operation of the economy. The rivers of debt, both public and private, still coursing through our economic system mean that we will have to grapple with constrained choices, at least for the foreseeable future. But what of the longer-term? Are we facing a future of diminished expectations? If we are drifting into stagnation, how might this affect our respective societies? How will this affect the life prospects of those growing up in such an environment? Such concerns can be assuaged, of course, by a return to strong growth. Can the growth model upon which both America and Britain have relied for the last three decades, guided by a free market ideology and heavily invested in the financial sector, again deliver the desired prosperity, and stability? If a new economic model is needed, what might it be? And what are the political implications of these economic trends? To date the traditional nostrums of neither the left nor the right have resonated strongly with American or British electorates, both of which remain deeply apprehensive toward the future. The major economic crises of the last 100 years – the Great Depression and the 'stagflation' of the 1970s – proved to be political watersheds, ushering in new eras. In this crisis, transformative political movements have so far been noteworthy for their absence. How will this current crisis alter the disposition of ideological and political forces? Are we on the cusp of another new political era, or will we see a return to the status quo ante? What will the politics of this age of austerity look like?

Speculating on the future trajectory of current trends is something of a fool's errand, to be sure. (Or, given the subject matter, it might be better to use the boilerplate of financial product advertising: 'past performance is not an indication of future results'.) The crisis that swept through global financial markets in the fall of 2008 has undoubtedly had social, political, and economic affects that are both profound and long-lasting. Some of these are identifiable in the three years that has elapsed since the crash. Others remain obscured by our own proximity to events and will only be revealed with the passage of time. As such it is still too early for a volume like this to provide a truly comprehensive appraisal of the legacy of this crisis. At the same time, enough time has elapsed and enough dust has settled, as it were, to begin to start making an assessment of the aftermath, determining which elements of our political and economic systems remain stable, which have been changed indelibly, and which perhaps teeter on the brink of some still unforeseen transformation. *The Legacy of the Crash* is our attempt, through our individual and collective efforts, to provide a foundation for understanding these events as they continue to unfold in the years to come, with the hope that others may be guided as to how to best respond to these challenges. Without doubt, our two great nations have been tested much more severely in the past, but these are still great burdens. Let us hope that we may soon, to borrow Winston Churchill's inspirational words, find a way to again move our societies into the 'broad, sunlit uplands' of prosperity and stability.

Notes

1. The collapse of the Russian ruble undermined Long Term Capital Management (LTCM), the financial firm headed by Nobel Prize-winning economists Myron Scholes and Robert C. Merton. Overleveraged and unable to meet margin calls, LTCM was eventually bailed out by a consortium of other financial firms under the guidance (but without direct financial involvement) of the Federal Reserve. This served to reinforce the idea that markets could correct themselves.
2. Whether federal officials could have or should have bailed out Lehman Brothers remains a point of great controversy. In the immediate aftermath of their collapse, Paulson implied that it was a conscious choice to uphold market principles. Not so long after that, Ben Bernanke claimed that the Federal Reserve simply did not have legal authority to loan money to Lehman given their limited collateral. (The $85 billion bailout of AIG two days later was backed by its assets.) It should be noted that the thrust of informed opinion both in Washington and on Wall Street in the weeks leading up to Lehman's bankruptcy leaned against yet another bailout.
3. Written in haste, the original bill is only around 850 words long.
4. Even at this point, 108 Republicans and 63 Democrats voted against the bill.
5. Perhaps not so surprising if one assumes that Congress is effectively 'in Wall Street's pocket'. In a less conspiratorial vein, the uncertainty of the causes of the crash and the much more certain effects of heavy handed regulation may have blunted the drive for greater market controls.
6. A 2010 Congressional Budget Office study suggested that unemployment was lowered from 0.7 percent to 1.8 percent as a result of Obama's stimulus package (CBO, 2010, p. 2). Even so, whether this was sufficient return on investment is debatable.
7. The concept implies that every dollar of government spending will increase economic output by some increment greater than one.
8. There has also been aggressive and ongoing monetary stimulus from both the Bank of England and the Federal Reserve. See Chapter 3.
9. While beneficial overall, the nomination of Tea Party-backed candidates hurt the Republicans in some significant Senate races, most notably in Alaska, Delaware, and Nevada. See Chapter 6.

10. Even while converging on goals, differences remain on the means. The Conservatives have boosted taxes, notably value added tax (VAT), to try to move the budget into the black. Republicans so far (June 2011) refuse to countenance any tax hikes.
11. The alternative vote system involves the ranking of candidates. The candidates receiving the lowest number of votes are eliminated and their second choice votes distributed to the other contenders. This process continues until someone has received 50 percent or more of the vote.

References

Barro, Robert J. (2009) 'Demand Side Voodoo Economics', *The Economists' Voice*, 6(2), Article 5.

Brooks, Arthur (2010) *The Battle: How the Fight between Free Enterprise and Big Government will Shape America's Future* (New York: Basic Books).

Cassidy, John (2009) *How Markets Fail: The Logic of Economic Calamities* (New York: Farrar, Straus and Giroux).

Coates, David (2010) 'Separating Sense from Nonsense in the US Debate on the Financial Meltdown', *Political Studies Review*, 8(1), 15–26.

Congressional Budget Office (2010) *Estimated Impact of the American Recovery and Reinvestment Act on Employment and Economic Output from April 2010 through June 2010*, August (Washington, DC: CBO).

Crouch, Colin (2009) 'Privatized Keynesianism: An Unacknowledged Policy Regime', *British Journal of Politics and International Relations* 11(3), 382–99.

Friedman, Jeffrey (2009) 'A Crisis of Politics, not Economics: Complexity, Ignorance, and Policy Failure', *Critical Review*, 21(2–3), 127–83.

Gallup (2011) 'In U.S., 46% Favor, 40% Oppose Repealing Healthcare Law', 7 January, www.gallup.com.

Hall, Peter A., and David Soskice (eds) (2001) *Varieties of Capitalism: The Institutional Foundations of Comparative Advantage* (New York: Oxford University Press).

Jablecki, Juliusz and Mateusz Machaj (2009) 'The Regulated Meltdown of 2008,' *Critical Review*, 21(2–3), 301–28.

James, Harold (2009) *The Creation and Destruction of Value: The Globalization Cycle* (Cambridge, MA: Harvard University Press).

Lindblom Charles E. (1977) *Politics and Markets: The World's Political and Economic Systems* (New York: Basic).

Posner, Richard (2009) *A Failure of Capitalism: The Crisis of '08 and the Descent into Depression* (Cambridge, MA: Harvard University Press).

Stiglitz, Joseph (2010) *Freefall: America, Free Markets, and the Sinking of the World Economy* (New York: W.W. Norton).

Taylor, John B. (2009) *Getting Off Track: How Government Actions and Interventions Caused, Prolonged, and Worsened the Financial Crisis* (Stanford, CA: Hoover Institution Press).

Wallison, Peter J. (2009) 'Cause and Effect: Government Policies and the Financial Crisis', *Critical Review*, 21(2–3), 365–76.

Part I

The Causes and Consequences of the Crash

2

Was there Ever an Anglo-American Model of Capitalism?

Wyn Grant

When the Obama administration and Cameron government took office, their principal challenge was dealing with the aftermath of the global financial crisis (GFC). They had to deal with a range of potentially contradictory objectives. An overriding priority was to prevent a 'second wave' of the GFC which could fatally damage already weakened institutions and the whole model of Anglo-American capitalism. Quite what this model was and how it influenced decision-making after the crisis is a central theme of this chapter.

Beyond the task of seeking to prevent a renewed crisis in the financial system, which required effective coordination between countries through arrangements such as G20, the two governments had more immediate domestic tasks to tackle. Both countries had substantial budget deficits, but taking drastic action to eliminate the structural budget deficit, largely through public expenditure cuts and the initiation of a new age of austerity, was a more central concern for the Cameron government. Because of the continuing status of the dollar as an international reserve currency, American governments can print money to help fund their deficit. This, of course, can have an inflationary effect elsewhere in the world, which is exactly the complaint of China against the United States.

Both countries faced the dilemma of how to grow out of the recession induced by the global financial crisis. The Cameron government was criticized by the retiring head of the Confederation of British Industry (CBI), Sir Richard Lambert, for not having a coherent growth strategy to match its deficit reduction strategy. The last quarter of 2010 saw a 0.5 percent fall in gross domestic product (GDP) in the UK, although this was largely the result of exceptional winter weather. The Obama administration had been more willing to commit large sums of public money to prop up American companies in danger of failing, particularly in the motor industry. However, unemployment in the US remained at a stubbornly high level, even higher than in the UK. By the beginning of 2011, there were signs of returning consumer confidence in the US, but it remained very fragile in the UK, not least because of falls in real wages and a fear of unemployment.

The UK also faced persistently high levels of inflation, well in excess of the Bank of England target. In part this was a consequence of the depreciation of sterling after the GFC, which did help to boost exports, but it also reflected rising world commodity prices, notably of cotton, food and oil. However, there were also domestic factors at work. It was possible that the output gap was less than had been estimated, meaning that there was less spare capacity to take up as the economy recovered. The effectiveness of the Bank of England's Monetary Policy Committee (MPC) was called into question. The Bank had been pumping money into the economy through quantitative easing and was fearful of increasing interest rates and choking off any recovery, but it faced increasing pressure to take action to bring inflation under control. There was a concern that if consumer expectations of higher inflation became entrenched, this would feed through to wage settlements, triggering spiraling inflation. Of course, such inflation would have the by-product of reducing the debt burden.

Both countries therefore faced a series of difficult short-run challenges, although given the election timetable, the Obama administration had a more pressing electoral imperative to restore the economy. The Cameron government took the view that pain inflicted in the first two years of its period in office would be offset by the benefits of a recovering economy later. However, in the medium term, the Cameron government faced a likely increase in the 'misery index', the sum of the rate of inflation and the rate of unemployment. In the US there were prospects that the misery index would ease. Short-term pressures aside, both governments operated in economies that were characterized as 'Anglo-American'. In what ways did this model constrain and shape their objectives and policies?

The Anglo-American model

Any Anglo-American model of capitalism is a construction of reality undertaken for a variety of purposes. As Andrew Gamble (2003, p. 87) reminds us, it 'is a political space, an "imagined community"'. Opponents of what they see as an Anglo-Saxon model of capitalism may exaggerate its coherence in order to construct an account of what it is they are opposed to. The model of capitalism is nested in a wider set of relationships and narratives: 'It is a military alliance, a model of capitalism, a form of government, a global ideology and a popular culture' (ibid., p. 86). One form of discourse in particular has been associated with this model: 'Globalization from its inception has been predominantly an Anglo-American discourse and an Anglo-American project' (ibid., p. 104). One immediate reaction to the GFC was that it heralded the end of globalization, but despite a short-run fall in levels of world trade, the paradigm displayed considerable resilience.

The essential features of the model include a primacy of the market over the state with the state performing a largely enabling role: 'removing the barriers to free market exchange and sustaining the institutions which could define and defend individual property rights'. This role in turn gives rise to the salient characteristics of the model: 'in particular its voluntarism and short-termism, as well as the liberal character of its welfare system and corporate governance, and the relative importance of its financial institutions, particularly its stock markets' (ibid., p. 105).

In any model such as that provided in the 'varieties of capitalism' literature a basic methodological criterion is that the within-category variation should be exceeded by the between-category variation. In Terrence Casey's attempt to construct a comparative capitalism index, 'the usual liberal suspects' including Britain and the United States 'hover in the lower left' (Casey, 2009, p. 269). However, 'These figures show a greater variation among Anglo-Saxon economies than their European counterparts' (ibid., p. 270).

One escape route is to portray the UK as a hybrid model so that 'in much of the literature concerning international economic positioning the United Kingdom is still treated as an entity balanced somewhere between America and Europe, reflecting both political orientations but also a still recognisably European welfare system' (Coffey and Thornley, 2009, p. 2). In the interests of parsimony, this chapter does not consider the welfare system: its focus is on the economy. In a broad strategic sense, 'the purpose of the special relationship was to allow Britain to act as a broker between the United States and Europe' (Gamble, 2009, p. 98). A hybrid political economy could, however, be seen as a sign of weakness rather than strength (Gamble, 2010a) in so far as it tries to bring together incompatible principles.

One response to the question what variety of capitalism is British capitalism is to state that 'the most reasonable short answer would have to be that it is a very complex one' (Coffey and Thornley, 2009, pp. 152–3). This may be a correct assessment, but it is an inherently unsatisfactory one. Societies and economies are complex and are possibly becoming more so, but it is the task of social scientists to try and order that complexity so that we can better understand it. Such understandings will be contested and rightly so. However, we need to stand back from that complexity to see if there are patterns that we discern that can enable us to provide some coherent account of the processes at work.

To be fair to Coffey and Thornley, following work by David Coates they argue that 'the United Kingdom has managed to sit somewhere between America and Europe, while scoring poorly on both comparisons. The British variety of capitalism may therefore be a complex one, but it is not impressive' (ibid., p. 153). Perhaps so, but some of the European examples are not particularly impressive in terms of rates of growth or levels of unemployment.

The broad argument presented here is that the UK does conform to a liberal model of capitalism, not least in terms of the centrality and mode of organization of the financial services sector, but that the terrain in Britain is more contested than in the US. This is for two main reasons. First, when the British model is under pressure, as in the GFC, there is an alternative model that can be resorted to in a way that is not possible in the United States, or at least has not been possible since the days of the New Deal. This is what might be termed 'the dirigiste temptation'. The reference to dirigisme is deliberate because it is France that is often turned to for an alternative model in such circumstances.

Second, Britain is a member of the European Union (EU). Gamble (2003, p. 230) is unambiguous in seeing this as the direction of travel: 'The most promising future governing strategy for Labour would be to embrace Europe both as a model for capitalism and for welfare and democracy.' The Coalition government has placed an emphasis on a different route to either Atlanticism or one Europe, seeing emerging countries such as India with their growing middle class as an outlet for British exports and diplomatic and political assets have been deployed in that direction.

One has to be careful about what means by Europe (or America for that matter). As subtle a writer as Gamble recognizes (ibid., p. 220) that 'Europe and America are not monolithic, but highly complex and differentiated political spaces. There is not one Europe or one America but several, and the differences between liberal and conservative America, or between social democratic and conservative Europe are wide.' The EU operates the highly interventionist and protectionist Common Agricultural Policy, and espouses 'European champions', but it also has a state aids policy which has been used to curb interventionist excesses during the global financial crisis.

The United States is, of course, a federal state and this has permitted individual states at various times to take their own initiatives to attract foreign investment, to improve training or to promote employment, although depleted state coffers have made this more difficult in the recent past. The UK has devolved administrations and the Scottish government in particular is enlarging the political space in which it can operate and is more prone to interventionist responses. It has created agencies to stimulate innovation in the Scottish economy such as Scottish Enterprise, Scottish Development International, and the Scottish Investment Bank. The latter body has, however, been slow to start work, its budget is £150 million and it has reportedly been engaged in turf wars with Scottish Enterprise. Over time this Scottish political space is likely to become more significant, particularly if significant fiscal powers are devolved, but the analysis here focuses on the UK as a whole. That requires an historical analysis of how understandings of the government-business relationship in Britain have developed over time.

The dirigiste temptation

The First World War and its aftermath

Before the First World War what was perceived as an increasing challenge to Britain's economic hegemony drew a protectionist response. (Williams, 1896). The First World War brought a number of businessmen into government and thus gave the political class a new dimension through the formation of a network of 'industrial politicians' who had experience of both business and government. At the end of the war, the 'productioneers' movement, associated with such figures as Dudley Docker, the founder of the Federation of British Industries, and Christopher Addison, the Minister for Reconstruction, sought to take British economic policy down a new path, aimed at creating a high-wage, high-output economy with a measure of government intervention and an emphasis on co-operation between employers and labor (Davenport-Hines, 1984).

The First World War shook up traditional approaches to economic management but 'despite the advances in industrial techniques achieved in consequence of state intervention, and a full appreciation of the competitive power of German and American enterprise, state-sponsored modernization was stillborn'. In explaining the failure of industrial reconstruction, 'historians have traditionally cited the post-war resurgence of political and economic orthodoxy as evidence of an unshaken faith in the pre-1914 liberal order' (Kirby and Rose, 1991, p. 21). The explanation is more complex than the resurgence of a formerly dominant discourse. Once Germany had been defeated, reconstruction as a discourse which found institutional expression in the Ministry of Reconstruction was displaced, particularly if it could be presented as an advocacy of adopting the methods of the defeated foe. Macmillan (1933) later tried to revive the discourse of reconstruction, but with no perceptible effect on the debate at the time.

Nevertheless, the relationship between government and industry had been changed and this had a number of important consequences. The failings of the British chemical industry had been evident during the war and this led to the formation of ICI (Imperial Chemical Industries) as a 'chosen instrument' of government which received favored treatment. Britain's lagging position in electricity generation for industry was tackled by the formation of the Central Electricity Board. Civil aviation was promoted, the processing of agricultural products was tackled through the formation of the milk marketing boards and the British Sugar Corporation, and the London Passenger Transport Board was established.

Insofar as there was a unifying discourse in that period it was 'rationalization' exemplified by the Securities Management Trust set up by the Bank of England in 1928 followed by the Bankers' Industrial Trust. In practice, little rationalization was actually achieved and there was a tolerance for even state sponsorship of cartels. Policy took a protectionist turn so that British industries no longer faced the challenge of an open economy. The general protective tariff was supplemented by quantitative restrictions on imports.

Britain's traditional industries, not least the textile industry, were enabled to continue with outmoded structures and working practices. In practice, the government 'helped to reinforce old structures with a new layer of powerful institutions that embodied existing structural problems rather than counteracting them' (Tolliday, 1987, p. 336). This was exemplified by the iron and steel industry which was able to shelter behind a tariff wall and function within a state-sponsored cartel through the Iron and Steel Federation over which government had little control. There was little or no institutional innovation in terms of intermediation between government and industry, although the public corporation served as a model for post-war nationalization.

Divergences between the US and the UK

In the period after 1945, there were significant divergences in the management of the economy in the UK and US. The adoption of a commitment to full employment in 1944 by the UK government transformed both the goals and the mechanisms of economic policy. Keynesian demand management was seen as required to deliver full employment, although in practice the long post-war boom ensured that there was no major unemployment problem and the economy simply had to be fine-tuned to deal with successive balance of payments crises which put pressure on sterling. However, the more active involvement of government in the management of the economy led to a much closer working relationship with the trade unions and employers than had prevailed in the inter-war period. This particularly became the case as governments increasingly resorted to prices and incomes policies to cope with the inflation problem in a full employment economy. The deployment of this policy instrument was a dominant feature of the policies of both Conservative and Labour governments between 1960 and 1979.

In the US the Employment Act of 1946 established government responsibility for ensuring maximum levels of employment and set up the President's Council of Economic Advisers to advise on how this might be done. However, it should be noted that the word 'full' which was present in an earlier version of the bill was subsequently removed. Keynesian ideas never established the same ascendancy that they did in the UK, with some business interests seeing them as excessively interventionist. Moreover, the same government machinery did not exist to put policies into practice. There was a contrast between the way in which 'British economic policy was administered by a closed and hierarchical civil service, dominated by a powerful Treasury while US policy has always been made by a fragmented bureaucracy in conjunction with outside experts and the Congress' (Hall, 1989, p. 16). While President Nixon was able to proclaim in 1971 that 'I am now a Keynesian in economics' and the US did make some hesitant experiments with prices and incomes policy, the permeation of Keynesian ideas as a basis for economic policy was less complete than in Britain.

The contrast between a more regulatory approach in the US and a more interventionist approach in the UK is also shown by another divergence, that over nationalization. The network part of a utility is generally a natural monopoly, that is to say the most efficient producer is generally one firm, whether privately or publicly owned. In either case, there is scope for exploitation of the monopoly position, but in one case the solution is regulation and in the other case ownership. The US embarked in the inter-war period on a process of expanding the scope of its regulation of utilities, albeit largely through intermittent judicial decisions rather than by some coordinated federal effort. In Britain the central state acquired public utilities after the Second World War. 'In contrast in the United States utilities remained as investor-owned utilities (IOUs) mainly regulated at state level' (Chick, 2010, p. 688).

A variety of discourses surrounded nationalization in Britain. There was, of course, a socialist discourse, reflected in the adoption of Lenin's phrase about the commanding heights of the economy. 'There was an unvarying belief among British socialists, a belief that persisted well into the 1960s that, whatever else was wrong about the Soviet Union, its economic management was a great success' (Dell, 2000, p. 142). However, in practice, 'The Labour movement was becoming more interested in efficiency as a motive for nationalisation' (Chester, 1975, p. 385). Many of the utilities had been hit hard during wartime. They needed substantial capital investment if they were able to efficiently meet the demands of an expanding post-war economy and it was by no means clear that this would be available from private sources. What happened in practice was that the initial use of average cost pricing led to considerable cross-subsidization and the perpetuation of inefficiencies in the structure of production (albeit ones that were politically and socially convenient) while privately owned industries received key inputs at below their marginal cost.

In practice technological considerations may have been more important than political form. Britain nationalized its utilities as vertically integrated national monopolies, but in the United States 'vertical integration [was] the dominant structure of state-based Investor Owned Utilities' (Chick, 2010, p. 688). Similarly, in the United States the way in which regulatory arrangements specified the rate of return 'contained an important, averaging, cross-subsidizing component' (ibid., p. 689). Network industries involve high sunk costs and uncertainties about a credible return and 'Regulation and public ownership were but differing responses to these problems of uncertainty and commitment' (ibid., p. 699).

It is difficult in practice for government to withdraw entirely from industries like electricity and gas. They raise important issues of energy security when, as in the case of gas, much of the product has to be imported from politically uncertain regimes. They are classic bundled goods with the consumer purchasing not just the product but security of supply, but how does one price security of supply in the future to present consumers when the lead time of investments is long? There is also the question of climate change, leading companies in Britain to have to obtain some of their supplies of electricity from more expensive sources. In practice it is difficult to map out a purely liberal solution to these problems.

Nationalization and then privatization was an area of great political contestation in Britain from 1945 until the end of the 1980s. The public utilities were the main focus of this debate and in many ways it served as a convenient political differentiator for political parties that had moved closer together. There was no comparable debate in the US where there was no mixed economy in the British sense.

Brighton and its aftermath

The so-called 'Brighton Revolution' of 1960 signaled a more intervention-ist phase in British economic policy, stimulated by the realization that the growth rate in Britain was falling behind that of its continental competitors. Indicative planning in France was seen as offering an alternative model. In selling their planning model to the British counterparts, 'The Plan' was portrayed 'as being essentially a piece of market research on a national scale' so that 'the elements of compulsion involved in French planning were, if not actually denied, very considerably soft-pedalled' (Leruez, 1975, p. 88). As a consequence of being given a 'rather rosy picture of French planning', the British 'drew up two sound plans but gave little thought to how to implement them' (ibid., p. 89).

This period after 1960 saw the rise of industrial policy in the sense of a set of measures intended to encourage firms to take decisions that would lead to a more efficient and competitive industrial economy. In practice, industrial policy in the period from the late 1960s to the early 1980s was often a reactive response by sometimes reluctant governments to a major readjustment required in the economies of the western world. This was triggered by the two oil shocks and the consequent phenomenon of 'stagflation' (low growth, high inflation and rising unemployment) but it had deeper causes:

1. The exhaustion of the long post-war boom stimulated initially by the needs of reconstruction and rearmament (so-called 'Pentagon capitalism' in the United States). As Barry Eichengreen notes (2007, pp. 28–9), 'the share of profits in gross national product began to fall. And with declining profits came declining investment, reflecting the reduction in the rate of return on new capital.'

2. The emergence of 'newly industrializing countries' producing standardized manufactured goods using off-the-shelf technology and cheap labor while taking advantage of tariff reductions secured

through the General Agreement on Tariffs and Trade (GATT) process which then challenged established producers in the west.

3. The diminishing marginal returns obtained from Fordist modes of production, consumption and workplace organization and the emergence of new forms of technology which permitted niche production of quality goods aimed at more discerning consumers.

Even governments that were not disposed to intervene systematically in their economies, such as that of the US, found themselves acting to save declining industries or firms in jeopardy. Such interventions were usually influenced by perceptions of the importance of a sector or firm in a national or regional economy, for example Chrysler. However, as an attempt at systematic policy it was more developed in Britain than the US, particularly in the form of the 'Industrial Strategy' pursued by the 1974–79 Labour government. Britain moved, if rather reactively and hesitantly, in a more dirigiste direction.

A substantial academic literature grew up devoted to the analysis of industrial policy, (for a selection of key articles, see Grant, 1995). The general view that emerged from that literature was that it was a relatively dysfunctional form of policy in which the public money spent did not produce commensurate gains. It can be argued that industrial policy was really a form of social policy that slowed down the adjustment process, or at least mitigated its worst effects and thus made the process of adjustment more socially and politically palatable. If that was the case, then it can be argued that rather than directing the funds available at failing sectors or firms, it would have been better to direct the money to displaced workers to allow them to relocate or acquire new skills that would improve their employability. Training policy was, however, seen as a distinct activity from industrial policy and generally undertaken by different government departments.

A summary of the main findings of the literature from the period of active industrial policy suggests the following that it was very difficult for politicians or bureaucrats to 'pick winners' in terms of sectors of firms. Bureaucrats often lacked the requisite skills or the relevant knowledge, indeed knowledge was generally asymmetrically distributed between bureaucrats and industrial managers, not least in publicly owned industries. Neither politicians nor bureaucrats were able to forecast the future, for example the transformative impact of information and communications technology (ICT). Politicians often made decisions on electoral grounds, for example the political sensitivity of a particular constituency or region or even personal links with it ('bringing home the bacon'). One consequence was that larger companies were generally favored over smaller companies and policies favoring small business were relatively slow to develop (Moran, 2009), although small businesses have the greatest capacity to contribute to the growth of employment.

Multinational companies often played one country off against another or even one state of a federal unit against another (as happened over the location of car plants in the US) in the search for investment funding. They became expert at bending the rules to qualify for some unlikely projects. EU state aids policy was one attempt to counteract this tendency, but it has never been fully effective. Given the above considerations, it is not surprising that it was difficult to demonstrate 'additionality', that is, that the additional funds would lead to investment that would not otherwise occur. The projects that were funded were often highly capital intensive and generated little in the way of additional employment. Often plants were unnecessarily replicated in different regions of the country for political reasons, for example the steel and aluminium sectors in the UK.

Policy was highly gendered in the sense that it favored forms of industrial production that involved men in physically demanding forms of activity that fitted conventional definitions of masculinity, for example the steel industry. Industries that were characterized by high female levels of employment such as food processing tended to receive less aid. Industrial structures tended to be ossified, with preference given to established materials, products and technologies which had greater political displacement through their trade associations and political networks. Underlying problems of overcapacity were not tackled; indeed they were perpetuated and made worse by subsidizing surplus capacity to keep it in operation.

The liberal era

The Thatcher government quickly retreated from any form of industrial policy. One important policy innovation was the privatization of the nationalized industries, removing an importance difference between the UK and the US. The Thatcher government also gave primacy to the goal of combating inflation and effectively abandoned the full employment commitment, using control of the money supply as a policy instrument in place of the traditional Keynesian techniques. Given that the Reagan administration in the US was simultaneously taking a market-oriented stance, there was significant convergence between economic policies in the two countries, although the US ran a much bigger budget deficit. The Thatcher government effectively introduced a new post-war settlement, the main features of which were subsequently adopted by New Labour which in particular saw any notion of industrial policy as a reversion to Old Labour thinking or old-style social democracy. 'There is no known alternative to the market economy any longer; market competition generates gains that no other system can match' (Giddings, 2000, p. 164).

Manufacturing industry declined more rapidly under the Labour governments after 1997 than during the Conservative governments of Margaret Thatcher. Under her governments the manufacturing share of output declined from 25.8 percent to 22.5 percent. When Labour came into office in 1997, manufacturing accounted for more than 20 percent of the economy. By 2007, that share had declined to 12.4 percent (Gibbs, 2009).

New Labour tended to adopt more stringent tests to assistance to industry than in the US. Under the Treasury's Green Book rules, government intervention was permissible only when there was a demonstrable market failure and even then a business case had to make for intervention. The US tended to be guided by more pragmatic, national interest considerations, although it should be noted that the US did not experience the additional constraint of satisfying EU state aid rules. In areas such as the development of biocontrol agents as environmentally friendly replacements for synthetic pesticides, the US provided more external support to the industry (Grant, 2010).

New Labour and the conversion of Lord Mandelson

There was no stronger advocate of market friendly policies within New Labour than one of its principal architects, Peter Mandelson. His transformation into someone who took a more interventionist stance is testimony to the strength of the dirigiste temptation in Britain and in particular the example of France. An equivalent temptation does not exist in the US. It also marked the way in which New Labour edged away from market-oriented policies under Gordon Brown.

Following his return to British politics in 2008, Lord Mandelson changed from a frequent critic of French industrial policy, particularly its designation of casinos and yogurt manufacturers as strategic sectors to be protected from foreign takeovers, to an increasingly vocal supporter of a 'smart' industrial policy. It was noted, 'Lord Mandelson is a changed man. While Britain's business secretary used to scorn many aspects of French industrial policy – which he once saw as a byword for state meddling and protectionism – he has become the champion of a more interventionist approach in the UK' (Parker, 2010). How did Lord Mandelson succumb to the dirigiste temptation?

Following the GFC, and substantial assistance given to the banking industry, the government faced lobbying for assistance from industry, especially from the automotive industry. Some of this was simply faced down. Tata Motors, the owner of Jaguar Land Rover, was reported to be initially asking for as much as £1 billion, but this was scaled down to £800 million, although £340 million of this would come in the form of a loan from the European Investment Bank. The UK government offered only to guarantee a £175 million bridge loan and Tata then decided that it could find commercial funding on less onerous terms.

Lord Mandelson initially set out his approach in a series of interviews and speeches in December 2008. He made it clear that there would be no 'blank check' for troubled firms and that the government would act as lender of last resort. It was up to individual companies to sort out their own future if they ran into trouble: 'We will not be supporting companies with flawed business plans and companies with no prospect of recovery' (*Sunday Times*, 7 December 2008). Big government was not back and there would be no return to the interventionist approach of the 1970s. However, the business secretary was prepared to support a market-led 'industrial activism' with significantly improved state support for growth sectors and green technologies (*Financial Times*, 3 December 2008).

As Lord Mandelson explained his approach, 'We are focusing on cross-cutting technologies and Britain's capability to test and develop innovative products.' The concept of market failure was extended beyond what a rigorous economic analysis would imply: 'We have focused on doing only what the market alone won't – usually because the benefits cannot be captured by a single company.' The intention was to invest in national capabilities, not national champions. Thus, 'As far as capital for industrial innovation is concerned, we see the role of government as making sure smart investments get made, not turning itself into an investment bank.' (Mandelson, 2009).

Mandelson freely admitted in his autobiography that this approach involved 'a stronger role for government than I had envisaged in my 1998 Competitiveness White Paper' (Mandelson, 2010, p. 457). What he had in mind 'was a broader, strategic industrial activism.' (ibid., p. 456). This was 'Not the old Labour practice of "picking winners", which had ended up more often than not with the losers picking government. Not a renewed government role in owning, or running, businesses, or using protectionist tariffs to skew the rules of open international competition' (ibid.). Nevertheless, Tony Blair had to be reassured that 'this was about making markets work better, not replacing them' (ibid.,

p. 457). Mandelson's approach is very similar to what Gamble (2010a) describes as the 'social investment model' as distinct from the 'Anglo Saxon' (or Anglo-American) model entailing strategic investment in economic competitiveness, including human capital, the research base and infrastructure.

Mandelson argued that Britain 'could learn from France in the way it invested in or rescued French high-tech companies, allowing them to flourish in new markets.' (*Financial Times*, 15 January 2010). In March 2010 he made a pilgrimage across the Channel to discuss state inter-ventionism with French business leaders. He reported that 'We have something to learn from continental practice without falling into the pitfalls of second-guessing business.' He made it clear that 'we are not talking about public ownership nor are we talking about centralised planning of business'. But he took the view that France was better 'at setting strategic goals and objectives'. Britain was quite good at setting up a regulatory system, 'but we have always assumed the supply side would take care of itself' (*Financial Times*, 14 March 2010).

There were limits to the shift in policy. As Gordon Brown explained, 'We don't want to be picking winners, which is so often picking losers' (quoted in Parker, 2010). The initiatives taken by the Labour government fell far short of the Trades Union Congress (TUC) calls for a £5 billion French-style fund to make strategic long-term investments in manufacturing companies. Lord Mandelson set up a £950 million strategic investment fund which was dwarfed by President Sarkozy's €20 billion (£17.7 billion) fund which also took minority stakes in companies rather than giving grants or loans.

In many ways the British response also paled in comparison with what was done in the US. There 'President Obama set up a US Treasury Automotive Task Force with a very wide membership which has undertaken a rapid restructuring on the US automotive sector including, of course, huge state aid, nationalisation, Chapter 11 bankruptcies and rationalisations of Chrysler and GM, the Fiat/Chrysler merger and the closure of many factories and dealerships. The reaction in Europe was far less coherent' (Wilks, 2009, p. 281). President Obama found $60 billion for Chrysler and General Motors out of a global total of around $100 billion of aid, leading to critics of the administration to complain of the arrival of 'Government Motors'. However, restructuring was required and the effective removal of the head of GM led Wilks to argue that 'the limits of industrial intervention appear to have been redefined' (ibid., p. 280).

The Coalition government's policy

Coalition government policy was necessarily driven by the priority accorded to tackling the structural budget deficit. This meant cuts in the budget of the business department on top of the initial £836 million of 'efficiency savings' initially identified by Business Secretary Vince Cable. However, the notion of 'rebalancing' the economy, 'less financial engineering and more real engineering', as Lord Mandelson (2010, p. 456) had defined it, was not abandoned. It was referred to by the Chancellor in his Budget speech in terms of the balance between the financial and the manufacturing sectors, and it was referred to by Vince Cable in terms of wealth being spread around the regions. What was not clear was what policy instruments would be available to achieve these objectives.

What Vince Cable did make clear was that direct grants would be given to individual companies only in exceptional circumstances, focusing instead of creating a better climate for business through lower taxes and promoting training. 'We're moving away out of an emergency time, and support will come in more indirect ways', Vince Cable explained. 'Not in direct support for companies – we don't have the funding to do that, and it isn't good policy anyway' (*Financial Times*, 29 June 2010). The government made it clear that it was unwilling to fight other countries in a 'subsidy war' (*Financial Times*, 1 July 2010).

The government did agree that a £21 million grant to Nissan to produce its Leaf electric car in the North East would go ahead. Nissan put some pressure on the government, pointing out that other governments, notably Spain, were willing to offer support (*Financial Times*, 10 June 2010). The government also confirmed a Labour government pledge for £360 million of guarantees for a £415 million European Investment Bank loan to Ford to support £1.5 billion of investment in low-carbon 'Eco-boost' engines and other new technologies in the UK. The government seemed reluctant, however, to lend support to GM's plans to produce the Ampera at Ellesmere Port on Merseyside. The government proceeded with plans for a green investment bank but it is expected to receive only a small amount of public funding with most of its money being raised in the private sector. The limitations of the bank became a source of tension between the coalition parties.

However, the government did not proceed with a loan to Sheffield Forgemasters to enable it to expand into the nuclear sector. This proved to be politically contentious as the government gave as one reason for its decision that the directors were not prepared to dilute their shareholdings, but this subsequently appeared not to be the case. The more general question the government no doubt asked was why, if the project was a viable one, it could not proceed with a commercial loan.

Assessment and future trends

It is difficult to disentangle the effects of the policies of the two administrations from the structural situations of the two economies. For all its problems, the US remains the leading world economy. Many individual American states, not just California, have GDPs larger than significant developed countries. The American economy remains an engine house of innovation, particularly in advanced technologies. It enjoys a large internal market that delivers economies of scale. The dollar is not going to disappear as the world's reserve currency any time soon. All this means that the US has a greater capacity to recover quickly from the recession than the UK. Its international position means that it can be relaxed about what is in fact a much more serious and chronic budget deficit.

A central question for the UK remains how far its private sector is dependent on contracts from the public sector. If there is a substantial dependence, recovery will be difficult. There are clearly particular challenges for the construction industry where much work depends on public sector contracts, although the Cameron government has continued to issue controversial Private Finance Initiative (PFI) contracts, and where house building has been slowed down by the lack of availability of mortgage finance. There are, however, some indications of a recovery in manufacturing and some success in boosting exports to emerging countries. What is less clear is whether the Cameron government has a coherent growth strategy covering such areas as skill formation, transport infrastructure and research and development. However, the liberal Anglo-American model does not encourage it to think in those terms and indeed its own terminology emphasizes boosting enterprise with a revival of Mrs Thatcher's enterprise zones.

Moran (2009) is more skeptical than other authors about the existence of an Anglo-American model. He notes 'some striking differences in political patterns that might make us doubt whether we are looking at a single model of capitalist democracy' (Moran, 2009, p. xii). Moran comes to the conclusion that in Britain a system that was once very different from the US has been transformed, not by any process of 'Americanization' but through the growing influence of the EU and the breakdown of the pre-democratic regime. The British system 'is now shaped more than in the past by legal regulations, it now involves more formal relations between regulators and regulated than in the past, and it is now more often characterised by an adversarial, punitive approach to enforcement than in the past' (ibid., p. 170). However, in both systems 'democratic politics is under great pressure from business power' (ibid., p. 171).

The two systems are very similar in the structural displacement of the financial sector in economic and political terms (although work in progress by Moran suggests that its contribution to the economy whether in terms of employment or tax revenues is often overstated). As Gamble (2010b, p. 10) observes, 'The power of the financial sector was indirect and structural rather than direct. Bankers had few political allies and little political trust, but their main advantage was that governments recognised the vital importance of a successful financial sector to economic performance, did not have an alternative growth model and so were wary of introducing reforms that could permanently damage the ability of the financial sector to recover.' Although reforms have been introduced in both countries, an acid test will be whether the investment and retail functions of banks are separated in Britain. The Chancellor has indicated support for the recommendation in principle of the Vickers Commission to ring-fence investment and retail functions of banks, but the devil will be in the detail.

In Britain there is a recurrent dirigiste temptation in the sense of looking to French models in times of crisis which has no American equivalent: Canada is seen either as an irrelevant comparison or an example of what to avoid. This chapter has also noted variation over time as well as variation between countries. British policy became much more interventionist between 1945 and 1979 regardless of which party was in office. Moves in a more interventionist direction in the US were more spasmodic and more hesitant and the economic and political establishment never succumbed wholeheartedly to Keynesian orthodoxy, as proclaimed by the self-appointed disciples of Keynes in the way that it did in Britain.

In practice, however, both countries, but especially the US, gave substantial assistance to their auto industries in the midst of the GFC because the economic and political costs of not doing so were seen to be too high. The auto industry has a central role in both economies with a substantial 'multiplier' effect. For Mandelson (2010, p. 455), a key consideration was that the car industry was 'on its knees'. In this sense the 'new' industrial policy was very similar to the old one with its emphasis on Fordist mass production.

The extent to which the Anglo-American model is an imagined space is illustrated by the case of BP (British Petroleum). In many ways it is a prototypical Anglo-American company: shareholdings in Britain are only one percentage point ahead of American Depositary Receipts held in the

US and its main market is in the US. Yet criticism in the US following the Gulf oil spill centered on the notion that it was a British company and much of the political rhetoric seemed to be driven by American nationalism. The appointment of an American chief executive was seen as an attempt to assuage American political opinion.

Perhaps the main function of the model is to provide a target for those who seek to assign blame for the GFC to a deficient Anglo-Saxon approach to the economy. It does not imply a unity of approach. As is evident from the policies of the Obama administration and Cameron government, there are important differences, and British membership of the EU is a factor of increasing importance in shaping relevant policies in the UK. Contrary to predictions in the immediate aftermath of the GFC, liberal capitalism has not disappeared. In many ways one can expect a reversion to 'business as usual' and the restoration of the Anglo-American model as a frame for policy. However, deficient economic performance and growing electoral concerns may produce 'ad hoc' initiatives from the Cameron government which mimic those of the Obama administration at the height of the crisis.

References

Casey, T. (2009) 'Mapping Stability and Change in Advanced Capitalisms', *Comparative European Politics*, 7, 255–78.

Chester, N. (1975) *The Nationalisation of British Industry, 1945–51* (London: HMSO).

Chick, M. (2010) 'Network Utilities: Technological Development, Market Structure and Forms of Ownership', in D. Coen, W. Grant and G. Wilson (eds), *The Oxford Handbook of Business and Government* (Oxford: Oxford University Press), pp. 684–702.

Coffey, T., and C. Thornley (2009) *Globalization and Varieties of Capitalism* (Basingstoke: Palgrave Macmillan).

Davenport-Hines, R.P.T. (1984) *Dudley Docker: The Life and Times of a Trade Warrior* (Cambridge: Cambridge University Press).

Dell, E. (2000) *A Strange Eventful History: Democratic Socialism in Britain* (London: HarperCollins).

Eichengreen, B. (2007) *The European Economy since 1945* (Princeton: Princeton University Press).

Gamble, A. (2003) *Between Europe and America: the Future of British Politics* (Basingstoke: Palgrave Macmillan).

Gamble, A. (2010a) 'The 2010 Spending Review: Implications for the State and its Reach', British Academy Forum, London, 30 July.

Gamble, A. (2010b) 'The Political Consequences of the Crash', *Political Studies Review*, 8, 3–14.

Gibbs, C. (2009) 'Decline in Manufacturing Greater under Labour than with Thatcher', *Financial Times*, 3 December 2009.

Giddens, A. (2000) *The Third Way and its Critics* (Cambridge: Polity Press).

Grant, W. (ed.) (1995) *Industrial Policy* (Cheltenham: Edward Elgar).

Grant, W. (2010) 'Environmental and Food Safety Policy', in D. Coen, W. Grant and G. Wilson (eds), *The Oxford Handbook of Business and Government* (Oxford: Oxford University Press), pp. 663–83.

Hall, P. (1989) 'Introduction', in P. Hall (ed.), *The Political Power of Economic Ideas* (Princeton: Princeton University Press), pp. 1–26.

Kirby, M., and M.B. Rose (1991) 'Productivity and Competitive Failure: British Government Policy and Industry, 1914–19', in G. Jones and M.W. Kirby (eds), *Competitiveness and the State: Government and Business in Twentieth-Century Britain* (Manchester: Manchester University Press), pp. 20–39.

Leruez, E. (1975), *Economic Planning and Politics in Britain* (Oxford: Martin Robertson).

Macmillan, H. (1933) *Reconstruction* (London: Macmillan).

Mandelson, P. (2009) 'Best "Industrial Policy" Britain has Developed', *Financial Times*, 30 July 2009.

Mandelson, P. (2010) *The Third Man: Life at the Heart of New Labour* (London: Harper Press).

Moran, M. (2009) *Business, Politics and Society: An Anglo-American Comparison* (Oxford: Oxford University Press).

Parker, G. (2010) 'Endorsing the French Model', *Financial Times*, 21 January.

Tolliday, S. (1987) *Business, Banking and Politics* (Cambridge, MA: Harvard University Press).

Wilks, S.M. (2009) 'The Impact of the Recession on Competition Policy: Amending the Economic Constitution?', *International Journal of the Economics of Business*, 16, 269–88.

Williams, E.E. (1896) *Made in Germany* (London: Heinemann).

3
Capitalism, Crisis, and a Zombie Named TINA

Terrence Casey

The financial crash that hit in September 2008 was more than a downturn in the business cycle. It was a 'crisis of capitalism – a much rarer event, potentially giving rise to new politics, policies, and even the reorganization of capitalist economies' (Gamble, 2009a, p. 7). This chapter explores the implications of this crisis for the political economies of America and Britain. Has this crisis of capitalism led to a fundamental transformation of Anglo-American capitalism? After a brief tour of the Anglo-American model of capitalism, the causes of the crisis and the major policy responses of both states are reviewed. Surprisingly, the neoliberal growth model has (so far) largely survived this crisis intact. More than anything else, the liberal model seems set to survive because no viable alternative growth model has been advanced by a political coalition with realistic electoral prospects.

Anglo-American capitalism before the crash

Both the US and UK are characterized as ideal-typical 'liberal market economies' (Hall and Soskice, 2001). The 'neoliberal revolutions' of Margaret Thatcher and Ronald Reagan included the deregulation of product, labor, and capital markets; the privatization of state-owned industries and the outsourcing of public services; fiscal retrenchment, reducing overall state spending and slicing marginal tax rates to increase private investment; and a general belief in the self-regulation of markets. Neoliberal reformers were, for the most part, successful on all of these fronts, with their gains consolidated by the ostensibly left-wing governments of Bill Clinton and Tony Blair in the 1990s. The one draw was state spending, which, after shrinking for two decades, was basically the same in 2007 as in 1980 (see Figure 3.1). Despite the commonalities, differences between Britain and America abound (see Moran, 2009). Britain has a unitary system with power concentrated in the core executive. Powers are separated (and shared) in the US between the executive, legislature, and judiciary, all of whom are involved in economic regulation, and the federal system allows states to exercise independent fiscal and regulatory policies. Division provides more direct openings to organized interests in the US, although the structural influence of business, especially of the City, weighs heavily on British policy-making. Organized labor has declined substantially in Britain since the 1970s, yet unions remain even weaker in the US. The exceptions in both states are public sector unions, which remain significant political forces. The greatest differences come in public policy. Social democracy never gained a beachhead in America. The British state does more – and is expected to do more – for its citizens. Nowhere is this more vividly illustrated than in health care. The National Health Service (NHS) is so sacrosanct that the Conservatives were compelled to protect it in their budget-cutting 2010 manifesto. In America even the inclusion of a 'public option' in the Obama administration's health care legislation was considered beyond the pale.

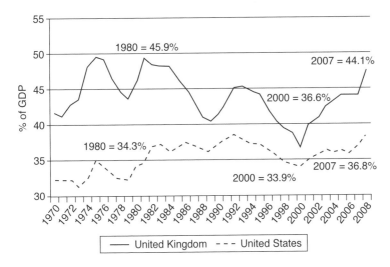

Figure 3.1 US and UK total government expenditure, 1970–2008

Source: OECD (2011).

Understanding the crisis

The concurring and dissenting opinions of the US Financial Crisis Inquiry Commission (FCIC) illustrate that there is little consensus on the causes of the crisis (see FCIC, 2011). The following analysis focuses predominantly on the US, the epicenter of the meltdown. On one level this is all very simple: asset market crises are common in capitalist economies and in 2008 the US housing market bubble burst (Reinhart and Rogoff, 2009). Yet the near collapse of the international financial system and the deepest recession since the Great Depression is well beyond common. Why was this crisis so much worse? How did the collapse in house prices in the US lead to an international financial crisis? Finally, were the sources of the crisis the same in the UK as in the US?

Macro-economic conditions created the conditions for a crisis, specifically the expansionary monetary policies of Federal Reserve Chairman Alan Greenspan and his successor Ben Bernanke. To keep the economy growing after the dot.com bust and 9/11, the Federal Reserve kept interest rates low: 2001–04 was the longest sustained expansionary monetary policy since the early 1950s (Gjerstad and Smith, 2009, p. 277). The federal funds rate fell from just under 6 percent in 2001 to 1 percent by mid 2003, not rising again for another year. The widely used 'Taylor Rule'[1] suggested that rates should have ascended starting in 2001 (Taylor, 2009, pp. 2–3). The steady flow of easy money encouraged institutions and individuals to take on riskier credit, including subprime mortgages, and fed the housing bubble. The Case-Schiller National House Price Index doubled from 2000 to its peak in the second quarter of 2006. Yet the Fed did not see the danger early enough. Greenspan expressed concern about house prices in mid 2005, but suggested it was 'froth' in the market rather than a bubble (*New York Times* (online edition), 21 May 2005), a position reinforced by Bernanke later that year (Posner, 2009, p. 90). Even in August 2007, the Federal Reserve's Open Market Committee, responsible for setting interest rates, expressed greater concern with economic overheating and inflation than a collapse in asset prices (ibid., p. 121).

Nor was the regulatory structure attuned to identify systemic problems. Both the UK and the US systematically deregulated financial transactions, the 'Big Bang' deregulation of the City in 1986 and the repeal of Glass-Steagall in 1999 under President Clinton (which separated commercial and investment banking) being the major milestones along the way. On both sides of the Atlantic policy-makers believed innovation and growth were nurtured through minimal regulation. Nor was this only a right-wing policy. New Labour bragged of their 'light touch' regulation of the City, whose place as an international financial center was a pillar of economic policy. Gordon Brown claimed the era of boom and bust was over because of the sophistication and flexibility of finance (Gamble, 2009b, p. 454). Clinton's Treasury Secretary Lawrence Summers, in agreement with Greenspan, spiked a plan to regulate credit default swaps in the late 1990s (Friedman, 2009, p. 158). The conventional wisdom was that 'private regulation' of financial markets was optimal (Greenspan, 1997). Financial firms pursuing imprudent strategies would be punished by the market, providing a warning to others. The speed of financial innovation, moreover, meant that regulators would always be 'behind the market'. Markets were best left to correct themselves.

The organization of regulatory institutions exacerbated matters. The UK was governed under a 'tripartite system' wherein the Bank of England, the Financial Services Authority (FSA), and the Treasury were all responsible for financial stability. The FSA regulated individual banks while the Bank of England monitored the system as a whole, but communication and coordination between them was wanting. US regulation was even more divided:

> The existence of multiple federal financial regulatory bodies – including the Federal Reserve, the Federal Deposit Insurance Corporation, the Securities Investor Protection Corporation, the Securities and Exchange Commission, the Commodity Futures Trading Commission, the Federal Housing Authority, the Federal Housing and Finance Administration, the Office of Housing Enterprise Oversight, the National Credit Union Administration, the Treasury Department and its agencies, such as the Comptroller of the Currency and the Office of Thrift Supervision – and fifty state banking and insurance commissioners – has led to a fragmentation of regulatory authority, a lack of coordination, turf wars, yawning regulatory gaps with respect to hedge funds, bank substitutes, and novel financial instruments, and an inability to aggregate and analyze information about emerging problems in financial markets. (Posner, 2009, pp. 289–90)

The most obvious failing in both systems is that no single entity had the responsibility, authority, or powers to monitor the system as a whole, spot destabilizing trends, and take preventive action in response (HM Treasury, 2010a, p. 4).

Financial deregulation is seen by many as the primary culprit in this crisis. Yet a note of caution is warranted. Firms unquestionably took on excessive risk without regulatory interference. Policy-makers had tools available to them, however, not the least of which was tightening monetary policy, to constrain market behavior if they chose to do so. They fully expected that markets would correct themselves, precluding any systemic crisis. Deregulatory ideology was thus more significant than the legal incidence of deregulation. Secondly, the impetus for bad behavior derived not only from the lack of regulation, but also from the perverse incentives created by (some) regulations.

Cheap credit and light touch regulation were necessary, but insufficient, conditions to produce an explosion in subprime lending. Further impetus came from the two government-sponsored enterprises (GSEs): Fannie Mae (formally the Federal National Mortgage Association, founded during the Great Depression) and Freddie Mac (Federal Home Loan Mortgage Corporation, created in 1970). Fannie and Freddie operated in the secondary mortgage market, buying mortgages from banks so as to encouraging more lending. The initial push for greater subprime lending came from the Community Reinvestment Act's (CRA's) (1977) goal of increasing affordable housing for poorer, often minority, homeowners. Following a Boston Federal Reserve Bank study on discrimination in mortgage lending, the Clinton Administration tightened the CRA so that banks would be evaluated on performance rather than the standards they used in lending. Extending loans to those otherwise unqualified for a standard (prime) mortgage meant reducing lending standards; hence 'subprime loans'.[2] Banks might have balked had not Fannie and Freddie loosened their underwriting standards to buy up these loans. Private sector actors looking to expand profits during an unprecedented housing boom pushed the growth of subprime lending, but their ability to do so was facilitated by the GSEs. By 2009, Fannie and Freddie had guaranteed $1.6 trillion in subprime and Alt-A[3] loans, about 40 percent of all outstanding value (Wallison, 2009a, p. 370). Attempts were made during the Bush years to rein in the GSEs, but all were blocked in Congress, including by key Democrats who would later lead the charge on financial reform – Barney Frank (D-MA) and Chris Dodd (D-CT). That being said, government policies to boost homeownership, including the activities of the GSEs, received strong, bipartisan support for decades.

Asset bubbles popping, even the stock market crash of 1929, are not in themselves sufficient to engender systemic financial crisis (Friedman, 2009, p. 162). What transformed the housing collapse into a financial crisis was the securitization of subprime mortgages. Securitization is when assets are bundled into various types of financial instruments and sold to other actors; in this case, mortgage-backed securities (MBSs). Ironically, the rationale for securitization is to reduce risk through diversification. By bundling mortgages from different regions, you reduce the risk that a housing downturn in one area will wipe out your investment. Risk can be further reduced through credit default swaps (CDSs), a form of insurance transferring the risk of default to a third party for a premium (see Wallison, 2009b). Securitization decreases banks' incentives to properly scrutinize loans, however, pursuing instead an 'originate and distribute' strategy (Coates, 2010, p. 21). Big institutional investors should have been sufficiently savvy to avoid such a 'sucker's bet'. In reality, the major banks were heavily invested in subprime MBSs. Rather than diversifying risk, securitization served to concentrated it. Why did the proliferation of MBSs backfire so spectacularly?

This occurred, perversely, because of financial market regulations, specifically the capital-adequacy guidelines under the Basel Accords. With banks regulated nationally, the Bank of International Settlement's Basel Committee on Banking Supervision's job is to establish common guidelines across national regulatory structures. Under the Basel rules a bank was 'well capitalized' if it maintained 8 percent capital against assets (Jablecki and Machaj, 2009, p. 305). The rules also gave different risk weights to different classes of assets. Commercial loans received a 100 percent risk weight; government bonds were zero. Mortgages fell right in the middle at 50 percent. Securities issued by government-sponsored entities, including Fannie Mae and Freddie Mac, received a 20 percent risk weighting,[4] as did asset-backed securities, including MBSs with an AAA or AA rating (Friedman, 2009, pp. 143–4). Shifting into MBSs meant decreasing capital minima and increasing profitable investment potential. Banks did not plunge into MBSs in order to diversify risk, they did so to make an end-run around capital adequacy requirements, increase their leverage and boost profits (Acharya and Richardson, 2009, p. 197). Bear Stearns' borrowed to equity capital ratio was 35 to 1 before they collapsed; UBS's was 50 to 1 (Posner, 2009, p. 221). Fannie Mae and Freddie Mac had a whopping 75 to 1 ratio in 2007 (FCIC, 2011, p. xx). Not all banks were so imprudent. JP Morgan, Capital One, and Wells Fargo, for example, did not get overly leveraged (Friedman, 2009, p. 153). Mortgage-backed securities were paying very favorable returns, so for many companies leveraging into MBSs made good business sense. Even when bankers recognized they were riding a housing bubble, competition created an incentive to stay with the crowd, hoping to jump at the right time. Citigroup's CEO Charles Prince famously told the *Financial Times* in July 2007, 'As long as the music is playing, you've got to get up and dance.' That executives like Prince were handsomely compensated based on short-term profits rather than long-term solvency further encouraged this behavior.

Leveraging required highly rated (AAA or AA) securities. How did subprime MBSs, by definition high-risk investments, end up with AAA ratings? Partly it was the nature of the rating system. Beginning in the Depression era, banks are prohibited from investing in speculative securities (below a BBB rating), as determined by recognized rating manuals. Bankers had to rely on third-party risk assessment, whose pronouncements now attained the force of law. In 1975 the Securities and Exchange Commission (SEC) solidified this by declaring that securities firms could only use the ratings of 'nationally recognized statistical rating organizations'. By the late 1990s this meant Moody's, Standard & Poor's, and Fitch, giving them a government sanctioned oligopoly over securities ratings (White, 2009, pp. 390–2). In addition, they operated an 'issuer pays' business model – the company for whom they issued the bond rating paid the fees. This created a conflict of interest; securities firms that did not like the rating of their bonds could take their business to one of the other three. Rather than serving as neutral arbiters of the quality of the securities, these firms worked with companies to reconfigure their offerings so that they could receive a favorable rating (White, 2009, p. 394).

The financial alchemy of transforming subprime mortgages into AAA securities occurred by dividing these securities into segments, or 'tranches'. Investors in each tranche received dividends from the repayments of the mortgages from the entire MBS. Purchasers of junior tranches (rated BB and lower) received a higher payoff, but were first to lose their money if the mortgages went under. Senior tranche purchasers only saw a loss after all of the junior tranches were wiped out. The rating agencies, using probability formulas, deemed the likelihood of all the mortgages in these securities going under to be very low. Since the risk of senior tranche investments was low, they were given a AAA rating – even though all of the mortgages in the MBSs may be subprime (Friedman, 2009, pp. 136–8). Add to this that many subprime mortgage-backed investments were held in structured investment vehicles (SIVs) – informal entities connected to the banks through lines of credit. This 'shadow banking system' was not subject to the capital requirements and other regulations of their parent banks. Thus MBS purchases by SIVs entailed zero capital requirements, allowing the parent bank's capital minima to be reduced even further. If the major banks had just passed these shabby investments on to others, they might be more hated, yet still solvent. In fact, the major purchasers of MBSs were the banks that issued them or the SIVs they sponsored (Acharya and Richardson, 2009, p. 200). Rather than diversifying risk as is intended, securitization served to concentrate a huge amount of risk right back on the balance sheet of major financial institutions. All was well, of course, as long as the value of the underlying assets continued to grow. When the US housing market collapsed, they were seriously overexposed.

Across the Atlantic, the crisis was both homegrown and imported. The financial sector plays an even larger role in the British economy than in America. Financial intermediation accounted for five percent of gross value added (GVA) in 1970. By 2008 it accounted for 8 percent of GVA and 15 percent of whole economy profits (Haldane, 2010, p. 4). From 1987 to 2007, the UK financial services sector grew at 4.7 percent per annum while the whole economy grew at 2.6 percent (Weale, 2009, p. 4). As a global financial hub, the performance of the City was intimately linked to trends in wider financial markets, including the US. Many British firms, moreover, pursued strategies similar to their American counterparts, starting with Northern Rock, the first major British bank to collapse. Nor was this merely a banking problem. The entire British economy became overleveraged during the 2000s, with a massive increase in private debt, much of it tied to a booming housing market. Average total household debt increased from 105 percent of income in 2000 to 160 percent in 2008 (McKinsey, 2010, p. 24). This was matched by a sharp rise in public debt. The reputation for economic prudence developed by Gordon Brown in the first Blair government was thrown aside after 2001, when the spending taps were turned wide open for the next five years. As revenue slowed, net public debt rose from 30.7 percent of gross domestic product (GDP) in 2000 to 36.5 percent in 2007 (HM Treasury, 2010b). Taken together, the UK experienced the largest rise of total debt to GDP of any of the major economies, from just over triple GDP in 2000 to 469 percent in 2008, *before* having to deal with the fallout of the crisis (McKinsey, 2010, p. 18). The crisis in America was entirely homegrown. The UK imported much of it, but once the contagion hit the British shores, it found an agreeable host.

Responses to the crisis

US housing prices peaked in late 2006 and deflated throughout 2007. As they did, the structure of securities and the interconnections between financial firms that relied upon their value began to unravel also. Northern Rock was nationalized, Bear Stearns was taken over, and Fannie Mae and Freddie Mac were formally absorbed by the US government. If there is a culminating point in the events of the crisis it was the collapse of Lehman Brothers on 14 September 2008, when it became clear to all that disaster loomed. London and Washington intervened in unprecedented ways to avert systemic collapse, provided economic stimulus to revive growth, and implemented regulatory reforms to prevent future catastrophes. Policy also influenced politics, and both countries have seen a change of government since the crisis hit. Cumulatively, these policies may have staved off depression, but both economies continue to struggle well into 2011.

After Lehman's collapse, the global financial system seized up entirely. The British and American governments then ignored the boundaries of free market ideology altogether. In October 2008, Congress approved the Emergency Economic Stabilization Act establishing the Troubled Asset Relief Program (TARP) authorizing the Treasury to spend up to $700 billion dollars to purchase the 'toxic assets' of failing banks. The original plan was to then sell these assets at some form of auction, an idea which quickly proved a non-starter. The complexity and opacity of these instruments made it difficult to determine any meaningful values (Posner, 2009, p. 61). Plus the market for these assets had dried up. The Treasury thus shifted from asset purchases to capital injections, purchasing $205 billion in preferred stock from 707 financial institutions (CBO, 2010a, p. 2). Three institutions received the lion's share of the funding. Citigroup and Bank of America (having swallowed up Merrill Lynch) each received $40 billion with Citigroup receiving an additional $5 billion in guarantees against losses. AIG got $70 billion – $40 billion in stock purchases and a $30 billion line of credit (CBO, 2010a, p. 4). President Bush also invoked his executive authority in December 2008 to extend TARP funds to automakers Chrysler, GM, including GM's financing arm, GMAC. The program was expanded by the incoming Obama administration to $82 billion all told, giving the government majority ownership in GM and a substantial minority stake in Chrysler. TARP also established a $50 billion program to help homeowners avoid foreclosure through mortgage modifications and created a Special Master to review the executive compensation for companies receiving substantial bailouts. By early 2009, the US government owned stakes in major banks, was the majority owner of America's largest automaker, was modifying mortgages, and was rendering judgement on executive salaries.

TARP wound down in October 2010 with the government having dispersed $388 billion of the $700 billion available. By that time $204 billion has been repaid, including 78 percent of the capital injected into financial institutions (US Department of the Treasury, 2010, p. i).

Citigroup and Bank of America are no longer under the TARP, although AIG has only repaid about one-fifth of the capital advanced. By early 2011 the government's share of GM was down to one-third with the automaker looking to buy back additional shares, and Fiat was set to purchase the remaining shares of Chrysler. In both word and deed the Obama administration has established that it intends to liquidate government holdings in these companies as soon as possible. When combined with revenues raised from stock sales, the Treasury estimates that the total cost of TARP to be around $50 billion, as well as an additional $30 billion loss on AIG (US Department of the Treasury, 2010, p. 3). At about 0.5 percent of GDP, this is well below both the $350 billion initial estimates for the TARP and comparably much lower than the savings and loan bailouts of the 1980s, which cost the taxpayers the equivalent of 2–3 percent of GDP.

The Brown government moved with similar speed to shore up the banks. Following Lehman's collapse, and with direct intervention from the prime minister, Lloyds TSB purchased HBOS, the UK's largest mortgage lender, in a £12 billion shares swap. Two weeks later the government nationalized Bradford & Bingley, taking over its £50 billion mortgage unit. Following America's lead, Brown and Darling announced a rescue package of their own, including £50 billion of cash for equity swaps, £100 billion in short-term loans from the Bank of England, and another £250 billion in loan guarantees (*Guardian* (online edition), 8 October 2008). Five days later it was announced that the Royal Bank of Scotland, Lloyds TSB and HBOS were to receive £37 billion between them in exchange for equity stakes of roughly 60 percent for RBS and 40 percent for the merged Lloyds TSB and HBOS (BBC News Online, 13 October 2008). Whitehall would also now have a say in how the banks were run, including questions of executive compensation.

Having blocked financial collapse, attention turned to reviving growth. The 'era of big government' came roaring back to life as both nations implemented massive stimulus packages. American stimulus began before the crisis broke in earnest, with a $168 billion package in February 2008. Bush's lame-duck status precluded additional stimulus before 2009. Just after being sworn in President Obama signed the $787 billion American Recovery and Reinvestment Act, including immediate aid to states and localities, extended unemployment benefits, and tax cuts. Longer-term commitments included an array of infrastructure and transportation projects, R&D grants, and nearly $90 billion for clean energy development (Grunwald, 2010). Chancellor Darling sought to jump-start the British economy with a £21 billion stimulus package in November 2008. The bulk of the stimulus came through a 2.5 percent

VAT reduction applicable through 2009, necessitating a vast increase in public borrowing, up to £175 billion in 2009.

Monetary policy was also unleashed with full force. The Fed began aggressively cutting rates at the end of 2007, with the Bank taking a more conservative approach. Once the crisis hit full force, both central banks quickly slashed rates to near zero. With nowhere else to go on interest rates, Mervyn King and Ben Bernanke moved to boost the money supply through 'quantitative easing'. This involved purchasing assets and then transferring credits to institutions reserve accounts – a more subtle and sophisticated equivalent to printing money. In March 2009 the Bank, with the Chancellor's approval, purchased £75 billion of government securities (gilts) and some high-quality private assets. Three additional rounds raised the total amount of assets purchased to £200 billion. The MPC decided in February 2010 to hold at that level, reviewing the need for further purchases at each meeting (Bank of England website). The Fed was even quicker on quantitative easing, buying up $1.4 trillion in assets (GSE securities, private MBS's, and commercial paper) between the fall of 2008 and August 2010 (Federal Reserve website). With the economy still struggling and core inflation flat, the Fed initiated a second $600 billion round of quantitative easing (quickly dubbed 'QE2') in the fall of 2010. Purchases of new assets under QE2 came to an end with the second quarter of 2011, with the Fed continuing to buy new bonds as existing investments mature, thus not withdrawing any money from the economy. In the first ever press conference by a Federal Reserve Chairman in April 2011, Bernanke gave no indication as to when that policy would change.

Fiscal and monetary stimulus did not produce recovery, however. Following a sharp downturn in 2009, both economies saw the return of modest growth in 2010 (see Table 3.1). The OECD's May 2011 *Economic Outlook* makes similar projections for the next two years. Even these numbers may prove optimistic as the US housing market again declined and the May jobless rate tipped above 9 percent. The UK economy saw a 0.5 percent contraction in the last quarter of 2010 followed by an equivalent uptick in the first quarter of 2011. The refrain from the Labour government (when they were still in power) and the Obama administration was that without aggressive intervention the economy would be vastly worse, a politically and economically difficult counterfactual. Whatever gains were made, they came at a terrible cost to public finances. Deficits skyrocketed to 11.3 percent of GDP in the UK and 11 percent in the US in 2009. CBO projections do not see the US deficit dipping below $500 billion for the rest of the decade. National debts have concurrently ballooned (Figure 3.2), doubling in the US and increasing over 150 percent in Britain.

Table 3.1   GDP growth and unemployment rates in the US and UK

	GDP (% change)		Unemployment (%)	
	US	UK	US	UK
2006	2.7	2.8	4.6	5.4
2007	1.9	2.7	4.6	5.4
2008	0.0	−0.1	5.8	5.7
2009	−2.6	−4.9	9.3	7.6
2010	2.9	1.3	9.6	7.9
2011*	2.6	1.4	8.8	8.1
2012*	3.1	1.8	7.9	8.3

* Projections (from May 2011).

Source: OECD (2011).

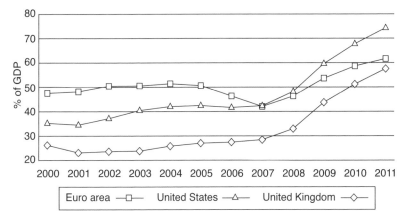

Figure 3.2   Public debt levels

Source: OECD (2011).

Faced with this abysmal fiscal situation, Chancellor George Osborne's 2011 budget aimed to eliminate the structural deficit within the term of this Parliament. Given the Tory's manifesto commitments on the NHS, other departments will see 19 percent cuts on average. Up to half a million public sector jobs may be shed by 2015 and additional contributions (£3.5 billion total) required by public employees for their pension schemes. Cost control in general state pensions would be achieved by hastening the increase in the retirement age to 66 and indexing pensions to the consumer price index (CPI) rather than the (generally higher) retail price index (RPI). An additional £7 billion in savings will come from reductions in welfare budgets through changes to incapacity, housing benefit and tax credits (BBC News Online, 20 October 2010). New revenue would be generated through a VAT increase from 17.5 percent to 20 percent, purported to raise an additional £13 billion per year. The overall corporate tax rate was cut while new levies will be imposed on North Sea oil producers and banks. Even with this the deficit will remain at 9.5 percent of GDP for the 2010/11 fiscal year (ONS, 2011). Whether this increases market confidence and private investment is a point of speculation. What is certain is that the pain will be felt in the near term. With flat wages, declining public benefits, and rising inflation, the Office of Budget Responsibility (OBR) forecasts that the real standard of living for most British families will fall through 2013 (*Daily Telegraph* (online edition), 24 March 2011). The coalition is betting that strong growth will return by then.

The fiscal quandary is equally severe in the US, driven by the big entitlement programs: Social Security, Medicare, and Medicaid, accounting for 43 percent of federal outlays between them. Other mandatory spending and interest on the debt account for an additional 17 percent; defense spending and non-defense discretionary spending account for about 20 percent each. With rising healthcare costs and aging baby-boomers, the fiscal burden of all three entitlement programs will increase exponentially without reform. The steep rise in the debt combined with the lack of a credible reduction plan was sufficient to draw an admonition from the International Monetary Fund (IMF) (*IMF Fiscal Monitor*, April 2011).

America's separation of powers and divided government complicates matters. Following big Republican gains in the 2010 midterm congressional elections, the two ends of Pennsylvania Avenue are at loggerheads. The Republican position is built on House Budget Committee Chairman Paul Ryan's proposals (Ryan, 2011), calling for $6.2 trillion in spending cuts over the next decade and bringing overall federal spending below 20 percent of GDP, having risen to 24 percent in 2010. Domestic spending would be cut to 2008 levels and frozen for five years, Medicare transformed into a voucher program, and Medicaid shifted to block grants to the states. Having staked a forward position on Medicare and Medicaid – and remembering George W. Bush's failures – the plan offers no reforms of Social Security. The Republican plan also would reform the tax code, reducing the top rates for individual and corporations, and closing various tax breaks and loopholes. The balance of adjustments fall on the spending side and, adopting supply side arguments, is premised on tax cuts increasing revenue by stimulating growth.

President Obama countered in April 2011 with a plan for $4 trillion in cuts over the next 12 years – despite having submitted a budget in December that increased spending and foresaw a $1.65 trillion deficit. Obama's proposed savings come mainly through cuts in discretionary domestic and defense spending, as well as raising revenue through repealing tax benefits aimed at upper income Americans. Republican Speaker John Boehner immediately declared tax increases a 'non-starter' (*Washington Post* (online edition), 14 April 2011). Also included is a proposed 'debt failsafe', a triggering mechanism that would automatically cut spending across the board if deficits are not stabilized by 2014 – but excluding Social Security, Medicare, and other programs for low-income Americans (Bloomberg (Online edition), 13 April 2011). Indeed, Obama's proposal offers no significant changes to the major entitlement programs other than some general proposals to seek greater efficiencies within Medicare.

The first skirmish in this war ended with an eleventh hour compromise in April 2011 to cut $38 billion from the fiscal year (FY) 2011 budget. The battle shifted in the summer to the need to raise the debt ceiling, which will be reached by August 2011. Conservative Republicans vowed to vote against this unless matched by serious deficit reductions. As of this writing, negotiations were ongoing.[5]

The final major element of recovery was the re-regulation of the financial system. With health care dominating the legislative agenda in Obama's first year, the Dodd-Frank Wall Street Reform and Consumer Protection Act was not passed until July 2010. Under this legislation the Federal Deposit Insurance Corporation (FDIC) is granted powers to unwind failing firms deemed a threat to financial stability. The Act also implemented a watered down version of the 'Volcker Rule' (named for former Fed Chairman Paul Volcker), intended to stop banks from proprietary trading (playing the market with their own money) and investing in hedge funds and private equity. Banks are also required to spin some riskier derivative swaps (commodity, equity, and non-investment grade credit contracts) off to separate affiliates (with higher capital margins) while retaining interest rate, exchange rate, and higher-quality credit swaps (*The Economist*, 2010, 3 July, p. 66). It also requires standardized derivatives to be traded through clearing houses. Customized derivatives are not so restricted. To better spot the onset of systemic risk, the bill creates a Financial Stability Oversight Council, headed up by the Treasury Secretary and the Chairman of the Federal Reserve. For consumers the Act also created a broadly empowered Consumer Financial Protection Bureau (CFPB) housed inside the Federal Reserve.[6]

The final bill was an unwieldy 2,319 pages, criticized for being both too restrictive and too permissive. If the problem was giant firms taking giant risks in unregulated markets, the law provides only a partial cure, putting limited constraints on reckless behavior and providing a loose structure for liquidation when things go bad. In reality, many of those 'too big to fail' firms are even bigger than before the crisis. For those who see government as the problem, the legislation has a massive omission: it does nothing with Fannie Mae and Freddie Mac. A February 2011 Treasury White Paper presented three options for the government's role in the mortgage market: limit it only to Federal Housing Authority loans (for poorer borrowers only); providing guarantees for mortgages, but only at market-competitive standards (for example, higher down-payments); or serve as an insurer of mortgages only for 'catastrophic downturns' in the market. But the final choice was kicked to Congress and any transition would take five to seven years at least (US Department of the Treasury, 2011). All three proposals foresee a substantial withdraw of the government from the mortgage market over the long term. Overall, the biggest issue with the Dodd-Frank Act is that nobody really knows how it will work. The legislation requires hundreds of rules to be written by dozens of agencies. How agencies will translate the legislation and what ability lobbyists have to blunt the process remains to be seen. Beyond this, a more Republican Congress will be less inclined to authorize funding for increased government regulation of financial markets, which may gut the rules regardless of how they are written.

In the UK, within the pre-crisis tripartite system, the Bank of England focused on macro-economic stability, the Treasury on the budget, and the FSA on individual financial institutions. Systemic risk fell between the cracks (HM Treasury, 2010a, p. 4). In the wake of the meltdown, the Labour government passed the Banking Act of 2009, giving the Bank a statutory obligation to maintain stability, managed by a new Financial Stability Committee and creating a Special Resolution Regime to allow authorities to manage distressed institutions (Bank of England website). For the Coalition government, these reforms did not go far enough (Hoban, 2010). In June 2010 they appointed an Independent Banking Commission headed by Sir John Vickers. The main issue for the Vickers's Commission is whether to separate retail and investment banking along the lines of the old US Glass-Steagall Act. Their final report is not due until September 2011, but an interim report in April suggested only putting a firewall between retail banking operations and riskier trading operations (Independent Commission on Banking, 2011), rather than formally breaking up universal banks.

In July 2010 the Treasury released a White Paper (HM Treasury, 2010a) outlining its other proposed reforms. The tripartite system, it argued, failed to identify problems as they were developing, did not mitigate them before dangerous instabilities built up, and had difficulty dealing with the crisis once it broke. To better identify and counter systemic threats – 'macro-prudential regulation' – the White Paper proposes creating a new Financial Policy Committee (FPC) chaired by the Governor of the Bank and made up mainly of Bank representatives. Operational responsibility for regulating individual banks was transferred from the FSA to a new Prudential Regulation Authority (PRA), also under the Bank. As the FSA was said to rely too heavily on 'tick-box' regulation rather than risk analysis, the PRA is intended to follow rules less and judgment more (HM Treasury, 2010a, p. 23). This structure combines macro- and micro-prudential regulation in the Bank, closing the gaps in responsibilities and giving regulators tools to ensure systemic stability, such as countercyclical capital requirements, capital buffers during upturns, leverage limits, and variable risk weights (HM Treasury, 2010a, pp. 15-16). Centering these controls in the Bank will additionally allow monetary policy and financial regulation to work together. As in the US, the Cameron government proposes creating a Consumer Protections and Markets Authority (CPMA) to take over the business regulation responsibilities of the FSA (itself being dissolved into the new PRA and CPMA). Following consultations, the new regulatory framework is not expected to be in place until the end of 2012, however.

Concurrent with national reforms are a new set of international rules, the so-called Basel III rules, which increase and tighten the definition of banks' capital requirements. This renders finance more solvent, but may reduce profitability and national growth. A 2011 OECD study estimated that the new requirements might reduce aggregate output by –0.05 per cent to –0.15 percent per annum (Slovnik and Cournède, 2011). Of greater concern is that banks moved into mortgage-backed securities because their lower risk-weight allowed them to reduce capital minima. The new rules leave risk-weights unchanged. As these rules are being phased through 2019, moreover, the details of implementation may substantially affect their actual impact.

Our current economic woes grew out of the financial sector. One would expect major reforms in response to the crisis. Nevertheless, neither Britain nor America attempted a major structural reform of finance. While there will be new limitations and controls, they do not look to be especially onerous. More importantly, given delays in rule-making and implementation, we will not know how any of this will really work until at least 2013.

The stability of Anglo-Saxon capitalism

In the homelands of neoliberalism, the financial crisis of 2008 produced the unthinkable: nationalization, market intervention, and a revival of Keynesianism. Given the scope and rapidity of this volte-face, it seemed an era had ended. Surveying the scene three years later, however, what is most striking is how little the political economies of the US and UK have changed. The retreat of the free market model appears to have been temporary.

This is quite a contrast from previous crises. The Great Depression saw the New Deal in the US, initiating a multi-decade rise in the scale and scope of the federal government. The Attlee Government went even farther, nationalizing major industries, undertaking demand management, and implementing cradle-to-grave welfare. The crisis of the 1930s thus moved the state to the center of economic management in both countries. As the postwar boom collapsed in the 1970s, the Thatcher and Reagan governments reversed course, arguing that the state *was* the problem and inaugurating three decades of neoliberal economic governance. However, if we look at the major policies in response to the 2008 crisis – bailing out the banks, fiscal and monetary stimulus, and financial market regulation – these are better described as ad hoc reactions in a moment of crisis rather than a coherent rejection of neoliberalism. The policies of Gordon Brown, George W. Bush, Barack Obama, and David Cameron have all in their own way sought to address the *specific* excesses of the recent past, not fundamentally restructure the political economy. The Obama administration may have run on 'change you can believe in', but they have not been able to deliver any structural change in American economic management. Even the health care plan has an uncertain fate. So far there is minimal indication that political elites in Britain and America are ready to abandon the core elements of a liberal market economy.

The same largely holds true for the general public, indicated first by the political success of the Conservatives and Republicans in post-crisis elections. In terms of economic attitudes, an October 2010 Rasmussen poll found that 75 percent of Americans think free markets are better than government management of the economy, with only 14 percent thinking government control of the economy is better (Rasmussen Reports, 2010).

The 2010 British Social Attitudes Survey showed a populace that was more economically conservative, less supportive of government spending and less supportive of policies of redistribution. Even among Labour supporters, only 49 percent still supported redistribution (*Guardian* (online edition), 26 January 2010). A clear majority (59 percent) supported the coalition's budget-cutting plans after they were first elected, although that support dropped to 48 percent a year later as cuts began in earnest (Ipsos MORI, 2011). It can only be suggested rather than substantiated here, but it appears that the liberal movement established an intellectual hegemony that, while shaken by the crisis, remains intact.

In policy terms the main hindrance to structural change is the parlous state of public finances. Having started the decade in excellent fiscal shape, the US and UK were overdrawn *before* the crisis broke. A high percentage of current deficits, moreover, are structural rather than cyclical and can only be tackled through reviewing basic spending commitments. A 2010 Congressional Budget Office report raised the alarm in rather stark terms (CBO, 2010b) and Moody's hinted at downgrading the US credit rating if the debt ceiling was not raised (*New York Times* (online edition), 2 June 2011) – a real economic danger given the number of Treasury bonds held in foreign hands. Economic policy in both states turns on finding ways to balance the books without squashing growth, a challenge at the forefront of British political debate. Even if expediency prevents them from making all of the cuts outlined, the Cameron government seems determined to stay the course on spending, a position reinforced – despite flat growth and rising inflation – by a supportive IMF report in June 2011. Riding the wave of midterm election success, the Republicans have the political initiative in the US, pushing the debate to how quickly, not whether, to cut spending. Even if the British and American governments had the means to expand their role, they lack the inclination. Despite the bailouts and nationalizations, the thrust of policies since then has been to disengage as expediently as possible. The majority of the bank bailout under TARP has been repaid. GM and Chrysler have restructured to the point of offering shares publicly and seeking to buy back shares held by the Treasury. By mid 2011 the Coalition government was actively seeking a private buyer for Northern Rock. Barring further systemic shocks, fiscal realities present substantial impediments to renewed state interventions for some time. In practice there has not been a broad shift in the economic management of either state.

At root crises of capitalism are political events and this crisis most assuredly impacted politics in both countries. Lehman collapsed just weeks before the 2008 presidential election, turning Obama's lead into a landslide. With solid majorities in both houses of Congress, Obama seemed poised for a Roosevelt-like first term. In terms of legislation, he was able to pass major initiatives: stimulus, health care, financial regulations. Yet the Obama administration made the political calculation that the stimulus package passed in their first weeks would induce recovery and turned their attention to health care, devoting an inordinate amount of time and political capital to that bill. The end product was a complicated mélange which lost popular support. Economic recovery meanwhile faltered, providing an opening for the Republicans. The result was one of the biggest midterm elections gains by an opposition party in American history, with the Republicans retaking the House. Both in Congress and on the presidential campaign trail, Republicans have coalesced again around the need to shrink the size of government. Regardless of what might happen in the 2012 elections, it is clear that the reformist moment of Obama's first term is over.

Gordon Brown portrayed himself a 'serious man for serious times', but his Labour Party governed during the collapse, ensuring a Labour defeat if not quite a Conservative victory in the 2010 general election. The electorate abandoned the party of socialism (itself having long abandoned socialism) in favor of the party of free markets (having shifted to the political center) – but not quite, forcing a coalition with the Liberal Democrats (themselves divided between liberal and social democratic wings). One year in, the coalition has held together, although not without fights, especially in regards to university tuition fees and the NHS. Cameron's ideas for a 'Big Society' present some intriguing possibilities for a social renovation, but they have yet to crystallize into coherent policies. Nor would they mean the abandonment of liberal economics. Labour for its part opted for the more left-wing leadership of Ed Miliband over his older and more Blairite brother David, but the younger Miliband has yet to make any significant inroads into the Conservatives' support.

In sum, the political sands in Britain and American have not shifted a great deal and, to the extent that they have, they have shifted more toward those parties and interests most likely to want to reduce the role of the state and revive the free market model.

A zombie named TINA

Many presumed that the 2008 financial crisis dealt a fatal blow to the Anglo-Saxon model capitalism. As the above analysis shows, however, neoliberalism is not dead yet. Popular culture presents us with a useful image of that deemed dead yet still animated: a zombie.[7] To paraphrase Karl Marx, there is a zombie haunting the Anglo-Saxon economies: a zombie named TINA. TINA, of course, is the acronym made famous by Mrs Thatcher to justify her policies: *There Is No Alternative*. The neoliberal model lives on, despite manifold declarations of death, primarily because there are no alternatives. Certainly there are calls for reforms and logical alternatives modes of economic organization. Nevertheless, no politically powerful forces have rallied behind a clearly articulated set of alternatives to free market capitalism in either Britain or America. More than anything else, liberal capitalism will revive in these states because the left has no coherent alternative growth model to offer that has any traction among the broader voting public. Some economists, especially Paul Krugman and Joseph Stiglitz, have pushed for an aggressive Keynesian response to the downturn. Yet Keynesianism is problematic in open economies ('leaky Keynesianism', as James puts it (2009, p. 216)), politically backward-looking, and, when applied post-crisis, has done little to revive growth. Calls for even greater stimulus have the air of a Great War general demanding just one more big push to achieve victory. A green growth model is certainly the most original option for progressive forces. This was, indeed, the first point listed in a letter sent to Chancellor Osborne by a group of left-leaning academic economist urging him to change course (*Guardian* (online edition), 6 June 2011). Fundamentally the purpose of green development, however, is to solve environmental problems not economic problems. The promise of a future full of green development and material prosperity – economies that are both clean *and* growing as rapidly as before – still seems a long way off, if it is even viable. Without being able to deliver policies without material trade-offs, green growth alternatives continue to offer a limited electoral appeal. This crisis of capitalism, in short, has yet to produce a counter-liberal coalition in either Britain or America, let alone one that has maneuvered to a position of electoral success. Mrs Thatcher's axiom still rings true, at least for now.

Notes

1. Economist John Taylor's 'rule' predicts the optimal short-term interest rate based on levels of inflation and output.
2. A loan is deemed subprime because, for whatever reason, it is a greater credit risk. For example, if a standard (prime) loan requires a 20 percent down payment (hence a 'loan to value' (LTV) ratio of 80 percent), mortgages requiring 10, 5 or 0 percent down would be considered subprime. By 2000, Fannie and Freddie were buying mortgages with 100 percent LTV ratios (Wallison, 2009a, p. 370).

3. Standing for 'Alternative A-paper', a mortgage whose risk is between prime and subprime.
4. A bank would thus have to maintain $8 in capital for every $100 of commercial loans, $4 for every $100 in mortgages, and $0 capital reserves for government bonds. With their 20 percent risk weight, mortgage-backed securities required $1.60 in capital for every $100 put into MBSs.
5. Both sides largely ignored the recommendations of the bipartisan debt commission headed by Republican Alan Simpson and Democrat Erskine Bowles calling for a mix of spending cuts, tax increases, and moderate entitlement reform (for example, increasing the Social Security retirement age).
6. Controversy erupted with the appointment of Elizabeth Warren to head of the new CFPB as a 'special adviser' to the president rather than as the formal head, skirting the constitutional necessity of submitting her to nomination hearings or requiring her to report directly to Congress.
7. Zombies have broken out of the horror genre, invading popular comedies like *Shaun of the Dead* and *Zombieland*, as well as reworking classic literature, most notably Seth Grahame-Smith's *Pride, Prejudice and Zombies*. Even scholars have gotten into the act, with books like *Zombie Economics* (Quiggin, 2010) and *Zombie Capitalism* (Harman, 2010), Daniel Drezner's 'Night of the Living Wonks' in the July/August 2010 *Foreign Policy* explained how different international relations theories would handle a zombie apocalypse.

References

Acharya, Viral V., and Matthew Richardson (2009) 'Causes of the Financial Crisis' *Critical Review*, 21(2–3), 195–210.

Coates, David (2010) 'Separating Sense from Nonsense in the US Debate on the Financial Meltdown', *Political Studies Review*, 8(1), 15–26.

Congressional Budget Office (2010) *Federal Debt and the Risk of a Fiscal Crisis*, 27 July (Washington, DC: CBO).

The Economist (2010) 'Not All on the Same Page', 3 July, pp. 65–7.

Friedman, Jeffrey (2009) 'A Crisis of Politics, Not Economics: Complexity, Ignorance, and Policy Failure', *Critical Review*, 21(2–3), 127–83.

Gamble, Andrew (2009a) *The Spectre at the Feast: Capitalist Crisis and the Politics of Recession* (Basingstoke: Palgrave Macmillan).

Gamble, Andrew (2009b) 'British Politics and the Financial Crisis', *British Politics*, 4(4), 450–62.

Gjerstad, Steven, and Vernon L. Smith (2009) 'Monetary Policy, Credit Extension, and Housing Bubbles: 2008 and 1929', *Critical Review*, 21(2–3), 269–300.

Greenspan, Alan (1997) 'Fostering Financial Innovation: The Role of Government', in James Dorn (ed.), *The Future of Money in the Information Age* (Washington, DC: Cato Institute), pp. 45–51.

Grunwald, Michael (2010) 'How the Stimulus is Changing America', *Time* (online edition), 26 August, accessed 26 August 2010.

Hall, Peter A., and David Soskice (eds) (2001) *Varieties of Capitalism: The Institutional Foundations of Comparative Advantage* (New York: Oxford University Press).

Haldane, Andrew (2010) 'The Contribution of the Financial Sector: Miracle or Mirage?' 'Speech given at the 'Future of Finance' Conference, 14 July.

Harman, Chris (2010) *Zombie Capitalism: Global Crisis and the Relevance of Marx* (Chicago: Haymarket Books).

HM Treasury (2010a) *A New Approach to Financial Regulation: Judgment, Focus and Stability*. Cm7874 (London: The Stationery Office).

HM Treasury (2010b) Public Sector Finances Databank, 21 July, www.hm-treasury. gov.uk/psf_statistics.htm, accessed 22 August 2010.

Hoban, Mark (2010) Speech by the Financial Secretary to the Treasury at the London Stock Exchange, 26 July.

Independent Commission on Banking (Vickers Commission) (2011) Interim Report, April.

Ipsos Mori (2011) 'The Budget 2011' www.ipsos-mori.com/Assets/Docs/Polls/ Budget2011briefing.PDF, accessed 3 June 2011.

Jablecki, Juliusz, and Mateusz Machaj (2009) 'The Regulated Meltdown of 2008', *Critical Review*, 21(2–3), 301–28.

James, Harold (2009) *The Creation and Destruction of Value: The Globalization Cycle* (Cambridge, MA: Harvard University Press).

McKinsey Global Institute (2010) *Debt and Deleveraging: The Global Credit Bubble and its Economic Consequences* (McKinsey).

Moran, Michael (2009) *Business, Politics, and Society: An Anglo-American Comparison* (Oxford: Oxford University Press).

OECD (2011) *Economic Outlook 89* (Paris: OECD).

Office of National Statistics (2011) *Public Sector Finances* (Statistical Bulletin), April (London: ONS).

Posner, Richard (2009) *A Failure of Capitalism: The Crisis of '08 and the Descent into Depression* (Cambridge, MA: Harvard University Press).

Quiggin, John (2010) *Zombie Economics: How Dead Ideas Still Walk Among Us* (Princeton: Princeton University Press).

Reinhart, Carmen M., and Kenneth S. Rogoff (2009) *This Time is Different: Eight Centuries of Financial Folly* (Princeton: Princeton University Press).

Ryan, Paul (2011) *The Path to Prosperity: Restoring America's Promise*, House Committee on the Budget, Fiscal Year 2012 Budget Resolution (Washington, DC: GPO).

Slovik, Patrick, and Boris Cournède (2011) 'Macroeconomic Impact of Basel III', OECD Economics Department Working Papers, No. 844 (Paris: OECD).

Taylor, John B. (2009) *Getting Off Track: How Government Actions and Interventions Caused, Prolonged, and Worsened the Financial Crisis* (Stanford, CA: Hoover Institution Press).

US Department of the Treasury (2010) *Troubled Asset Relief Program: Two Year Retrospective* October (Washington: GPO).

US Department of the Treasury (2011) *Reforming America's Housing Finance Market: A Report to Congress* (Washington: GPO).

Wallison, Peter J. (2009a) 'Cause and Effect: Government Policies and the Financial Crisis', *Critical Review*, 21(2–3), 365–76.

Wallison, Peter J. (2009b) 'Credit Default Swaps are Not to Blame', *Critical Review*, 21(2–3), 377–87.

Weale, Martin (2009) 'Growth Prospects in the Financial Sector', *National Institute Economic Review*, 207, January, 4–9.

White, Lawrence J. (2009) 'The Credit-Rating Agencies and the Sub-Prime Debacle', *Critical Review*, 21(2–3), 389–99.

4
A Tale of Two Cities:[1] Financial Meltdown and the Atlantic Divide

David Coates and Kara Dickstein

The 2008 financial meltdown was a genuinely global affair. By the time it was over, the global banking system had lost up to $4.1 trillion of its value, the world fiscal deficit had risen from 2 percent to over 10 percent, and economies worldwide had seen a spike in unemployment that totaled at least 50 million (Skidelsky, 2009, pp. 13–16). These enormous numbers stand comparison to those generated by the depression of the 1930s, and like that depression, the one which began in 2008 threw a long global shadow. But the shadow was not the same everywhere. It was deepest where the crisis originated and the meltdown first occurred – in the United States and the United Kingdom. And even where it was deepest, there we can still see significant variations of gray. The purpose of this chapter is to chart and explain both the shadow and the variation.

US financial meltdown

The credit crisis began in the US housing market in 2006 and 2007. After a decade in which house prices had effectively doubled and in which many homeowners had remortgaged their houses to sustain high levels of immediate consumption, two Bear Stearns hedge funds heavily engaged with subprime loans unexpectedly collapsed in July 2007. Concern then spread rapidly through the entire US financial system about the widespread sale of such loans to house buyers on low incomes, and about the associated danger of a foreclosure tsunami; and with good reason. In 2001 new subprime and home equity loans had totaled $330 billion, just 15 percent of all new residential mortgages. Five years later the equivalent figures were $1.4 trillion and 48 percent of all new residential mortgages. This would not have mattered – outside the housing sector at least – had not these mortgages also been securitized. But they had. Securities collateralized by mortgages increased in the US financial system from $18.5 billion in 1995 to $507.9 billion in 2005. The two dates were divided by what the President's Working Group on Financial Markets called 'a dramatic weakening of underwriting standards for US subprime mortgages' (Winant, 2008). That weakening was so dramatic that by November 2007 Merrill Lynch was obliged to write off $8 billion in losses on mortgage-backed securities, and by the end of 2008 one house in ten in the United States was either in or on the edge of foreclosure (Coates, 2010a, p. 231).

This deepening foreclosure crisis spread rapidly through the entire US banking and insurance system, leaving key players unsure about their own viability and the viability of others, and bringing down a number of leading US financial institutions. 2008 witnessed first the January sale to Bank of America of Countrywide Financial (the main private provider of subprime loans) followed in September by the seizure by federal regulators of Washington Mutual, the nation's largest Savings & Loan institution. The complete collapse of Bear Stearns followed in March 2008 and then, in a single terrifying week in September, the swallowing up of Merrill Lynch by Bank of America, the first of many Treasury bailouts of insurance giant AIG, and the allowed collapse of Lehman Brothers. The spreading financial crisis broke the confidence of banks in each other, and dried up the supply of credit from bank to bank, and from bank to consumer. What had begun as a financial problem in the housing market then rapidly became a credit-shortage problem for firms and households alike. The US gross domestic product (GDP) fell at an annualized rate of 6.2 percent in the last quarter of 2008, a year in which 2.6 million Americans lost their jobs. 2009 was worse – 6 million more jobs gone, including 1.2 million lost in the US manufacturing sector. The Federal Reserve cut interest rates effectively to zero in a vain attempt to blunt the recession, yet the US economy still moved into recession in December 2007 and stayed there throughout 2008 and the first half of 2009.

The initial Bush administration response to difficulties in the US housing market was simply to allow market forces to play themselves out. The Republican administration's initial argument was that 'a federal bailout of lenders would only encourage a recurrence of the problem. It is not the government's job', President Bush said in September 2007, 'to bail out speculators or those who made the decision to buy a home they knew they could never afford' (*Financial Times*, 1–2 September 2007, p. 2). As mortgage lenders themselves then began to default, the

Bush administration initially restricted itself to quietly orchestrating private-sector rescues designed to contain the spreading fire. Only at the eleventh hour did the Bush administration see the need for unprecedented public intervention; but when it did, it went in for bailouts on the grandest of scales. The two main Government Sponsored Enterprises (GSEs), Fannie Mae and Freddie Mac, were already in federal hands by the time Lehman Brothers fell, taken into full 'conservatorship' (that is, effectively nationalized) by the hitherto entirely free-market Republican administration. The subsequent response of Treasury Secretary Hank Paulson to the September 2008 credit crisis was a $700 billion rescue package aimed at locating and absorbing mortgage-backed securities whose value was in freefall. The Troubled Asset Relief Program (TARP) bill that passed early in October 2008 included a congressionally-imposed $150 billion of tax breaks, limits on executive pay in bailed-out companies, and powers to ease mortgage terms to prevent foreclosure. Paulson used TARP money in the last months of the Bush administration not to buy toxic assets (quickly finding and valuing them proved too difficult) but to recapitalize commercial and investment banks, and the largest of the insurance companies and hedge funds, hoping in that way to restore inter-bank confidence and the large-scale flow of credit again.

By the time the Obama administration came to power, the US Treasury had made available $125 billion in aid to nine major banks, an additional $125 billion to smaller banks and an extra $40 billion to AIG. Alongside the moves to stabilize individual institutions, monetary policy too quietly eased, with Federal Reserve-financed injections of yet more credit guarantees and central bank-orchestrated expansion programs for the financial industry worldwide. $900 billion in loans to banks was made available by the Federal Reserve as early as December 2007, followed by a further $250 billion in March 2008 to encourage mortgage lending, $29 billion to smooth the sale of Bear Stearns to JPMorgan Chase in March 2008, eventually $123.8 billion to bail out AIG, $620 billion in October to help foreign central banks trade foreign currency for dollars, $1.8 trillion to buy commercial paper, and $540 billion to buy assets from money market mutual funds short of cash – these last two again in October 2008. In the last 15 months of the Bush presidency, breathtaking amounts of money were poured into the financial system on a regular basis to keep institutions viable and credit creation intact.

The incoming Obama administration quickly followed up on all four fronts of the crisis: housing, banking, unemployment and global recovery. On the *housing* front, and sharply reversing the Paulson policy of not using TARP money to directly help struggling mortgage holders, within a month of being in office the Obama administration put aside $75 billion of the bank bailout fund to help up to 4 million homeowners renegotiate their primary mortgages. That same month, the administration put an extra $200 billion into Fannie Mae and Freddie Mac, and then later (Christmas Eve 2009) quietly announced that the Treasury would provide unlimited financial assistance to both the main GSEs. By that point too, the Federal Reserve (with administration support) had purchased from Fannie and Freddie hundreds of millions of dollars of mortgage-backed securities, with the ultimate aim of owning $1.25 trillion of such securities.

The *banking* story was more complicated: a matter of initial support and long-term regulation. The administration continued the Bush policy of giving TARP loans to major institutions: in March 2009 taking up to a 36 percent stake in Citigroup and making a fourth injection of capital into AIG; and in May putting TARP money into six major insurance companies. TARP money was still being distributed, to GMAC among others, as late as December 2009, although by then other temporary support measures were being allowed to expire on schedule. Individual bank bailouts were supplemented during the early months of the Obama administration by a three-month-long stress test to establish the financial viability of 19 major US banks; and by the launch of a toxic assets plan that had the Treasury partially financing a series of public-private investment funds to buy up unwanted mortgage-backed securities. New legislation to tighten federal and state regulation of US financial institutions took much longer to implement: first proposed by the Obama administration in May 2009, financial reform was finally enacted in July 2010. That legislation created, among other things, a new financial stability oversight council and a consumer protection bureau, and new rules on derivatives trading (details in Coates, 2010b).

What the Obama administration brought new to the table, when compared to its Republican predecessor, was a *stimulus package* aimed at alleviating the general recessionary impact of the credit crisis. The $787 billion American Recovery and Reinvestment Act included $276 billion in tax cuts for low- and middle-income Americans and for small businesses, and over $500 billion in a series of spending programs. The Obama White House rendered specific assistance to the US auto industry, even taking partial temporary ownership of GM; and like the Bush administration in its brief post-crisis moment, continued to press other major industrial economies to adopt similarly loose fiscal and monetary policy. US pressure for fiscal largesse met increasing resistance over time, particularly from the German government. In 2008, every major government had briefly been fiscally liberal. By 2010 that was no longer the case.

UK contagion

As in the US, the financial problems experienced in the UK in 2008–09 had their domestic origins in the local housing market where – as in America – subprime mortgage loans had become increasingly common and mortgage-backed securitization had been accompanied by declining underwriting standards (Stephens and Quilgars, 2008, pp. 199 and 205). In the UK as in the US, as more people received loans to finance home purchases, the demand for homes had increased and house prices had soared. By 2007, the total value of housing assets in the UK was 3.5 times as large as the total value of housing debt. In London as in New York, housing and finance markets had become intertwined as consumers borrowed more based on their home equity, and as lending secured on dwellings had drastically increased. The warning bells of an impending financial crash began to sound in the UK just after they were heard in the US. In September 2007, Northern Rock, a mortgage lender, was forced to turn to the Bank of England for cash. When banks increased the cost of inter-bank lending in response to concerns about bad loans in the US, the inter-bank money markets on which Northern Rock depended for funding dried up. Concerns about Northern Rock's liquidity led to a run on the bank, the country's first in more than a century.

Initially Northern Rock seemed to be a localized and isolated problem caused by a reckless business model; over time, however, as US-exported uncertainty hit the inter-bank lending markets in London, lending by UK-based banks and building societies occurred more slowly and at higher interest rates for both banks and consumers. Demand for houses decreased and the price of homes fell, cutting into the equity on which consumers had heavily borrowed. Climbing interest rates for consumers increased the pain of homeowners and debtors who had to pay off their various loans. Repossessions began to rise, and increasing numbers of borrowers began to default on their loans. As in the US, securitization then spread these problems to even more institutions. September 2008 was a traumatic month in London no less than in New York. Amid the blows to their finances and the growing uncertainty, London-based banks also began to shut their doors to new mortgage customers and to decrease their loan availability. The frozen banking system and resulting lending slump led to a credit crunch in the UK which affected not only the ability of consumers to borrow and spend but also the ability of firms to obtain the funding necessary for their growth. So, as in America, unemployment rapidly rose in the UK, from 5.3 percent in 2007 to 7.6 percent in 2009. UK GDP declined at an annualized rate of 2.8 percent in the last quarter of 2008 and by 3.7 percent in 2009. The Bank of England cut its interest rates in an attempt to stimulate the economy; however, it did so more slowly than the Federal Reserve. While the Bank incrementally decreased its rates from 5.75 percent in December 2007 to 0.5 percent in March 2009, the rates were still as high as 3 percent in November 2008, and the economic contraction, despite rate cuts, lasted throughout 2009.

Unlike the Bush administration, the Brown government never left the resolution of the UK's growing financial and economic problems simply to market forces. Instead, the members of the tripartite arrangement[2] took action even before the crisis of September 2008. They addressed the looming failures of important lending institutions, prevented further bank runs by protecting depositors' funds, and worked to restore liquidity and encourage lending. Only days after the run on Northern Rock, the Treasury guaranteed all of the bank's deposits. After several failed attempts to find a private buyer for the bank, Northern Rock was officially taken under temporary public ownership in February 2008. The New Labour government also orchestrated a rescue takeover of HBOS by Lloyds Banking Group in September 2008, and took Bradford & Bingley into partial public ownership. In November 2008, the government took a majority share in the Royal Bank of Scotland (RBS): that stake was later increased to 68 percent in return for the bank's pledge to extend more loans.

The Bank of England began its Special Liquidity Scheme (SLS) as early as April 2008, lending banks £50 billion in government bonds in return for collateral in the form of the banks' high-quality mortgage-backed and other securities. In October 2008, the Treasury began a recapital-ization scheme, initially purchasing £25 billion of Tier 1 capital from eligible institutions and spending a further £25 billion on preference shares. Through this scheme, the government invested £37 billion into RBS and HBOS/Lloyds. The government also proposed a £200 billion extension of the SLS, created a £250 billion credit guarantee scheme, and cut fees to banks in an effort to stimulate their lending. In February 2009, the Brown government proposed an Asset Protection Scheme (APS) through which the Treasury would underwrite a bank's toxic assets in return for an agreement to lend more to homeowners and businesses. In addition to pouring public funds into the bailout and assistance of banks, in October 2007 the government extended depositor protection to guarantee the first £35,000 of a depositor's savings. A year later, this guarantee was increased to cover the first £50,000 of savings. As in the

US, UK monetary policy was also eased to restore liquidity and encourage credit creation. In September 2007, the Bank of England announced that it would inject £10 billion into the money market to bring down the cost of inter-bank lending, and in December 2007, it participated in a coordinated international move by five major central banks to inject £50 billion into world money markets. In March 2009, the Bank of England began its Asset Purchase Programme (APP), or quantitative easing policy. The APP began at £75 billion. In August 2009, it was expanded to £175 billion, and it became £200 billion by 2010.

Additionally, the Brown government took medium- to long-term measures on the same four fronts on which the Obama administration also moved: housing, banking, the global recovery and the role of government stimulus. Far less was done in the UK than in the US directly to assist *housing*. In one of his few measures to help the housing market, the New Labour Chancellor, Alistair Darling, raised the value of residential property to which stamp duty land tax would apply, first to £175,000 in 2008 and then to £250,000 in 2010. In 2008, New Labour pressed major mortgage providers to extend the minimum period before commencing repossession and provided help to the unemployed with interest payments on their mortgages. In April 2009, New Labour also introduced a modest Homeowners Mortgage Support Scheme which, though directly helping only 34 households in its first year, was widely credited with 'a positive impact on mortgage arrears management, encouraging greater patience from lenders when borrowers missed payments' (Land, 2010). In contrast, the new Conservative–Liberal Democrat Coalition government elected late in the crisis (May 2010) capped housing benefits, scrapped regional house-building targets and reduced the housing budget. On the *banking* front, in August 2009 the Financial Services Authority (FSA) mandated that bankers' pay deals be linked more closely to their banks' long-term profitability. In November 2009, Darling required banks such as RBS and Lloyds to create and eventually sell new banks from their existing branch networks. In December 2009, the Treasury implemented a one-off punitive supertax of over 50 percent of bankers' bonuses; and in February 2011, bonuses for the directors of bailed-out banks were deferred over three years and restricted to shares. Both Darling and his Coalition successor, George Osborne, examined the efficacy of the tripartite regime. While Darling did not plan to change its fundamental structure, Osborne quickly transferred many of the FSA's powers to the Bank of England, essentially stripping the FSA of its responsibility and ending the tripartite system. In June 2010, Osborne announced a 0.04 percent tax of bank balance sheets, which would begin in 2011 and increase to 0.07 percent in

2012. He also presided over the successful participation of four UK banks in the European stress tests. Finally, in July, the Coalition government announced plans eventually to sell its state-controlled banking assets and to allow several of New Labour's liquidity schemes to be withdrawn in 2012 as planned.

The approach of the Coalition government to the question of *global recovery* differed from those of its New Labour predecessor and the Obama administration. While New Labour ministers had often spoken of the danger of ending fiscal stimulus programs prematurely, the Conservative Chancellor quickly joined the dominant voice within the European Union (EU) which was promoting a turn to fiscal moderation. These divergent views are illustrated by the differences in the measures taken by the two governments to *stimulate* the UK economy. In November 2008 New Labour launched a significant economic stimulus package: £20 billion of tax cuts and government spending. This followed a call by Brown for governments around the world to adopt similar measures, a call which briefly earned the beleaguered prime minister wide praise in financial circles on both sides of the Atlantic. In contrast, Osborne's first move was a £40 billion austerity budget that cut welfare spending, increased value added tax (VAT) to 20 percent and imposed a £2 billion levy on banks and building societies. As UK politics moved right, fiscal restraint became the new route to economic growth in the UK, the kind of fiscal restraint favored in the US by the Republican Party.

Similarities and differences

Housing

Herman Schwartz places both the US and UK in the 'liberal market' quadrant of his comparative typology of housing systems (Schwartz, 2008, p. 268). Liberal market systems share certain characteristics: relatively high levels of private ownership, relatively high levels of mortgage debt in relation to GDP, easy and relatively cheap refinancing of mortgages, and a significant degree of securitization of mortgage loans. In such housing systems, 'people are likely to see housing as a form of investment to a greater degree than in systems dominated by socially provided rentals' (Schwartz and Seabrooke, 2008, p. 244) of the sort common elsewhere in much of western Europe. Three shared features of the two housing markets stand out as particularly significant here: regulatory changes prior to the crisis, growing securitization and house price inflation. In the years leading up to the housing bubble, both countries experienced a shift from more regulated mortgage providers to private mortgage providers which were not bound by the same regulatory standards.[3] In the US, 'at its peak in 2005, more than $1.1 trillion in residential mortgage-backed securities were issued and sold to investors' (Zandi, 2009, p. 116), 40 percent of which were subprime and near-prime loans. In the UK a third of all new mortgages contracted between the second quarter of 2005 and the third quarter of 2007 were similarly subprime or near-prime. In the US, house prices which had been virtually flat for four decades prior to 1995 then effectively doubled in a decade. In the UK, the pattern of house prices was more volatile over time, but similarly exploded in the years following financial deregulation.

There were and remain significant differences on both the demand and supply sides of each housing market. The supply-side differences are the more visible. The UK is a small island with a large population, extensive planning controls and limited building land; by contrast, except in its urban centers, the US is not. The supply of housing in the latter in the last decade has been far more buoyant than it has in the former. 'Between 2001 and 2006, the United States built more new homes than would have been required by the growth in its population. In contrast, countries such as … the United Kingdom … barely managed to build enough homes to keep up with growth in the number of households' (Ellis, 2008, p. 3). On the demand side, the manner in which house purchases are financed in the two economies also differs. There is no tradition in the UK of the US fixed-rate 30-year amortized mortgage of the kind generalized by Fannie Mae; the purchase of most UK houses is still financed through bank/building society-provided adjustable-rate mortgages of variable length. In addition, the tax regimes in the two systems are very different. The UK phased out tax relief on mortgage interest payments in the 1980s, the very time that the US was extending tax relief to take in not simply first mortgages but also second ones. The UK levies a substantial stamp duty on house purchases; in the US, such taxation occurs only at the state level and is generally lighter. There was no UK equivalent to the US Savings & Loan crisis of the late 1980s; rather, there was a slow and incremental demutualization of UK building societies, made possible by the 1986 Building Societies Act. In the run-up to the crisis, the UK housing market had a lower level of subprime lending than did the US housing market; and after the crisis (and in spite of its more onerous tax regime) the UK initially saw a more rapid return to stable or rising house prices.

Finance

There are striking similarities between New York and London as financial centers, and very strong linkages between the two. US-owned and headquartered financial institutions have a real presence in the City of London; British banks are minor but real players in New York. In both economies, the financial sector is a key contributor to GDP, a key conduit of foreign (and bountiful) investment flows, and a key contributor to the trade balance. Both financial centers experienced systematic deregulation in the years after 1980. Both came to be dominated by a handful of major institutions (commercial banks, investment banks, hedge funds and insurance companies) committed to organizational growth and enhanced profits. These were institutions that were increasingly involved in (and actively hungry for) the buying and selling of mortgage-backed securities, and ever more linked together in a shadow banking network of new financial instruments operating below the regulatory radar. In both financial centers, cultures developed of banking superiority, high and expanded bonus payments, and increasingly breathless speculation. At the start of the crisis, each financial center contained rogue institutions that had allowed themselves to become excessively leveraged. At the start of the crisis too, each financial center contained institutions that were considered both too big to fail and yet too insolvent to continue without government assistance. At the end of the crisis – and in large measure because of that assistance – each financial center, to differing degrees, contained institutions that were even bigger (and so even less able safely to be allowed to fail), that were once more extremely profitable, were paying out generous bonuses to senior staff and were resisting calls for tighter financial regulation.

Though the relationship between New York and London as financial centers is a close one, it is in no sense an equal one. Nor are the regulatory structures and philosophies operative in each exactly the same. In a very real sense the US exported the financial crisis of 2008, and the UK imported it. It is true that many UK financial institutions were enthusiastic importers of US-generated financial instruments; but it remains the case that the instruments they imported were US-made. It was subprime mortgage securitization from the US housing market, not from the UK housing market, that infected the global (including the London) financial networks with toxic assets in the years up to 2008. It was US-based credit-rating agencies that gave those assets Triple-A ratings they did not warrant. It was major US financial institutions that drove the subprime frenzy; and it was US-based companies (especially Lehman Brothers and AIG) who were key players in the escalation of leverage rates to unsustainable heights in London no less than in New York. UK banks were not innocent in the process. Most followed suit. Some, like Northern Rock, followed suit with internally generated enthusiasm.

The Northern Rock business model was voluntarily adopted though still Lehman-backed. But the space within which to develop and generalize that business model, and in which to enshrine a culture of speculation and high-risk profit taking, was far greater in the US than in the UK. It was far greater partly because, in the US, the regulatory structure was so complex relative to the single UK oversight exercised by the FSA. It was also far greater because – though light regulation was the norm in both cities – the people heading the US regulatory agencies were *so* committed to regulating with only the lightest of touches. In the US, as the FSA was being empowered in London, Congress was dismantling Glass-Steagall and even the Clinton administration was declining to regulate the new financial products then emerging.

Crisis and responses

In both the US and UK, the period of rising house prices and thriving financial institutions came to a definite end during a shared September 2008 shock. At this time, house prices fell, inter-bank lending rates rose, repossessions and defaults on loans increased, and a credit-crunch ensued as lending slowed. These conditions led to a serious destabilization of the banking system, and triggered a common set of policy responses that were simultaneously institutional, fiscal and monetary. On the institutional front, policy-makers in both countries exhibited a shared willingness to save the banking system from collapse by guaranteeing bank deposits, buying toxic assets, recapitalizing banks and subjecting them to stress tests. On the fiscal front, policy-makers in both countries proposed big initial spending programs – quickly in the UK, slightly later in the US. On the monetary front, both central banks cut interest rates and utilized internal and globally coordinated quantitative easing. In addition to these common political responses, which were initially geared toward the national and global stabilization of the banking system, the countries experienced a common popular response. Both saw growing antagonism to bankers, increased calls for tighter regulation, and an at least temporary acceptance of the key role of public policy in lifting the economies out of recession. These popular responses propelled further reforms, as policymakers worked to create new regulatory structures, to rekindle economic growth and job creation, and to deal with soaring levels of public debt.

Yet because the underlying dynamic of the crisis was so fundamentally different in the two economies, the policy response that it generated differed too: differed in width, differed in sequence and differed in trajectory. In the UK, as we have just seen, much of the financial crisis was imported into the banking system via the purchase of US financial products. The housing problems in the UK made the crisis worse, certainly, but the housing market did not create the financial crisis to the same extent that it did in the US. Policy was therefore *narrower* in the UK; since housing was not as central to the crisis, UK policy was less focused on the foreclosure dimension than was policy in the US. The *sequence* of immediate policy responses also varied in the two countries: the UK went from bank guarantees to recapitalization, to nationaliza-tion, to toxic asset isolation, to stress tests, to bank surcharges, to belated minor regulatory change. While the US also began with bank guarantees, policy there focused on absorption of toxic assets before sequentially turning to recapitalization, stress tests, bank surcharges, and eventually, extensive re-regulation. The US saved its banking system (though not its housing finance system) without nationalization; the UK did not. Finally, the *trajectory* of policy differed between the two. While both countries were initially committed to fiscal stimuli, the UK now definitely is not. The Obama administration's current fiscal strategy is less clear, though it definitely remains opposed to the austerity budget strategies favored by both the Coalition government in London and its Republican opponents in Washington, DC.

Shaping forces

Similarities

Both economies shared a level of exposure to the impact of the credit crisis which set them apart from other major economies. All major economies were affected – the crisis was genuinely global – but none were affected so deeply as the US and UK. All were (through their banking systems) to some degree culpable, but none were as responsible as the US (and the UK) for the origins and dissemination of the crisis. So there is something special and different about the modern US and UK economies that set them apart. Superficially, the similarity seems rooted in a shared growth model, one anchored in debt. The US, for its part, has known two sustained periods of economic growth in the post-war era. The first, from 1948 to 1973, rested on a capital-labor accord that regularly raised the wages of blue-collar unionized northern male workers. It was a growth model based on rising labor productivity and strong internal sources of consumer demand. The second, from 1992 to 2008, was similarly based on rising labor productivity, but this time growing income inequality (and weak labor unions) left internal consumer demand dependent on rising levels of personal debt (Coates, 2010a). The slightly more sustained UK growth experience from 1992 to 2008 contained a stronger internal wage dynamic, but it too ultimately depended for its capacity to raise living standards on the willingness and ability of people to deploy (via credit) wages they had not yet earned. By 2009, the volume of consumer credit outstanding in the US had reached $2.48 trillion. By June 2010, total UK personal debt stood at £1.46 trillion – the consumer credit part being £218 billion. In such a context of debt, it is hardly surprising that any substantial expansion of home ownership should require subprime lending, or that the growing wealth of the financial sector should have become such a source of popular resentment.

The ability of people to borrow on this scale tells us that the financial institutions in each economy had grown to play a critical intermediating role between producers and consumers. The growing weight of finance relative to manufacturing was similarly marked in both economies: outsourcing and the decline of home-based manufacturing was a feature of both. But banks cannot lend what they do not first borrow: and the other common feature of the financial institutions in both economies was their enhanced capacity to do this. That capacity was itself partly the result of growing income inequality – the accumulation of surpluses by the super-rich had to be put somewhere. But mainly the capacity of Washington/New York and London to attract capital was the product of the global role played now by the US and previously by the UK as imperial powers. Foreign capital flowed into the US in vast volume in the years after 9/11. It flowed into London in smaller amounts, but still far more plentifully than into Frankfurt or Tokyo. It was when it stopped flowing – when confidence broke down in September 2008 – that the crisis began; and because it was into the US and UK that foreign investment funds had flowed so easily, the impact there was disproportionately great.

Money flows of this volume made the creation and proliferation of ever more complex financial instruments both possible and profitable. The flows also kept interest rates disproportionately low, helping to fuel the housing boom and the purchase of houses by people further and further down the increasingly unequal income ladder. The flows were a response to a new global pattern of surplus and deficit through which the US and UK became major debtor economies. The US quite simply followed a path which the UK had trodden long before. It stopped being the manufacturing center of the global system. Instead, the US became the world's consumer of last resort and the system's dominant borrower. In 2006, the US's current account deficit was $857 billion. The UK's was $68 billion – far smaller than that of the US but still qualitatively inferior to the current account surpluses of established economies like Germany and Japan and of the new emerging giants (China in particular). Oil economies and export-led growth economies drew revenues to themselves. Those revenues flowed back as foreign investment to the US and UK. The US and UK became debt-soaked, functioning at their existing levels of output and consumption only so long as the flows continued. In September 2008, briefly, those flows stopped.

Differences

Despite the above similarities between the US and UK, their different experiences during and after the financial crisis were shaped by undeniable variations between the two countries. These variations come on several levels: political, economic, and global.

Some accidental political differences arose as the crisis unfolded, the source of these differences being the timing of the crisis in relation to the electoral cycles in the two countries. In the US, a presidential election took place just as the crisis was hitting its stride; this election placed a moderate center-left government into power in Washington, replacing a more conservative party. In the UK, in contrast, such a moderate center-left government was replaced late in the crisis by a center-right one. Thus at different stages, the trajectory of policy changed course, leading the US to go slightly 'left' during the crisis, and the UK slightly 'right'. These changes indicate the popular dissatisfaction in both countries with the governments that were perceived to have steered the country into crisis in the first place. The political differences between the two countries also had deeper institutional and historical roots which affected the speed and focus of the policy measures enacted. The US and UK have completely different political systems: one is federal, the other is non-federal; one is presidential, the other is parliamentary. The non-federal, parliamentary system in the UK was bound to generate a greater coherence and speed of policy implementation than any of which the US was capable. Furthermore, the center of gravity of political debates varies either side of the Atlantic. While the legitimacy of a statist response to a crisis is a common dimension of UK conservative thought, it is not heavily present in American conservatism. The US political debate contains a libertarian strand of argument which does not appear in the UK (again, allowing state intervention to be more acceptable in the latter country), while the UK must consider the voice and policy measures of the EU as the US need not.

Both economies are post-industrial, in the sense that service employment and output have long replaced manufacturing as the key source of GDP growth and labor utilization. UK manufacturing employment peaked at 8.6 million in 1966, and is now in the region of 4 million. The US peaked later – at 19.6 million in 1979 – but is also now down: to 11.7 million. But finance still makes a significantly smaller contribution to US GDP than to UK GDP – 8 percent in one, perhaps as high as 30 percent in the other – it is the UK and not the US that has acquired what Vince Cable called 'the Icelandic disease': an over-reliance on finance that makes City success so critical to overall government performance (Cable, 2009, p. 164). Certainly City concerns were evident in the UK's maintenance of higher interest rates than those ruling in Frankfurt and New York prior to the onset of the crisis. Investment funds have to be *attracted* to London. There is nothing self-evident about why they should flow there, whereas New York has still the automatic cache of being the financial hub of the dominant global power (still commanding the main reserve currency) and the system's largest economy. Yet, paradoxically, the greater contribution of UK-based financial institutions to UK economic performance does not make the London government as subservient to City interests as Washington can be to the interests of Wall Street. This is partly because UK financial institutions are long used to government-led oversight through the Bank of England. It is also partly because the structures of financial regulation are so different in the two countries: the single-focused FSA automatically generated a more coherent code of behavior than any that could possibly be expected from the myriad of regulatory agencies that exist in the US at both the federal and state levels. The greater subservience of Washington to Wall Street is also partly the product of the porous nature of the US political system. Washington is much more easily penetrated (and dominated) by well-placed lobby pressure. Finally, the revolving door that carries major financial figures into and out of the US administration has no easy parallel in a UK world of career politicians, an independent civil service, and tighter ethic rules. There is elite movement between government and finance in London, but not on the Washington scale.

Many of the differences between the US and UK are the products of *domestic* political and economic variations, as we have seen. However, the policies and characteristics of both countries are also shaped by *global* forces reflective of their relative positions in the international community. US administrations, regardless of political color, are critically concerned with the US role as the global hegemon. US leadership on the world stage has had several effects. It brings capital flows to the US by default, and it helps maintain foreign confidence in the US dollar in the face of fiscal deficit, confidence which would be denied to the currency of a lesser power. The UK, in contrast to the US, possesses only the memory of its former global dominance. As such, its government's focus – again regardless of political color – is invariably one of maintaining the UK's relevance among global economic leaders. Throughout the crisis, and in the face of US and German competition, the UK government was determined to maintain London's supremacy as a financial center, a determination which contributed to New Labour's light-touch regulatory policies and to its emphasis prior to the crisis on strengthening the financial services sector above all others. The UK must find ways to draw speculative capital to the City of London through its financial policy, while the US simply attracts such monetary flows by virtue of its dominant global role. The positions of the two countries on the world stage differ as well. While the US stands alone in its globally hegemonic role, the UK is critically concerned with its position on the edge of Europe. Despite its decision to remain out of the euro zone, the UK, as a member of the EU, is constantly obliged to filter global policy concerns through this European lens. Unlike in the US, certain policies in the UK have been influenced by European concerns: the Greek and Irish debt crises, for example, spurred calls for fiscal austerity and deficit reduction on the Continent, calls with which the UK has also latterly concurred.

Conclusion

In both economies, it was predominantly the small business sector that bore the immediate brunt of the credit dearth: a dearth that quickly brought in its wake layoffs, falling consumer demand and diminishing business confidence. In both countries, a crisis that had begun in one part of the economy rapidly became a crisis of the whole economy. As it did so, the value of financial assets dropped dramatically – hitting small savers as well as large ones, triggering (among other things) an entirely unexpected crisis of private pension provision for baby-boomers on both sides of the Atlantic. The parallel collapse of consumer demand hit the labor market equally potently: and as jobs were lost in both the US and UK, a housing crisis which had originally been rooted in subprime lending morphed into one rooted in large-scale involuntary unemployment. The generalized recession that each economy acquired so quickly and so unexpectedly then became one that neither economy could easily shed. Indeed and instead, the recession incrementally spread from the private sector into the public sector, as the capacity of local and state government to finance basic welfare services was systematically undermined by the falling tax revenues generated by private sector layoffs. In that way, in each economy, a crisis initially characterized by private debt became, ironically, a crisis characterized by public debt – one in which the public spending made necessary by bank collapse and its ramifications reached a volume that the revitalized banking system was increasingly unwilling or unable to finance.

In such a climate the housing market did not recover rapidly in either the UK or the US. UK house prices did briefly revive in 2009 – reflecting perpetual house-supply limits and unusually low interest rates – but fell back again in 2010 and were forecast to fall further in 2011/12 (Stewart, 2011). Indeed, by December 2010 both house prices and house sales had been falling in the UK for six unbroken months, as demand for homes fell, underwriting standards tightened and first-time buyers in particular found entry into the housing market progressively more difficult. The American housing market was similarly flat, as the foreclosure crisis persisted. Foreclosures encompassed 5 million homes by December 2010 (one in ten mortgaged homes) as unemployment and lack of consumer confidence persisted and as banks moved to clear the backlog of homes they had come reluctantly to own. The number of US homes 'underwater' (with a bigger mortgage debt than their current value) did ease slightly in the third quarter of 2010, but still constituted at least a fifth of all US mortgaged homes (Coates, 2011). Major American banks entered 2011 with more than half a trillion dollars of second-lien mortgages on their books and still vulnerable to court-imposed damages for the inadequate paperwork associated with many of the original subprime mortgages.

But the banking sector in both economies had in general moved back into good times by the end of 2010, to the immense irritation of many of the victims of the 2008 financial tsunami – not least those many small businesses still struggling to raise credit. The worst excesses of the banking system that fueled the growth and distribution of toxic assets were by 2011 under tighter regulation in both economies, major financial institutions were being fined (if only modestly) for the worst of their previous practices, and in the UK at least banks were facing an annual levy of £2.5 billion. Such changes did not, however, stop major Wall Street institutions from reporting record profits in 2010. They did not prevent the distribution of major bonuses to senior staff; and nor did they remove the exposure of major banks – particularly in the UK – to the possibility of sovereign debt default by weaker euro-zone economies. Indeed, it remains one major irony of the fallout from the 2008 financial crisis that institutions then thought too big to fail were the very ones which, for all the regulatory initiatives put into play, emerged by 2011 even bigger than before and even more susceptible to system-wide collapse.

Add to that irony the other one – that the only sector of either economy that moved quickly from recession to growth (the financial sector) was the one whose bad practices had caused the recession in the first place – and you see why electorates in both the US and the UK still struggle to understand what has actually hit them. With both governments and governed trapped between high levels of debt (both public and private) and low levels of income (taxation revenues and wages), a new politics of austerity has come to dominate public policy on each side of the Atlantic. The opening lines of Charles Dickens' *A Tale of Two Cities* therefore have a new and a tragic resonance. In Washington and in London, as politicians, business leaders, workers and voters struggle to return to the certainties and affluence of an earlier age, the end of the first decade of the new century has indeed proved to be for them both the best of times and the worst of times – with the danger remaining that the worst of times is still to come.

Notes

1. Actually three cities – Washington and New York, and London. London is the site of both governmental power and City institutions. In the US, the centers of government and finance are geographically separate, hence the importance of the 'Washington–New York nexus'. The title is Dickens' fault. A fuller version, with chronological appendix, is at www.davidcoates.net/publications/non-fiction/american-politics-and-society/.
2. The tripartite members were the Financial Services Authority (FSA), the Bank of England and the Treasury. Each had a different responsibility: the FSA controlled micro-prudential (day-to-day) regulation of financial firms; the Bank of England monitored overall financial stability and set interest rates; and the Treasury maintained the overarching legal and institutional framework and controlled public funds.
3. In the UK, mortgage markets that had been dominated by building societies faced an influx of banks and centralized lenders. The 1981 abolition of the Supplementary Special Deposit Scheme loosened credit controls and allowed banks to lend on a greater scale; and the 1986 Financial Services Act allowed centralized lenders to enter the UK market. These new actors had access to more funds through the wholesale markets and were better equipped to utilize securitization. Thus they were able to issue more mortgage loans, including to subprime lenders. For the details of the US story, see the FCIC report (2011, pp. 79, 88–92 and 101).

References

Cable, Vince (2009) *The Storm* (London: Atlantic Books).
Coates, David (2010a) *Answering Back* (New York: Continuum Books).

Coates, David (2010b) 'US Senate Finally Passes Financial Reform', www.davidcoates.net/2010/06/01/u-s-senate-finally-passes-financial-reform/.

Coates, David (2011) 'Obama and Housing – is Anybody Home?', www.davidcoates.net/answering back/chapter 10.

Financial Crisis Inquiry Commission (FCIC) (2011) Report (New York: Public Affairs).

Giles, Chris (2010) 'Daunted by deficits', *Financial Times*, 23 June.

Land, Jon (2010) 'Shapps to Keep Labour's Mortgage Help Schemes – For Now', 24dash.com, posted 20 July.

Skidelsky, Robert (2009) *Keynes: The Return of the Master* (London: Allen Lane).

Schwartz, Hermann (2008) 'Housing, Global Finance and American Hegemony: Building Conservative Politics One Brick at a Time', *Comparative European Politics*, 6(3), September, pp. 262–84.

Schwartz, Hermann, and Leonard Seabrooke (2008) 'Varieties of Residential Capitalism in the International Political Economy: Old Welfare States and the New Politics of Housing', *Comparative European Politics*, 6(3), September, 237–61.

Stephens, Mark, and Deborah Quilgars (2008) 'Sub-prime Mortgage Lending in the UK', *European Journal of Housing Policy*, 8(2), 192–215.

Stewart, Heather (2011) House Prices to Fall by 20%', *Guardian*, 19 February.

Winant, Gabriel (2008) 'Private Sector Sparked Subprime Crisis: Fed', *Newser*, 12 October.

Zandi, Mark (2009) *Financial Shock* (Upper Saddle River, NJ: Pearson Education).

5
Fiscal Policy Responses to the Economic Crisis in the UK and the US

Edward Ashbee

Despite the many references to an 'Anglo-Saxon model' bringing countries such as the US, the UK, Australia and New Zealand together there were, as the financial crisis unfolded, important economic policy differences between the US and the UK. In particular, discretionary fiscal policies took very different forms. While the formation of the Conservative-led Coalition government in Britain in May 2010 and its commitment to large-scale retrenchment made some of these differences very visible, there were policy cleavages between the two countries throughout the crisis period.

This chapter considers the reasons for these differences. It assesses the part played by agency and contingency and the extent to which policy was shaped by the size of budget deficits and longer-run debt levels. However, the chapter emphasizes the causal importance of underlying economic variables and the institutional arrangements in pulling the US towards large-scale fiscal expansion and the UK towards relative restraint.

Stimulus policies in the US and the UK

Although there were regional variations, real house prices began to fall during 2005–06 in the US and towards the end of 2007 in the UK. Against this background, the consequences of credit expansion and overleveraging for the financial sector quickly became evident. Household names, most notably Bear Stearns and Lehman Brothers, collapsed. Merrill Lynch sold itself to the Bank of America. The US federal government took control of

Fannie Mae and Freddie Mac. In Britain, there were long lines at branches of Northern Rock leading to the provision of government guarantees to savers and the eventual nationalization of the bank. In September 2008, in a deal said to have been brokered by Gordon Brown personally, LloydsTSB took over HBOS (Halifax Bank of Scotland) so as to avert its collapse (Skidelsky, 2009, p. 10).

The 'credit crunch' (that took place as bank lending was sharply reduced) inevitably spilled over into the 'real economy'. Consumer confidence tumbled and unemployment levels rose. Although Lord Young, policy adviser to David Cameron after the 2010 election and Trade and Industry Secretary during the Thatcher years, pointed out in comments that cost him his job that those with outstanding mortgages gained from the fall in interest rates, many households and firms were compelled to cut their spending plans.[1] World trade flows contracted. On 29 September 2008, the Dow Jones Industrial Average lost 777 points, the index's largest-ever one-day fall (Keeley and Love, p. 18). When the upswing came, it was, particularly in the UK, slow, anemic and at times barely perceptible. There was frequent talk of a 'double dip' recession particularly after publication of the figures showing negative growth in the last quarter of 2010.

Faced by these developments, both the US and the UK exploited the possibilities offered by monetary policy. While interest rates had been raised in both countries during 2007, they were, by the beginning of 2009, at an unprecedented low.[2] Indeed, the reduction of the Bank of England's base rate to one percent in February 2009 was, as the *Guardian* noted, 'the lowest level in its 315-year history' (Seager, 2009). The term 'quantitative easing' entered political discourse as the Bank of England and the Federal Reserve purchased Treasury bonds on a large scale.

For commentators such as Paul Krugman of the *New York Times*, the scale and extent of the crisis required more. The US would otherwise risk a 'lost decade' of low growth and high unemployment. The crisis, Krugman argued, demanded the proactive use of discretionary fiscal policy: 'the Fed, having cut rates all the way to zero, has run out of ammunition to fight this slump' (Krugman, 2009). Although only limited numbers backed calls for a fiscal stimulus on the scale that Krugman proposed (and his later calls for a second stimulus), his critique of monetary policy was widely shared at the end of 2008 and during the early months of 2009. Furthermore, as Gordon Brown noted, governments could not credibly seek export-led recoveries if other nations were cutting spending levels (Brown, 2010, p. 130). While the G20 had concerns about the impact of the borrowing that would be required on long-term government debt levels, it placed increasing emphasis upon the importance of proactive fiscal policy. In mid November 2008, the Washington, DC, G20 summit called for the use of 'fiscal measures to stimulate domestic demand to rapid effect, as appropriate, while maintaining a policy framework conducive to fiscal sustainability' (*New York Times*, 2008).

Nonetheless, whereas the size of the package adopted in the UK was very modest indeed (totaling about £25 billion), the US package was (once the $787 billion American Recovery and Reinvestment Act (ARRA) had been passed in February 2009) the largest in the 30 countries surveyed by the Organization for Economic Co-operation and Development (OECD) in a March 2009 report (*OECD Economic Outlook – Interim Report*).[3] Table 5.1 shows the differences as a proportion of each country's 2008 gross domestic product (GDP).

Table 5.1   Total projected size of stimulus packages (spending and tax measures) in the UK and US, 2008–10

	2008–10 total net effect on fiscal balance (as % of 2008 GDP)
United Kingdom	–1.4
United States	–5.6
Weighted OECD average	–3.4

Source: Adapted from OECD (2009a, ch. 3, p. 110).

The relative size of the stimulus packages adopted in the US and the UK is, however, only one consideration. If the time distribution of the stimulus is brought into the picture, there are further differences between the two countries. In the UK, the Brown government concentrated almost all its projected stimulus funding (93 percent) on 2009. Indeed, 2010 and the years that would follow were to be a period of fiscal tightening and retrenchment as earlier spending was recouped (OECD, 2009a, p. 110). Speaking of Alistair Darling, the Chancellor of the Exchequer, Robert Chote, then serving as Director of the Institute for Fiscal Studies (IFS) put it in succinct terms: 'He will be pumping £16 billion of extra spending power into the economy next year and then taking all that out – plus a further £22 billion – just three years later' (Chote, 2008).

In contrast, US policy-makers based their projections on a longer time-frame and allocated over a third of overall stimulus spending (42 percent) to 2010 (OECD, 2009a, p. 110). Although President Obama spoke at the beginning of his period of office about deficit reduction, it only again became a top-line issue in the 2011 State of the Union

Address that was delivered in the wake of the 2010 midterm elections and the Tea Party movement's successes. In the address, Obama proposed that 'we freeze annual domestic spending for the next five years. Now, this would reduce the budget deficit by more than $400 billion over the next decade, and will bring discretionary spending to the lowest share of our economy since Dwight Eisenhower was President' (quoted in *National Journal*, 2011). Nonetheless, the President acknowledged that the cuts and savings that he sought shied away from specific proposals to address 'entitlement' spending (such as social security) and he matched his comments on the federal budget with calls for infrastructural projects, educational expansion, and a government commitment to innovation so as to boost American competitiveness. This was, he announced, 'our generation's Sputnik moment' (quoted in ibid.).

One further policy difference between the US and the UK should be noted. Whereas the US allocated (once the ARRA had been passed) more than 40 percent of the total stimulus on expenditure projects, the UK devoted almost all of its funding (beyond bringing forward some projects that had already been planned) to tax concessions (OECD, 2009a, p. 110).

Three interconnected questions should be asked about the policy gap between the US and the UK. First, why did the US adopt a far larger fiscal stimulus (as a share of 2008 GDP) than the UK? Second, why did the UK commit itself to fiscal retrenchment in 2010 whereas the US allocated the largest share of stimulus funding to that year? Third, why did the UK reject spending projects whereas they constituted a sizeable proportion of the US total?[4]

Political actors, agency and contingency

At first sight, these questions can be answered by considering the political preferences of office holders and the results of particular elections. Insider accounts of Gordon Brown's government suggest that there were tensions between Number Ten and Number Eleven Downing Street. Gordon Brown himself is said to have hoped for a larger-scale stimulus package while Alistair Darling successfully sought more limited measures. Darling's reluctance to commit himself to large-scale or sustained increases in public expenditure may have stemmed from his own immediate circumstances. He had only served as Chancellor since June 2007 (when Brown had succeeded to the premiership) and his period in office had been beset by difficulty. In October 2007, amidst much embarrassment, the Treasury lost the personal records it held on 25 million people and at the end of the summer of 2008, Darling's early warnings about the economic problems that lay ahead were swiftly repudiated by the Prime Minister's media team.

It might be said that policy developments in the US also owed much to political instincts, personality, accumulated 'political capital', and the fears associated with the specificities of the crisis period. Barack Obama's victory in the November 2008 presidential election, and the Democrats' gains in the congressional contests were, at least in part, a function of the economic uncertainties that defined the closing months of 2008 and they inevitably led to a significant reordering of policy priorities. They opened the way for the Obama transition team, the incoming administration, and the Democrats' congressional leadership to craft the $787 billion stimulus of the ARRA. Their thinking rested, at least in part, on the inclusion of 'twofers'. They not only sought to boost spending levels but also hoped to begin a process of longer-run structural change through public investment.

Nonetheless, it would be difficult to assert that agency-based variables are sufficient in themselves to explain the process of fiscal policy determination. It could hardly be said that fiscal expansion was an article of faith for either Obama or congressional Democrats. Indeed, throughout the 2008 election campaign, his campaign team had largely eschewed the economic radicalism that the conservative right ascribed to him. He had called for a 'middle-class tax cut' but also emphasized the importance of deficit reduction. Calls for a significant fiscal stimulus only moved center-stage during the weeks that followed the November election and the projected spending levels only began to approach $1 trillion towards the end of the year.

Furthermore, although partisan allegiances and the preferences of actors may permit the adoption of particular policies they do not assure it. There are constraints. In his account of Labour's later years in power, Andrew Rawnsley suggests that the Treasury was institutionally fearful of expansionary policies (Rawnsley, 2010, pp. 601–2). Its concerns appear to have been shared by the Bank of England. Indeed, in early 2009, the Bank's Governor, Mervyn King, warned publicly against a further fiscal boost (Fidler et al., 2009). In other words, although ideas and policy-makers are important in shaping the process of policy change, 'whether or not this happens still depends largely on whether key elites deem these ideas to be normatively acceptable and whether they can transport them through institutional channels into influential policy-making arenas' (Campbell, 2001, p. 162).

Budget deficits and debt

Other accounts have pointed to the size, structure and character of the government budget deficit and long-term debt levels in the US and the UK and the discourses that framed perceptions of them. In some respects, the UK faced greater fiscal strains than the US as the projected UK budget deficits were higher as a proportion of GDP. This having been said, the UK's longer-term national debt levels were comparatively modest. As Michael Devereux and Clemens Fuest conclude in an Oxford University Centre for Business Taxation briefing paper written in November 2008, UK government debt was, at 38 percent of GDP, relatively low by both historical and international standards. Japanese debt, they observed, represented more than 150 percent of its GDP (Devereux and Fuest, 2008, p. 2). Indeed, if budget deficits and debt levels are taken together, the UK and the US were in broadly similar positions. By the beginning of 2011, both were categorized by Bill Gross of the *PIMCO Investment Outlook* as 'red zone' countries within the 'ring of fire' in terms of budget deficit levels and public sector debt (as proportions of GDP). In such 'red zone' countries (in contrast with fiscally healthier nations such as Germany, Canada, Denmark and Australia), deficits and debt threatened to crowd out private investment and thereby constrain growth (Gross, 2011).

Even if government budget deficits are considered alone, the UK and the US were not in fundamentally dissimilar positions. Both faced significant *structural* budget deficits, in other words a budget deficit that is present throughout the business cycle and can be distinguished from the cyclical deficit which arises during periods of downturn.[5] These arose from tax cuts, rising expenditure levels, increasing 'entitlements' outlays brought about by aging populations, as well as the long-term impact of slow growth and a prolonged recession (Chote et al., 2009, p. 2).

Underlying variables and institutional arrangements

A larger part of the answer lies in a country's underlying economic variables and institutional arrangements. Both shape opportunities and constraints. They set the capacities of governments, mold the strategies adopted by political or economic actors, determine the distribution of power between those actors, and establish frameworks within which actors understand and represent their interests (Pontusson, 1995, p. 119).

Although perhaps neglected in some institutionalist accounts, underlying economic variables (or 'economic-structural variables') are of particular importance. As Jonas Pontusson notes, 'underlying structures shape the configuration and operation of political and economic operations' (Pontusson, 1995, p. 120). They include factor endowments, the distribution of income and wealth, the extent to which the economy is open (measured through the contribution of exports and imports to GDP), the occupational structure, the sectoral composition of industry, productivity rates, and despite some institutionalized features, the defining characteristics of many commodity and labor markets. Institutions are in contrast structured, rule-based and tied to mechanisms for the enforcement of such rules (ibid., p. 126). The following sections consider the ways in which such economic variables and institutional arrangements in both the US and the UK affected the use of discretionary fiscal policy.

Underlying economic variables

Underlying economic variables (or what might perhaps be termed the 'national economic architecture') shape the extent to which a national economy has 'automatic stabilizers' – non-discretionary and counter-cyclical tax revenues and forms of government provision that shift in size in response to the business cycle and thereby curb the excesses of the cycle. Although some accounts tie the economic impact of such stabilizers to overall state size, they are instead related to the size of public sector, the extent to which the tax regime has a counter-cyclical character, and the proportion of government spending that is devoted to social provision. Indeed, cross-country analyses published by the OECD suggest that because of the stabilizing role played by extended state provision in some countries there is an inverse correlation between the size and scale of social provision and the relative size of the discretionary fiscal packages that were adopted (OECD, 2009a, p. 117).

Nonetheless, the extent to which the relative size of automatic stabilizers explains the policy differences between the US and UK is open to question. As Christopher Howard has noted, estimates of government social provision as a share of GDP often neglect the distribution of social benefits in the US through tax expenditures (Howard, 2003).[6] Furthermore, insofar as overall changes in fiscal outcomes between 2007 and 2009 in the UK and the US provide evidence of stabilizers being brought into play, there were broadly similar drops in net fiscal balances. There was a 9.9 percent fall in the UK and an 8.4 percent drop in the US (Bénétrix and Lane, 2010, p. 31).

It may be more fruitful, therefore, to consider the part played by other underlying economic variables. They include, as Pontusson notes, a country's relative economic openness. Indeed, a national economy's exposure to international trade has significant consequences for the policy-making process. Economic management will be constrained, or be of more limited efficacy, in a relatively open economy within which a large proportion of GDP is derived from internationally traded goods and services. In particular, the value of projected multipliers for expansionary forms of fiscal policy will be lower in more open economies. A lower value multiplier might therefore be expected to inhibit or deter the use of discretionary fiscal policy whereas, conversely, higher value multipliers might encourage and facilitate fiscal expansion. Because of its size as a market and advanced industrial capacity, the US has a relatively closed economy. Whereas UK exports generally constitute over a quarter of GDP (28 percent in 2009), US exports amounted to just over a tenth (11 percent in 2009) (World Bank, 2010). Furthermore, during periods of downturn or at the beginning of an upswing, policy-makers in more open economies may well attach greater credence to the prospects of an export-led recovery. In the UK, there were still memories of the significant part played by exports in leading the economy out of the recession of the early 1990s. The steady depreciation of the pound sterling during the autumn of 2008 added further credibility to the hopes of those who thought in these terms. Underlying economic variables (and the value of projected multipliers) also incorporate the relationship between consumption and saving (as well as debt repayment) and anticipated shifts in the character of that relationship during periods of downturn and recessions. In the long run, the relationship owes much to cultural and social variables as well as 'real economy' indicators. At first sight, the level of debt owed by households and firms in the US and the UK was broadly comparable. It has been estimated at about 200–230 percent of GDP (*The Economist*, 24 June 2010). In both countries, it was said, households and firms would seek to rebuild reserves, restrain their spending levels because the assets they were holding had lost value, or would be unable to secure credit.

There were those, most notably John B. Taylor of Stanford University, who questioned the multipliers that some projected and have subsequently asserted that the stimulus policy pursued by the Obama administration had 'very little impact and not much to show for it except a legacy of higher debt' (Chan, 2010). Taylor and his co-authors suggested that the estimated multipliers and job projections underpinning ARRA were six times higher than those customarily used in new Keynesian modeling (Cogan et al., 2009, p. 22). Nonetheless, at least at the time ARRA was put forward, many of the Act's components appeared to offer significant multiplier values. Christina Romer and Jared Bernstein (and others such as Mark Zandi of Moody's Analytics who gave evidence before the House of Representatives Budget Committee) suggested that infrastructural spending would have a multiplier of 1.57 (Harding, 2010). Those elements within ARRA targeted at lower-income groups (such as an increase in food stamps) had higher projected multipliers.[7]

The character of the industrial structure (which in turn shapes the nature of business interests) should also be considered. The new and high technology sectors are proportionately larger in the US and thereby have greater weight within the business bloc. In 2007, the high-tech sector accounted for almost 10 percent (just over $1.4 trillion) of US GDP (Ministry of Technology, Trade and Economic Development and the Ministry of Advanced Education and Labour Market Development (British Columbia), 2008, p. 13). This had political consequences. The growing structural weight of new and high technology changed the center of political gravity within the US business bloc. As the 2008 elections approached, there were hopes that an Obama administration and a Democratic Congress would offer a boost to the new technology sector through public investment in broadband expansion, renewable energy, and the extended application of information technology in, for example, health care. Writing in *New Left Review*, Mike Davis has described a process of realignment whereby the new technology sector aligned itself with Obama's bid to secure the presidency:

> The near constant presence of Google CEO Eric Schmidt at Obama's side (and inside his transition team) has been a carefully chosen symbol of the knot that has been tied between Silicon Valley and the presidency. The dowry included the overwhelming majority of presidential campaign contributions from executives and employees of Cisco, Apple, Oracle, Hewlett-Packard, Yahoo and eBay ... The unprecedented unity of tech firms behind Obama both helped to define and was defined by his campaign (Davis, 2009, pp. 36–7).

Just as the new technology sector contributed to a partial reshaping of US politics, the character of the industrial structure has configured political processes in the UK. Indeed, the weight of financial capital has a long history. As Sidney Pollard argued, the pound sterling's return to the gold standard at pre-war parity in April 1925 reflected the relative strength of finance (or at least 'the section concerned with international finance, both long-term and short-term') and the corresponding weakness and subordination – as a class fraction – of industrial capital (Pollard, 1970, p. 13). Ed Miliband, who was elected as the Labour Party's leader after the 2010 election defeat, is among those who have noted that the financial sector still has disproportionate weight. One estimate suggests that financial services account for about 10 percent of UK GDP while, despite the visibility of Wall Street, the corresponding figure for the US is 7.5 percent (TheCityUK, 2011, p. 1). Against such a background, the calls of the 'bond vigilantes' for fiscal rectitude had resonance.

The structural differences between the US and the UK go some way towards explaining the contrasting attitudes towards fiscal expansion. In the US, the larger peak business groups backed both the Bush and the Obama stimulus. The US Chamber of Commerce said that the 2008 stimulus would 'spur business investment, consumer spending, increase productivity and put the U.S. economy back on track for long-term growth' (US Chamber of Commerce, 2008). A year later, Labor Secretary Hilda Solis publicly thanked the National Association of Manufacturers and said that its backing for ARRA 'was key to its passage on Capitol Hill' (quoted in *The Hill's Blog Briefing Room*, 2009).

In the UK, the peak business organizations were far less sanguine about calls for fiscal expansion. Towards the end of November 2008, just ahead of the Pre-Budget Report, the Confederation of British Industry (CBI) issued a press release calling for 'a fiscal boost' but then reined it in. The specific forms of fiscal boost that the CBI proposed were largely confined to modest business tax cuts, incentives to small and medium-sized enterprises to recruit apprentices, and a 'time-limited fiscal stimulus focused on employment through a temporary reduction in employer National Insurance Contributions' (Confederation of British Industry, 2008). Alongside this, the CBI also stressed the importance of the deficit and national debt:

> But given the poor state of public finances, any fiscal stimulus package will need to go hand-in-hand with a credible framework for getting back on track. This would prevent future generations being burdened with huge levels of debt (ibid.).

Underlying variables also incorporate a government's borrowing capacity. Although, as noted above, there were similarities between the US and the UK in terms of overall deficit and debt levels, they had different capacities. Having said this, fears were widely expressed in both countries. Much was said about the sovereign debt crises in some Mediterranean countries. In the UK, the issue became a rallying point for the Conservatives' efforts to win back the reins of power.

In the US, in the wake of the ARRA's passage, questions were asked about the bond sales necessary to fund the stimulus and the term 'bond vigilantes' began to be heard. The term was used to describe 'investors who pull the plug on governments they perceive as unable or unwilling to pay their debts' (Krugman, 2010). There were claims that should this happen, the US's credit ratings would be downgraded, upward pressure would be placed on interest rates, and there would be a process of 'crowding out' that would constrict growth in the private sector. Writing in the UK's *Daily Telegraph* at the beginning of 2010, Ambrose Evans-Pritchard cited reports suggesting that the US deficit and debt had reached a point where the US's AAA rating would be in serious jeopardy unless far-reaching budget-cutting measures were adopted within three to five years (Evans-Pritchard, 2010). Willem Buiter, a former member of the Bank of England's Monetary Policy Committee, suggested that there were, in the longer term, likely to be acute pressures leading to a loss of confidence and a flight from the dollar, causing 'the dollar in a couple of years to look more like an emerging market currency than like the US dollar of old' (Buiter, 2009).

Nonetheless, although the UK had in some respects greater latitude than individual euro-zone countries insofar as the pound could float downwards (and most of the UK's public debt was denominated in sterling and with a long maturity), the US had important structural advantages arising from its global position. As Alan Cafruny and Magnus Ryner have noted, whereas France found in the early 1980s that reflationary efforts could in a regime structured around floating exchange rates, trigger a speculative run on the national currency, the importance of the dollar as the world's leading reserve currency, the denomination of securities and other assets in dollars, as well as 'deep capitalization' in the US itself gave the US immense structural power. It could shape the preferences of both debtors and creditors (Cafruny and Ryner, 2007, p. 25).[8] As John Grahl concludes, 'From the point of view of macroeconomic policy, this kind of scale does not so much limit as practically eliminate external financial constraints on the United States' (John Grahl, quoted in ibid., p. 28).

Institutional arrangements and the political process

Underlying economic variables, particularly a national economy's relative openness, the value of projected multipliers, the sectoral composition of a country's output, and borrowing capacities, opened the way for fiscal policy variations. Nonetheless, while such variables created 'fiscal space' allowing expansionary forms of budgetary policy in the US, they were largely permissive in character and do not explain the outcomes in themselves. Other variables should therefore be considered; in particular, the institutional arrangements that govern political processes. Just as underlying economic variables mold institutional arrangements, such arrangements shape, facilitate but at the same time constrain the initiatives undertaken by political actors.

The federal character of the American state is particularly significant. Because the states spend and collect a relatively high proportion of total government expenditure and revenue, their actions have far-reaching fiscal and economic consequences. The 50 states are bound by their own laws, constitutions and budgetary procedures. Nearly all have balanced budget clauses in their constitutions or are constrained by statute.[9] As a consequence, *ceteris paribus*, state budgets have a pro-cyclical character. In a severe downturn such as that in 2008–09, the pro-cyclical pressures are severe. As the Center on Budget and Policy Priorities reported in July 2010:

> States already have faced and addressed extraordinarily large shortfalls as they developed and implemented spending plans…Every state save Vermont has some sort of balanced-budget law. So the shortfalls for 2009 and 2010 and most of the shortfalls for 2011 have already been closed through a combination of spending cuts, withdrawals from reserves, revenue increases, and use of federal stimulus dollars (McNichol et al., 2010).

Left unaddressed, state efforts to balance their budgets would have imposed a significant deflationary pull. This was in large part because expenditure by the individual states represented almost half of overall government spending in the US (44.9 percent in 2006). Local government expenditure in the UK was in relative terms, far more limited. Indeed, it spent only 28.4 percent of overall government spending in the UK (OECD, 2009a). Fear of a deflationary pull and the lobbying capacities of the states added to pressures for the 'bailout' which rescued many forms of state provision and constituted a significant part of ARRA. Fear of a deflationary pull and the lobbying capacities of the states added to pressures for the 'bailout' which rescued many forms of state provision and constituted a significant part of ARRA.

Other parts of the US institutional architecture may also have facilitated, and perhaps promoted, fiscal expansion while at the same time curbing or inhibiting the efforts of those who sought restraint or rallied around calls for a balanced federal government budget. It could be argued that the fiscal illusion hypothesis (which suggests that voters do not grasp the tax implications of spending decisions or recognize the effects of fiscal drag as inflation brings individuals into higher tax categories) may play more of a role in a political system that through biennial elections to the US House of Representatives and the direct election of those who the executive branch at both federal and state level offers significantly more opportunities for mass participation than parliamentary democracies such as the UK (Schultze, 1992, p. 26).

The institutional character of the American state also added to the pressures that opened the way for the passage of ARRA in other ways. Although accounts almost always focus on the barriers facing those who seek legislative reform (particularly in the US Senate), the many openings offered by a relatively fluid, inchoate and often porous state formation facilitate and encourage activity and lobbying by organized interests once opportunities for reform begin to emerge. As towards the end of 2008 it became evident that the incoming Obama Administration and the Democrats' congressional leadership would seek a large-scale stimulus package, a lobbying process among groupings and constituencies, many of which would gain directly from such a bill, began and quickly intensified. They argued for the passage of the Act while at the same time seeking to secure a significant share of the expenditure programs that it incorporated. The *Washington Post* noted the intensity of the lobbying processes and speculated on the extent to which these might trump economic priorities:

> The potential for massive new spending has touched off a frenzy among interest groups eager to claim their share of the expanding stimulus pie. The profusion of requests from governors, transportation groups, environmental activists and business organizations is spawning fears that the package could be loaded with provisions that satisfy important Democratic constituencies but fail to provide the jolt needed to pull the nation out of a deepening recession (Montgomery, 2008).

Although there were tensions between groupings and interests (particularly between environmental campaigns and those who sought traditional infrastructural projects such as road improvements) the coalition made its mark on the character of ARRA in its final form. In contrast, while there are many lobbying opportunities in the British political system, the institutional architecture has a more 'sealed' character. Access points are more limited and, as in the 1930s, the Treasury remains hegemonic.[10]

The porous character of the American state and ways in which this offered access to elite interests, particularly those tied to business, finance and commerce, has long been emphasized by scholars associated with

American Political Development (APD) and historical institutional-ism. Accounts have pointed to the penetration of the state through the character of those appointed to senior positions in the administration and the federal bureaucracy (many of whom are drawn from the larger corporations or Wall Street), the 'revolving door' between public service and the private sector; the degree of access that influential lobbies have to members of Congress and administration members (a process arguably facilitated by campaign contributions); the extent of 'producer capture' within particular departments, agencies and bureaus; the close associations between regulatory commissions and those that are the subject of regulation; and the extent to which the decision-making process (particularly the making of the annual budget) is subject to prolonged periods of uncertainty, instability and doubt. For Stephen Skowronek the American state is 'a hapless confusion of institutional purposes, authoritative controls, and governmental boundaries' (Skowronek, 1982, p. 287). Desmond King and Lawrence Jacobs refer to 'its consistent (though not uniform) lack of independent expertise to independently assess and respond to the behavior of markets and individuals; and multiple and competing lines of authority that stymie even necessary intervention' (King and Jacobs, 2010, p. 798). In a celebrated phrase, Skowronek spoke of the state as a 'hapless giant' (Skowronek, 1982, p. 290).

There are, however, further considerations. The relatively porous character of state boundaries is a variable rather than a constant. There is greater openness during both the early and closing phases of an admin-istration's lifespan. This is particularly the case as a new administration takes shape during the transition period and in its first few months.[11] James Pfiffner has captured the scale of the challenges facing the President-Elect. An incoming administration, he argues, has to staff the Executive Office of the President, build a cabinet, put forward appointees, establish a policy agenda, construct a relationship with Congress, and frame all of this in ways that can be conveyed to the broader public (Pfiffner, 2009a).

Furthermore, because the Senate confirmation process has become so slow and fractious, large numbers of political appointees remain unconfirmed during the early stages of an administration. There are often difficulties recruiting appropriate personnel. At the end of February 2009, over a month after Obama took office, Paul Volcker, former Federal Reserve Chairman and head of the Obama administration's Economic Recovery Advisory Board, noted the absence of support for Treasury Secretary Timothy Geithner within his own department: 'The secretary of the Treasury is sitting there without a deputy, without any undersecretaries, without any, as far as I know, assistant secretaries ... at a time of very severe crisis' (quoted in Kamen, 2009).

Although the Obama Administration was at this point ahead of the Bush and Clinton administrations in terms of appointments (and drew quite heavily on experienced Washington insiders who had served in the Clinton administration), the incoming administration formally nominated only six people during February 2009 and announced the names of 15 others who, it said, it intended to nominate (ibid.). Although it should be noted that there are significant numbers of permanent staff in, for example, the Office of Management and Budget, it has been said with some legitimacy that there is 'no institutional memory, no predetermined organizational structure, no adopted policies, no outline of their responsibilities, and no manual to show how the place works. In short, they arrive to an empty shell' (quoted in Pfiffner, 2009b, p. 90).

In such circumstances, there is a greater dependence upon external sources of expertise (including those on Capitol Hill as well as lobbies, think tanks and interest groups), than during periods when an administration has become 'bedded in'. At the same time, because lobbying relationships, access systems, and lines of communication between the incoming administration and external interests have yet to become solidified or are only partially formed, some of the relationships and structures that were formed during the primary and general election campaigns still remain in place. They are not at this stage displaced or superseded. In short, because of institutional circumstances, the transition team and the new administration will retain the ties and associations with the personnel, organizations and relationships that carried the winning candidate to victory. In particular, ARRA owed much to proposals developed and put forward by the Center for American Progress, a left-leaning think tank headed by John Podesta, who had served as President Bill Clinton's Chief of Staff and directed the Obama transition team during 2008–2009. Indeed, the Center stressed the extent to which the House of Representatives' version of the Act drew upon one of its reports, (*How to Spend $350 Billion in a First Year of Stimulus and Recovery*), which it had published at the beginning of December 2008.

> The Center for American Progress published a report last year setting out 'How to Spend $350 Billion in a First Year of Stimulus and Recovery.' Almost all of our proposals were included in the House plan – and many of these with increased funds to sustain spending for two years (Ettlinger and Straw, 2009).

Conclusion

This chapter has argued that the fiscal policy differences between the US and the UK during the economic crisis owed much to underlying variables and the character of the institutional architecture in the two countries. In particular, the relatively fluid, porous and inchoate character of the American state (features emphasized by scholars associated with APD and particularly pronounced during the early months of an administration) opened the way for established interests and constituencies, particularly those tied to the governing party, to secure spending commitments. The more centralized, hierarchical, and insulated character of the British state precluded capture in this way.

During the 1980s, comparative studies of policy responses to the Great Depression turned away from histories of economic thought and the 'Keynesian revolution', descriptions of the intellectual myopia of figures such as Ramsay MacDonald (Prime Minister, 1924 and 1929–35) and accounts of the interest-based blocs and coalitions that emerged in different countries. Instead, they turned to institutionalist explanations and considered, in particular, the character of state structures and the extent to which they permitted or constrained the emergence of policy alternatives. Although there is, as this chapter has suggested, a case for also considering the institutional structures that lie beyond the boundaries of the state apparatus and at the same time incorporating the part played by underlying economic variables, studies of the 'Great Recession' should make a similar turn.

Notes

1. Lord Young of Graffham echoed words attributed to Harold Macmillan (Conservative Prime Minister, 1957–63) when he told an interviewer that 'the vast majority of people in the country today' had 'never had it so good' (BBC News Online, 2010).
2. The realities of monetary policy were however rather different. When they were prepared to make loans available, commercial banks charged interest rates far above the base rate (OECD, 2009c, p. 12).
3. This chapter considers discretionary fiscal policy. It does not look at the fiscal costs of supporting the financial sector or non-discretionary or 'automatic' shifts.
4. It should be noted that there were also marked differences between the UK and other European countries. Many of the coordinated market economies such as Germany adopted, for example, work subsidy schemes so as to maintain employment levels. Such schemes, some commentators suggested, reinforced labor market rigidities.

5   The concept of a 'structural deficit' is contested because there are measurement problems and methodological difficulties distinguishing between the 'structural' and 'cyclical' deficits. Indeed, it could be argued that the concept of a 'structural' deficit is a political or ideological construct.

6. This, however, appears to limit the extent to which lower income groupings, which might be expected to have the highest marginal propensity to consume, secure gains (Kenworthy, 2010).

7. Christina Romer went on to serve as Chair of the Council of Economic Advisers. Jared Bernstein was appointed as Vice President Biden's Chief Economist and Economic Policy Adviser. There have also been suggestions based upon studies of the interwar years that realized multipliers might be higher in value. (See, for example, Almunia et al., 2009, p. 25.)

8. John Grahl recorded in 2005 that 90 percent of recorded foreign exchange transactions involved the dollar, and the capitalization of the New York Stock Exchange and NASDAQ amounted to about $11 trillion, half the world total (Cafruny and Ryner, 2007, p. 28).

9. The forms that balanced budget requirements take, and the roles in the process assigned to the governor and the legislature, differ from state to state.

10. To an extent, the British state still resembles the description given by Margaret Weir and Theda Skocpol in their account of comparative policy responses to mass unemployment during the 1930s. They argued that the structures governing civil service attitudes were relatively closed to new forms of thinking (and, in particular, Keynesian calls for public works programs). Much of the civil service was subject to the hegemony of the Treasury, the 'Treasury view' which stressed the importance of a balanced budget and market forces, and the Bank of England (Weir and Skocpol, 1986, p. 128). In an echo of the 'Treasury View', Mervyn King, Governor of the Bank of England, warned publicly against further fiscal expansion in early 2009 (Fidler et al., 2009). Furthermore, his concerns appear to have been backed within the Treasury itself. There were, Andrew Rawnsley argues, serious anxieties about debt levels and concerns that the exchange rate for the pound sterling might continue to fall (Rawnsley, 2010, pp. 601–2).

11. It would, of course, be a mistake to over-generalize about the character of transitions. There are, as James Pfiffner records, important differences depending upon the point at which preparations began, the size and character of the transition team, and the extent to which strategy is structured around well-chosen priorities (Pfiffner, 2009a). The character of a presidential campaign may also be a consideration. As Sidney Milkis and Jesse Rhodes record, the Obama campaign was, in contrast with Senator John Kerry's 2004 presidential campaign, a centralized 'national machine' largely structured around the Obama 'brand' (Milkis and Rhodes, 2009, pp. 8, 18).

References

Almunia, Miguel, Agustín S. Bénétrix, Barry Eichengreen, Kevin H. O'Rourke and Gisela Rua (2009) *From Great Depression to Great Credit Crisis: Similarities, Differences and Lessons*, National Bureau of Economic Research Working Paper 15524, (Cambridge: NBER).

BBC News Online (2010) 'Lord Young Apology Over "Never had it So Good" Remarks', 19 November, accessed 23 February 2011.

Bénétrix, Agustín S., and Philip Lane (2010) *International Differences in Fiscal Policy During the Global Crisis*, National Bureau of Economic Research Working Paper 16346 (Cambridge: NBER).

Board of Governors of the Federal Reserve System (2009) *Testimony – Chairman Ben S. Bernanke: Current Economic and Financial Conditions and the Federal Budget, Before the Committee on the Budget, U.S. Senate, Washington, D.C.* (Washington, DC: Board of Governors of the Federal Reserve System), 3 March, www.federalreserve.gov/, accessed 1 March 2011.

Brown, Gordon (2010) *Beyond the Crash: Overcoming the First Challenge of Globalisation* (London: Simon & Schuster).

Cafruny, Alan W., and J. Magnus Ryner (2007) *Europe at Bay: In the Shadow of US Hegemony* (Boulder: Lynne Rienner Publishers).

Campbell, John L. (2001) 'Institutional Analysis and the Role of Ideas in Political Economy', in John L. Campbell and Over Kaj Pedersen, (eds), *The Rise of Neoliberalism and Institutional Analysis* (Princeton: Princeton University Press).

Chan, Sewell (2010) 'In Study, 2 Economists Say Intervention Helped Avert a 2nd Depression', *New York Times*, 27 July.

Chote, Robert (2008) *Opening Remarks for Post-PBR Briefing*, Institute for Fiscal Studies, www.ifs.org.uk, accessed 2 January 2011.

Chote, Robert, Rowena Crawford, Carl Emmerson and Gemma Tetlow (2009) *Britain's Fiscal Squeeze: The Choices Ahead,* Institute for Fiscal Studies, IFS Briefing Note BN87, www.ifs.org.uk, accessed 2 January 2011.

Cogan, John F., Tobias Cwik, John B. Taylor and Volker Wieland (2009) *New Keynesian versus Old Keynesian Government Spending Multipliers*, www.stanford.edu/~johntayl/CCTW_100108.pdf.

Confederation of British Industry (2008) *News Release – CBI Calls for Immediate Government Action to Protect Jobs*, Confederation of British Industry, www.cbi.org.uk/, accessed 10 December 2010.

Davis, Mike (2009) 'Obama at Manassas', *New Left Review*, 56, March–April, 5–40.

Devereux, Michael, and Clemens Fuest (2008) *A Fiscal Stimulus Package for the UK?* Oxford: Oxford University Centre for Business Taxation Policy Briefing, 18 November.

The Economist (2010) 'World Debt', *The Economist (Online Edition)*, 24 June, accessed 23 November 2010.

Ettlinger, Michael, and Will Straw (2009) 'Recovery Plan Offers Needed Change', *Center for American Progress*, 16 January, www.americanprogress.org/, accessed 1 August 2011.

Fidler, Stephen, Joanna Slater and Matthew Cowley (2009) 'U.K.'s Brown Denies G-20 Stimulus Split', *Wall Street Journal*, 26 March.

Gross, Bill (2011) 'The Ring of Fire', *PIMCO Investment Outlook*, 23 February.

Harding, Robin (2010) 'Struggle to Prove Stimulus has Worked', *Financial Times*, 27 July.

The Hill's Blog Briefing Room (2009) 'Solis Doesn't Mention Union Bill at Business Group Breakfast', *The Hill's Blog Briefing Room*, http://thehill.com, accessed 14 October 2010.

HM Treasury (2008) *Pre-Budget Report – Facing Global Challenges: Supporting People through Difficult Times* (London: HM Treasury).

Howard, Christopher (2003) 'Is the American Welfare State Unusually Small?', *Political Science and Politics*, 36, 411–16.

Kamen, Al (2009) 'Good Thing All's Quiet at Treasury These Days', *Washington Post*, 2 March.

Keeley, Brian, and Patrick Love (2010) *From Crisis to Recovery: The Causes, Course and Consequences of the Great Recession* (Paris: OECD).

Kenworthy, Lane (2010) 'Social Spending and Poverty', 4 June, http://lanekenworthy.net, accessed 4 February 2011.

King, Desmond S., and Lawrence R. Jacobs (2010) 'Varieties of Obamaism: Structure, Agency, and the Obama Presidency', *Perspectives on Politics*, 8, September, 793–802.

Krugman, Paul (2009) 'The Stimulus Trap', *New York Times*, 9 July.

Krugman, Paul (2010) 'The Feckless Fed', *New York Times*, 11 July.

McNichol, Elizabeth, Phil Oliff and Nicholas Johnson (2010) *Recession Continues to Batter State Budgets; State Responses Could Slow Recovery* (Washington, DC: Center on Budget and Policy Priorities).

Milkis, Sidney M., and Jesse H. Rhodes (2009) 'Barack Obama, the Democratic Party, and the Future of the "New American Party System"', *The Forum*, 7(1), 1–26.

Ministry of Technology, Trade and Economic Development and the Ministry of Advanced Education and Labour Market Development (British Columbia) (2008) *Profile of the British Columbia High Technology Sector – 2008 Edition* (Victoria, BC: Ministry of Technology, Trade and Economic Development).

Montgomery, Lori (2008) 'Obama Team Assembling $850 Billion Stimulus', *Washington Post*, 19 December.

National Journal (2011) 'Obama Declares "The Rules Have Changed"', 25 January.

New York Times (2008) 'Statement from G-20 Summit', 15 November.

O'Grady, Sean (2009) 'Public Finances: Darling's Impossible Battle to Climb a Mountain of Debt', *Independent*, 10 December.

OECD (2009) *OECD Economic Outlook – Interim Report*, 'Chapter 3 – The Effectiveness and Scope of Economic Stimulus' (Paris: OECD), www.oecd.org/, accessed 7 April 2011.

OECD (2009a) *OECD iLibrary – Government at a Glance 2009 – General Government Expenditure by Level of Government*, www.oecd-ilibrary.org/, accessed February 25 2011.

OECD (2009b) *OECD Economic Surveys – United Kingdom* (Paris: OECD).

Pfiffner, James (2009a) 'Presidential Transitions', in George C. Edwards III and William G. Howell (eds), *The Oxford Handbook of the American Presidency* (Oxford: Oxford Handbooks Online), pp. 85–107.

Pfiffner, James (2009b) *The Strategic Presidency: Hitting the Ground Running* (Homewood: The Dorsey Press).

Pollard, Sidney (1970) *The Gold Standard and Employment Policies between the Wars* (London: Methuen).

Pontusson, Jonas (1995) 'From Comparative Public Policy to Political Economy: Putting Political Institutions in their Place and Taking Interests Seriously', *Comparative Political Studies*, 28(1), 117–47.

Rawnsley, Andrew (2010) *The End of the Party* (London: Viking-Penguin).

Schultze, Charles L (1992) 'Is There a Bias Toward Excess in US Government Budgets or Deficits?', *Journal of Economic Perspectives*, 6(2), 25–43.

Seager, Ashley (2009) 'Borrowing Cost at Historic 1% – But Will it Ease the Pain?', *Guardian*, 6 February.

Skidelsky, Robert (2009) *Keynes: Return of the Master* (New York: Public Affairs).

Skowronek, Stephen (1982) *Building a New American State: The Expansion of National Administrative Capacities, 1877–1920* (Cambridge: Cambridge University Press).

Weir, Margaret, and Theda Skocpol (1985) 'State Structures and the Possibilities for "Keynesian" Responses to the Great Depression in Sweden, Britain, and the United States', in Peter B. Evans, Dietrich Rueschemeyer and Theda Skocpol (eds), *Bringing the State Back In* (Cambridge: Cambridge University Press).

TheCityUK (2011) *Economic Contribution of UK Financial Services 2010*, www.thecityuk.com/, accessed 9 March 2011.

World Bank (2010), *Data – Exports of Goods and Services (% of GDP)*, http://data.worldbank.org/, accessed 9 March 2011.

Part II

Post-Crash Political Trends

6
Divided in Victory? The Conservatives and the Republicans

Tim Bale and Robin Kolodny

Introduction

Although its provenance is uncertain (being variously attributed to Oscar Wilde, George Bernard Shaw and Winston Churchill), the observation that the US and the UK are two nations divided by a common language is often – perhaps too often – repeated. When it comes to politics, however, it is easy to see why. Anyone delving into conservative commentary on the challenges posed (and the opportunities presented) by the current financial and economic crisis finds plenty of transatlantic lessons being drawn. Whether the shining examples and dire warnings to which they direct our attention would recognize themselves as such is another matter. For instance, according to one American conservative (Buchanan, 2010):

> Before the Tea Party philosophy is ever even tested in America, it will have succeeded, or it will have failed, in Great Britain. For in David Cameron the Brits have a prime minister who can fairly be described as a Tea Party Tory. Casting aside the guidance of Lord Keynes – government-induced deficits are the right remedy for recessions – Cameron has bet his own and his party's future on the new austerity. He is making Maggie Thatcher look like Tip O'Neill.

This is not quite how things are seen on the other side of the Atlantic. Indeed, according to one of the shrewdest and best-connected conservative commentators in the UK, it is imperative that Cameron, and those supporting him, not fall into the temptation that they have anything to learn from (let alone anything to teach) the populists across the pond. Writing at around the same time (D'Ancona, 2010), he reminded his readers that:

> The Tory tradition owes more to chipper decency than to glassy-eyed state-smashing: this is the country of [former Monty Python member turned travel writer] Michael Palin, not Sarah. Yes, the Tea Party is a riveting spectacle, and, one suspects, a gift that will keep on giving. But as a model for political action, fiscal reform or electoral strategy it is about as much use as the proverbial chocolate teapot.

Clearly, the two commentators are at opposite ends of the conservative continuum. Nevertheless, their very different takes on the same situation remind us that we cannot take the supposed affinity between the US Republicans and the UK Conservatives for granted. This chapter sets the electoral performance and the broad policy platforms of the two parties since 1979 in the context of the so-called special relationship between the two nations in which they operate. It then focuses on how and on what the parties campaigned in 2010, as well as on the results of that campaigning, before finishing with a discussion of what their responses to the age of austerity do and don't have in common.

Maybe special but rarely partisan: the US–UK relationship up to 1979

The so-called special relationship between the US and the UK neither is, nor ever has been, inevitable, but it has been significant (Dumbrell, 2006). The quality of that relationship does not seem to have been affected much by which party was in power on either side of the Atlantic. Even after the Cold War confirmed the two states as allies, there were still tensions, but they were rarely if ever complicated by partisan considerations. The Americans (then under a Republican president) refused to back the British (then governed by the Conservatives) during their ill-conceived adventure to snatch back the Suez Canal in 1956. The British (by that time governed by Labour) did the same to the Americans (initially under a Democratic president) when it came to Vietnam. Differences on individual issues, however, proved less important than a shared commitment to a liberal capitalist international order, underpinned, at least until the 1970s, by global institutions – the United Nations (UN), the North Atlantic Treaty Organization (NATO), Bretton Woods, the International Monetary Fund (IMF), and the General Agreement on Tariffs and Trade (GATT) – that US and UK governments of whatever stripe had together helped to create. The Republican Party has seemed to have more in common with the Tories than with Labour, whose links with the trade unions and enthusiasm for welfare spending arguably mean they have more in common with the Democratic Party. However, as President John F. Kennedy and Prime Minister Harold Macmillan demonstrated, a Democrat in the White House could cooperate with a Conservative in Downing Street. Conversely, as Harold Wilson and Lyndon Johnson, and then Edward Heath and Richard Nixon, showed a few years later, there was no guarantee that prime ministers and presidents of supposedly like-minded parties would see eye to eye.

In sync? Thatcher, Reagan and beyond

Wilson's successor, Labour premier Jim Callaghan, seems to have got on particularly well with his Democratic counterpart, Jimmy Carter. But the rapport established between Callaghan's successor as prime minister, Margaret Thatcher, and the man who in 1980 snatched the presidency from Carter, Ronald Reagan, was something else altogether. United in their belief that government was more often the problem than the solution, and convinced that a tougher line needed to be taken against the Soviet Union, Thatcher and Reagan were cast as ideological soul mates. The relationship between the UK and the US, while it could never be one of equals, and while there were bound to be occasional tiffs (the American invasion of Granada perhaps the most embarrassing), became closer than it had been since the Second World War and at least as close as it was later to become during the Blair–Clinton and Blair–Bush eras.

The British, it should be said, had been under no illusion – especially after Suez – about who was boss, but understood, nevertheless, that they brought something to the party in terms of the legitimacy and support they could lend to American foreign policy. Thatcher, however, was much more of a true believer. Regardless of whether Reagan or any of his colleagues were completely convinced there was much more to the deal beyond mutual self-interest, Britain's first female prime minister was genuinely convinced that there was 'a union of mind and purpose between our peoples, which makes our relationship truly a remarkable one' (Thatcher quoted in Jones, 1997, p. 1). The substance of such remarks, if not their style, marked something of a return to the Churchillian tradition (the 'English-speaking peoples' and all that) after years of more authentically Tory pragmatism – pragmatism tinged, it must be said, with just a touch of condescension and even latent anti-Americanism, be it of the English nationalist variety personified by Enoch Powell or the European-destiny version exemplified by Edward Heath. Thatcher's line also reflected a growing conviction – ironically, one that first became evident among the young advisers who had helped Heath while in opposition in the mid 1960s – that the UK would be better off (both in the literal and the figurative sense) if it were more like the US. As Europe came to be seen by more and more Tory MPs and commentators as a sclerotic, pacifist, corporatist, even semi-socialist dinosaur, the United States – dynamic, flexible, low-tax, low-spend – was increasingly seen as a role model whose economic system, though not its political system, was the one not just to watch but to emulate. The defeat of the Soviet Union only served to confirm this impression, the fact that it had been achieved in part by budget-busting defense spending conveniently forgotten in the rush of mutual self-congratulation. After all, hadn't both the Republicans and the Conservatives managed to win three general elections on the trot?

Headline election results, however, can be misleading. In the UK, substantial parliamentary majorities can be won on a relatively low vote share, particularly if the opposition performs poorly, while in the US, legislative elections often tell a more nuanced story than the results of presidential races (see Table 6.1). Certainly, the early and mid 1990s should perhaps have given any overly-triumphant Republicans and Conservatives pause for thought. When the economic chickens came home to roost, George Herbert Walker Bush lost to Bill Clinton (thanks in part to Ross Perot who won 19 percent of the national vote – mostly at Bush's expense) and the Conservatives, having won a last gasp reprieve in 1992 by dumping Thatcher two years earlier, were soundly beaten by Labour in 1997. But rather than wondering whether the Reagan–Thatcher recipe was really right for a new era, both the Republicans and the Tories took a while to opt for a supposedly more centrist alternative. Before George W. Bush came along, posing as a 'compassionate conservative' in order to deny Al Gore a victory in 2000 that should have been his for the taking, the Republicans shifted more to the right, a strategy that worked for them in their previous legislative triumph in 1994. Before David Cameron came along, the Conservatives made no sustained attempt to do anything different (Bale, 2009). Consequently, they were out of power for 13 years. During those 13 years, however, America continued to be a source of fascination and inspiration for the Tories – this despite the close relationship enjoyed by their nemesis, Tony Blair, not only with Clinton (who was famously unimpressed by stories that the Conservatives had tried to help out the Republicans in 1992 by trying to dig up dirt on his time in the UK during the 1960s) but also, in the aftermath of 9/11, with Bush.

Table 6.1 Percentage of votes and seats by party, UK House of Commons, 1979–2010

Election	Conservatives		Labour		Liberals*	
	Votes	*Seats*	*Votes*	*Seats*	*Votes*	*Seats*
1979	44%	53%	37%	42%	14%	2%
1983	42%	61%	28%	32%	25%	4%
1987	42%	58%	31%	35%	23%	3%
1992	42%	52%	34%	42%	18%	3%
1997	31%	25%	43%	63%	17%	7%
2001	32%	25%	41%	63%	18%	8%
2005	32%	31%	35%	55%	22%	10%
2010	36%	47%	29%	40%	23%	9%

*Liberal/SDP Alliance 1983–87; Liberal Democrats from 1992.

The Conservatives: from Thatcher to Cameron[1]

Instead of seeing their victory (albeit with a small parliamentary majority) at the 1992 election as a lucky escape and a signal that the electorate were looking for 'a kinder, gentler' Conservatism to emerge in the wake of Thatcher's replacement by John Major, the Tories believed they had been given a green light to carry on where she had left off. Plans were unveiled to privatize state-run concerns that even she had considered best left in public hands, most notably coal, rail, and the postal service. Meanwhile, there would be no going back on the introduction of internal quasi-markets in health care and education. Such initiatives would almost certainly have attracted widespread public opposition anyway. In the autumn of 1992 speculative pressure on the pound sterling forced the UK government into a de facto devaluation against other European currencies – but not before it had sacrificed its credibility and billions of dollars trying to avoid the inevitable.[2] But when combined with the evident failure of the Major government to control and protect the value of the national currency, to beat the recession, and to persuade even its own supporters to back its foreign (specifically its European) policy, the loss of confidence in the Conservatives' competence, compassion and credibility was as profound as it was swift. Worse still, Labour had at last managed to light upon a leader – Tony Blair – who was not only capable of projecting all three of these vital qualities, but who had plenty of personal charisma too. By 1997, the economy had begun to recover strongly but only at the cost of increases in taxation and stringent control of spending on electorally crucial areas like schools and hospitals. In any case, it was, as far as most voters were concerned, too little, too late. The electoral mood had swung away from concern about an overweening state towards the need to shore up and renew vital public services. Labour, promising to combine economic dynamism and social justice, romped home to a landslide victory.

There had, for the best part of a decade, been a mismatch between the centrist instincts of the voters and the neoliberal convictions of the party – a mismatch that had been disguised by Thatcher's ability to synchronize the electoral and the economic cycles and Labour's inability to present itself as a credible alternative. This would have been obvious had the Conservatives conducted a proper post-mortem after their defeat in 1997. Instead, they blamed the latter on their internal divisions over Europe and the fact that they had been forced by economic necessity to stop cutting taxes and selling off state assets (and the fact that there was little left to sell). Convinced that voters would soon see through Blair and New Labour, the Conservatives threw themselves straight into a leadership contest out of which emerged William Hague – a right-winger who believed that all the party had to do was to stop arguing about Europe, distance itself from the financial and sexual scandals that had tainted its last few years in office and return to the Thatcherite true path. A handful of Conservative strategists, and a few colleagues, warned that this might not be enough, but their 'modernizing' and more centrist message fell on deaf ears, in part because those around Hague, fearing for their leader's position, regarded dissent as an ideological and personal betrayal. The modernizers were either sidelined or simply left politics altogether, reduced to watching what amounted to a slow-motion train crash as Hague tried to attract support by taking populist positions on immigration, crime, and Europe.

Another trouncing at the polls in 2001 terminated Hague's tenure, but things got no better under his immediate successors, Iain Duncan Smith, who lasted just over two years, and Michael Howard, who led the party to a third election defeat in 2005. Despite some fumbling nods by Duncan Smith to the 'compassionate conservatism' of George W. Bush – something Hague had briefly toyed with but never really developed (see Ashbee, 2003, pp. 43–4) – neither he nor Howard (both of whom were convinced Thatcherites) were able to convince skeptical voters that the party had moved away from the right-wing nostrums of the 1980s and 1990s. Though Blair's image had taken a battering after the decision to join the US in invading Iraq, and despite concerns that the huge amounts of cash that he and his Chancellor, Gordon Brown, had poured into health and education had not always provided value for money, voters still refused to take the Conservatives seriously.

Three election defeats finally persuaded the party that it could no longer go on like this. In December 2005 it elected a new leader, David Cameron, who, whatever his private beliefs about the role of government, was determined to signal to voters that the party would be moving back into the center ground where elections in Britain tend to be won or lost. Policies that smacked of contempt for the public sector were abandoned. The party's commitment to the state-funded National Health Service (NHS) was trumpeted. And, as part of this attempt to 'decontaminate the Conservative brand', Cameron, although proclaiming the importance of family values, stressed his commitment not just to the environment and to international aid, but to equal treatment for sexual and ethnic minorities. Old favorites like Europe, immigration and crime did not disappear altogether (they did, after all, resonate with large numbers of floating as well as Conservative voters) but they were spoken about in a new, self-consciously reasonable tone. Cameron encountered some resistance but not much – mainly because, after a temporary blip as Brown replaced Blair as Labour leader and prime minister, the strategy seemed to be paying off, at least insofar as opinion polls were a reliable guide.

The Republicans: from Reagan to the Tea Party Movement

The character of the contemporary American party system is set fundamentally by the different approaches each major party took over the nature of government intervention in the economy after the Great Depression. Franklin Delano Roosevelt and the Democratic Congress passed the New Deal legislative program, creating government jobs to reduce the debilitating unemployment caused by the economic crisis while shoring up the nation's infrastructure. The Democratic Party dominated the national government (with brief exceptions in the 1950s) until 1968. In this time period, Democrats became firmly identified with creating the modern American welfare state – especially social security for the aged, widowed and disabled, and Medicare, nationalized health insurance for the elderly. Democrats became the willing champions of working-class white Americans, and the more reluctant allies of lower-class African-Americans. Paradoxically, the southern region remained solidly Democratic until 1994, mostly out of the lingering anger toward the Republican Party over the Civil War in 1861–65. Republicans, in the meantime, were resistant to the idea that government could or should mitigate the business cycle, though by the 1960s most of them had embraced the spirit if not the form of social security and Medicare. Both programs could be seen as logical remedies to deficiencies in the marketplace, namely its inability to offer the elderly (and others unable to re-enter the workforce) economic remediation in dire circumstances.

In the middle of the Vietnam War and a crisis of social change, Republicans came down on the side of 'law and order' and won the presidency in 1968 in a close race with a third-party candidate. Republicans controlled the White House from 1968 to 1976 and from 1980 to 1992. If not for Richard Nixon's Watergate scandal in 1974, Republicans would likely have held on to the presidency for the entire 1968–92 time period. Curiously, from 1954 to 1994, and at exactly the same moment they were electing Republican presidents, Americans chose Democrats to control the US House of Representatives. Republicans in Congress had a highly conciliatory attitude toward their Democratic counterparts during much of this period, a stance that likely contributed to their seemingly persistent minority status (Jones, 1970).

This anomaly of divided party control of government makes sense if we consider that social and foreign policy issues were not at the heart of the differences between the two major American parties until Ronald Reagan emerged on the national scene and won the 1980 election. From the New Deal to Reagan, the parties differed on the size and location of government in American society. Democrats favored a larger, universal state (though not on the same scale as the Labour Party) while Republicans favored a small, locally-controlled state. In this era, major progressive issues like the Civil Rights Act of 1964 passed due to the cooperation of liberal Democrats and moderate Republicans and the fact that the president who implemented and enforced affirmative action hiring policies for the benefit of African-Americans was Republican Richard Nixon. While 1968 set the stage for the divergence of the two parties on social issues, Reagan sealed it.

In 1980, Democratic President Jimmy Carter faced a disastrous economy and an angry public watching helplessly as American embassy workers were held hostage for over a year in Iran. These feelings of 'malaise' created an opening for the conservative campaign of Ronald Reagan to take hold. Reagan Republicanism was different because of its open hostility to the state in economic regulation, taxation, and provision of services. It wasn't governmental priorities that were of concern; it was government itself as enemy. On the other hand, government should be used to inject some old-fashioned moral values back into public life such as banning abortion and reintroducing prayer in schools (Evans and Novak, 1981). Reagan was also ready to ignore Cold War détente and argued for a massive defense buildup aimed at challenging the Soviet Union. Reagan's victory in 1980 and landslide re-election in 1984 fundamentally changed the nature of debate over the role of the state in America. Still, throughout the Reagan revolution and first Bush administration, Americans selected a Democratic House and for half this period, a Democratic Senate as well.

Bill Clinton's plurality win in 1992 was due to the allure of independent candidate, H. Ross Perot, who criticized both major parties for not taking fiscal responsibility for the overgrown, ineffective administrative state. Indeed, Perot's activist supporters are credited with making the Republican takeover of the Congress in 1994 possible (Rappoport and Stone, 2005). However, the geographical and ideological base of the Republican Party in Congress shifted significantly in the 1980s and 1990s, becoming more active in the southern and western regions and less conciliatory in their conservative ideas (Connelly and Pitney, 1994). The Republican-controlled Congress made budget balancing, term limits for national legislators, and opposition to unfunded mandates the cornerstone of their early agenda. Right after, they moved on to welfare reform, reflecting their belief in a Conservative Opportunity Society over a Liberal Welfare State, declaring that cash welfare benefits encouraged individual dependency on the state which was unhealthy.

From 1995 to 2007, Republicans held majorities in both houses of Congress, though the size of these majorities fluctuated as Democratic fortunes increased and Republicans' waned in this period (see Table 6.2). Why the country re-elected Democratic President Bill Clinton in 1996 (after seemingly sending him a 'warning' in the form of a Republican Congress in the 1994 midterm elections) and also another Republican Congress is a moot point. A variety of explanations have been suggested, including incumbency advantage, regional variation in party strength, and the simply strange tendency of Americans to be comfortable with divided government – this being a reversal of the Reagan and Bush years with Republican presidents and Democratic Congresses. In the famously close 2000 election, Republicans won the presidency and retained control of Congress. Republicans controlled national government for the next six years – which may have had more to do with the desire to rally around the president after 9/11 and the ensuing invasion of Iraq than any 'natural' preference for unified government. But in the 2006 midterm congressional elections, with Bush's approval rating at a historic low, Democrats regained control of both Houses of Congress.

Table 6.2　Percentage of votes and seats by party, US House of Representatives, 1980–2010

Election	Republicans		Democrats	
	Votes	Seats	Votes	Seats
1980	48%	44%	50%	56%
1982	43%	38%	54%	62%
1984	47%	42%	52%	58%
1986	44%	41%	54%	59%
1988	45%	40%	53%	60%
1990	44%	38%	52%	61%
1992	45%	40%	50%	59%
1994	52%	53%	45%	47%
1996	48%	52%	48%	48%
1998	48%	51%	47%	49%
2000	47%	51%	47%	49%
2002	50%	53%	45%	47%
2004	49%	53%	47%	46%
2006	44%	46%	52%	54%
2008	42%	41%	53%	59%
2010	52%	56%	45%	44%

Source: Calculated by authors from Election Information, Office of the Clerk, US House of Representatives at http://clerk.house.gov/member_info/electionInfo/index.aspx.

In 2008, Democrats won both the presidency and the Congress, for the first moment of unified Democratic government since Bill Clinton and his first Congress in 1993–95. During this time, new president Barack Obama tried, and ultimately succeeded, at a domestic policy reform that eluded Clinton – health care reform. While the legislation started out with aspirations to emulate many aspects of the NHS in the UK, significant discontent from Republican leaders – and even independents and moderate Democrats – forced the Obama administration to scale back significantly their ambitions. Instead, the enacted reform bill largely preserves the status quo system while extending affordable private insurance options (potentially government-backed) to those whose employers do not provide it or who are not employed. The new law also regulates the private insurance industry more tightly so that it approximates universal care by forbidding companies from dropping customers with pre-existing or expensive medical conditions. This is a modest reform indeed by European standards of care. The Obama administration also inherited a large deficit from the Bush administration, including a substantial military presence in Iraq and Afghanistan that demanded a consistent financial commitment for the near term. The global financial crisis of

2008, while helping Obama get elected, also meant the income side of the budget equation was weak. Rising unemployment, bank foreclosures on home mortgages, and bank failures presented special challenges for the Democrats. Obama's response was to offer additional government money to states to stimulate immediate job creation (mostly through public works programs already identified as high priority needs), and to continue a government-backed 'bailout' program to save large banks, insurance companies, and the US auto industry from failure. The justification for these actions was to prevent a bad situation from becoming much worse, but the Republicans began to respond that the administration's actions were bankrupting the nation's future. By the end of 2009, several highly publicized 'town hall meetings' on health care reform clearly indicated that Republicans intended to make health care a campaign issue in 2010. Once the bill was passed, it also became clear that the theme of runaway spending for economic stimulation – in the face of a continued recession and economic stagnation – would be a major enticement for business-affiliated candidates to run on and for frustrated voters to respond to.

The 2010 campaigns

Conservative campaigning in 2010

Until the global financial crisis, the British Conservatives had assumed that the solid if not spectacular economic growth the country had experienced under Labour would continue. They therefore talked about 'sharing the proceeds of growth' between tax reductions and improvements to public services. But as the scale of the deficit became clear – a gap between revenues and outlays increased by Gordon Brown's determination not to allow a serious recession to turn into a full blown depression – the Tories shifted gear. Insisting that they would protect the vulnerable, and vital (and electorally crucial) areas like health and education, Cameron and George Osborne, the Shadow Chancellor of the Exchequer, stressed the need to reduce the deficit as soon as possible and even talked about an 'age of austerity'. Promises that 'paying down our debt must not mean pushing down the poor', that a Conservative government would pursue 'fiscal responsibility with a social conscience', that 'we are all in this together' failed to convince large numbers of voters that the party needed to win back, not least because there was a gap between the scale of the its aspiration to eliminate the deficit in the course of one parliament and its reluctance to spell out exactly what and how much it intended to cut back.

Fortunately for the Tories, it was also clear that voters were similarly unimpressed with Labour's plans. Once the election was called at the beginning of April 2010, the Conservatives did a good job of destroying the government's alternative (taking more time to balance the books and doing it by raising taxes as much as by reducing spending) before it could get off the ground. On the other hand, it quickly became obvious that there was little public enthusiasm for the positive side to the Conservative message – that they would work towards creating a 'Big Society' in which local and voluntary initiatives would take responsibility for services currently provided by a supposedly centralized, top-down and unresponsive state. The policy was seen as 'cover for cuts' and confirmation that the Tories' real agenda was to reduce the role of the state, especially in welfare, so that it more closely resembled the American rather than the European model. Or else voters, pollsters concluded, simply failed to understand what on earth the party was going on about – hardly surprising, the US consultants (Bill Knapp and Anita Dunn – both mainstream Democrats) that it brought on board during the campaign are said to have suggested, when the idea was sprung on the electorate without preparation or pre-testing. Cameron was also criticized on his own side for agreeing to participate in Britain's first televised leaders' debates without ensuring first that there would be no place in them for the leader of the UK's third party, the Liberal Democrats, whose impressive performance knocked the Conservative campaign completely off course.

The debates focused attention not just on the Lib Dems' highly personable leader but also their immigration policy, which seemed to imply an amnesty for many of those who had originally entered the country illegally. This allowed the Conservatives to remind voters that it had by far the toughest position on such issues. Other 'harder-edged' (that is, more right-wing) Tory policies with voter appeal, like crime and a skeptical attitude to European integration, however, barely saw the light of day: it was thought unlikely, given the overwhelming importance of the economy, that they would shift votes and might actually put off some of the middle-class liberal voters Cameron's decontamination strategy had been designed to attract. There was little attempt – unsurprisingly perhaps – on the Conservatives' part to remind those voters about the party's conversion to the environmental cause: earlier exhortations to 'Vote Blue: Go Green' were but a distant memory by May 2010.

Republican campaigning in 2010

The 2010 campaign in the US started with the passage of the Obama health care law, officially the US Affordable Care Act, in February 2010. The law has remained controversial since its passage; however, attention shifted once more onto the stagnant economy, government spending, and the federal budget deficit. And in the firing line were the politicians who had supposedly gotten the country into such a mess, the latter being a particular focus of the Tea Party movement which, outraged over the government bailout of Wall Street banks and the adoption of health care reform, championed a variety of conservative economic positions already favored by Republicans, only more so.

According to Zachary Courser, 'The Tea Party movement embraces protest over organization, and independence over party politics'(Courser, 2010). It has no central organization, clear leader, or clear political goals besides expressing outrage at incumbent politicians – and not just Democrats. Depending on the particular record of Republicans in their area, Tea Party groups might embrace or reject those Republican office-holders and candidates. For example, incumbent US House member Michele Bachman of Minnesota quickly claimed affinity with the Tea Party movement and declared she would form a caucus of like-minded members in the US House. She was embraced, but Republican establishment candidates in Utah, Kentucky, Alaska and Delaware were denied their party's nomination in favor of Tea Party-sponsored candidates who could plausibly claim to be reflecting real concerns among their fellow Americans. The Gallup Poll found that since July of 2010, at least 64 percent of Americans identified the economy as the most important problem facing their country today. Consequently, campaign themes and advertisements nationwide hammered home the support or opposition candidates showed towards Obama administration programs meant to stimulate an economic recovery ('the bailout'), the size of the deficit, job growth, and whether the candidate was responsible for 'politics as usual'. While some Tea Party-backed candidates were successful, many were not after defeating establishment Republicans whose support among independents and Democrats was underestimated by Tea Party supporters in the general election.[3] This put the Republican Party in the sometimes awkward position of rejecting a candidate they previously embraced (such as Senator Lisa Murkowski of Alaska) because of the elastic nature of party nominations in the US.

The 2010 results – incomplete governing positions

Conservative–Lib Dem Coalition, May 2010

Anyone who ever thought that the British Conservative Party would coast to victory in May 2010 forgot the size of the task confronting it. Its barely perceptible 'recovery' in 2005 had still left it with less than a third of the seats in the House of Commons, while the fact that Labour's vote was more efficiently concentrated in marginal constituencies meant that an overall Tory majority would require a Conservative lead in vote share at the general election of about ten percentage points. But once the Conservative leadership had taken the strategic decision to appeal to the electorate by stressing the party's determination to cut the deficit at all costs, an outright victory was never on the cards. Election and post-election polling showed clearly that voters were not generally drawn to core Conservative values (individual opportunity over equality, reduction of the state in favor of greater reliance on markets, and so on). They were not decisively convinced by the party's preference for an immediate program of debt reduction through spending cuts and they were not convinced that the party had changed its Thatcherite spots. Still, people were tired with the Labour government and Gordon Brown as premier, felt that the economy generally and the debt crisis in particular required a change at the helm, and figured that the Tory leader, David Cameron, was a competent and a credible candidate for the top job (see Bale and Webb, 2010, for more detail on pre- and post-election polling). Little wonder then, especially with support for the Liberal Democrats holding up (if not ballooning in the way they had hoped), that the election resulted in a 'hung parliament' – a situation in which the Conservatives were the largest party but without the overall majority that British governments habitually enjoy over their competitors.

While there was clearly huge disappointment among Conservatives that they were unable to secure an outright majority, most were determined, come what may, to be back in Number Ten Downing Street after 13 long years out of power. Cameron and his team quickly rejected the idea of a minority government: they would not have been able to claim a mandate, nor muster the votes required, for their deficit reduction plans; nor could they guarantee that a second general election a few months later would have seen them triumphantly re-elected with a bigger majority. After all, Labour had tried that tactic back in 1974 only to find itself back in office but with such a small margin over its opponents that it returned to a minority situation within a year or so. The only sensible option was to make 'a big, open, and comprehensive' offer to the Lib Dems, who – with an alacrity that surprised many of their voters and some of their members – accepted. The coalition agreement, hammered out in just a few days, appeared to give the Tories most of what they wanted, especially on economic policy, and (even more amazingly) left them in control of all the major ministries – not just the Treasury, but Foreign Affairs, the Home Office, Health, and Education. The Lib Dems, who hopelessly underplayed their hand, declared themselves content with the ill-defined (and traditionally fairly meaningless) post of deputy prime minister, a few minor departments, and a referendum on a reform of the voting system that might ensconce them as the kingmaker between Labour and the Tories in future elections – but only of course if it could be won. In the event, the referendum, which asked voters if they wanted to replace First Past the Post with the Alternative Vote (the system used to elect Australia's lower house) was lost – and heavily. Even more worryingly for the Lib Dems at least, most commentators agreed that the 70–30 margin of victory for the 'No2AV' campaign was in large part down to the fact that they were the main advocates of change, as well as reflecting what became an all-out campaign on the part of their coalition partners, the Conservatives, to kill the proposal.

From May 2010, then, Britain has had a Coalition government but one that, to all intents and purposes, looks, sounds and behaves like a Conservative administration, and this is unlikely to change. The Lib Dems reacted to the crushing of their plans for voting reform and their disastrous results at the local elections held on the same day by promising to be more assertive. However, their plummeting public support, together with a determination on the part of Conservative MPs that they not be given an inch, make it unlikely that Cameron – even though he would prefer it if the Lib Dems fell apart later rather than sooner – will provide them with too many concessions. There is certainly no sense in which Cameron has felt obliged, like Obama, to be bipartisan or to place people outside his party in those portfolios where trust in its good faith or competence was lacking. Indeed, it is possible to argue, given its plans to reduce public spending so far and so fast, that it could be the most radically right-wing government the country has ever seen. True, Prime Minister Cameron seems intent on sticking to his promises to ring-fence health and (parts of) education spending. True, too, that the rhetoric on Europe, crime, and immigration has been turned down. However, while few doubt that the party leadership at least is indeed determined to shed its traditional ambivalence toward ethnic minorities and alternative lifestyles, it also seems determined not to appear soft on Europe, crime, and immigration. The program as a whole then looks very much like an attempt to take up where Thatcher and Major left off rather than the more 'touchy-feely' and centrist 'one-nation' Conservatism that Cameron first stressed when he took over in 2005.

Republican takeover of US House – divided government, 2011–12

The results on election night 2010 were truly stunning. Since discontent about economic conditions was rampant, Republicans were expected to do very well, but not quite this well. Several political scientists forecast a 52-seat gain for House Republicans (Campbell, 2010; Bafumi et al., 2011) in October of 2010. Nearly every other academic prediction called for significant Democratic losses, but short of loss of control of the chamber. Pundits did no better. A few did predict the Republican takeover of the House, but most also seemed not to believe the Republicans could prevail in so many local contests. In fact, the Republicans gained an unpredicted 63 seats in the US House. While they also gained six seats in the US Senate, it was not enough to give them majority control there. The White House, of course, remained in Democratic hands. Divided party control of government had returned. The reason why so few had foreseen the extent of the change had to do with the belief that committed Democrats would not so easily abandon their new president's agenda in favor of the Republicans. In a sense they were correct. What they did not expect was very strong turnout by Republican voters and indifference, in the form of weak voter turnout, by Democratic voters. In 2008, Barack Obama had done an exemplary job of energizing critical constituencies – especially young voters – to become re-engaged. The lingering effects of Obama's Organizing for America organization (which never actually shut down after 2008) should have kept the newly activated engaged. Instead, turnout levels retreated to pre-Obama levels or worse. Independent and weakly aligned voters who did vote had no problem giving the other side a try at taking on the economic problems; they had given Obama the same chance in 2008 and after two whole years, expressed their disappointment at his inability to turn things around swiftly.

As is customary, the new legislative majorities began to organize themselves immediately after the election in preparation for their swearing in on 3 January 2011. The Republicans selected their minority leader, Representative John Boehner of Ohio, to be the new Speaker of the House in the 112th Congress. Boehner is a seasoned politician with a great deal of leadership experience. While he holds very conservative policy positions, Boehner is known for having an easygoing, pragmatic manner. On the other side of the aisle, former Speaker Nancy Pelosi very unusually chose to assume the role of minority party leader after the Democrats lost their majority. Complicating this process of leadership selection was the 'lame duck' session Congress (so-called because some portion of the members who would vote and conduct business were either just defeated or retiring) which reconvened in late November 2010 still under the control of the Democrats. More than 20 bills were on the agenda ranging from the tax cuts, immigration, environment, unemployment benefits, child nutrition and food safety, to foreign policy. Freed from the worries of the elections, members acted swiftly and decisively, earning them the label of the 'Do-Something Congress'(Chaddock, 2010). However, the Congress still did not pass a permanent budget for the remainder of the 2011 fiscal year, leaving the country instead with a series of temporary budget provisions known as continuing resolutions. The budget was not fully approved until April of 2011. While this may seem to indicate compromise and reconciliation between the two parties, as of May 2011, the House Republicans are threatening to oppose an increase to the US debt ceiling even though most economic experts fear this would plunge the US into a deeper economic crisis if it must default on some of its debt obligations.

The newly elected Republican House which began its session on 5 January 2011 immediately scheduled a vote to repeal the not-fully-implemented health care reform law referred to by them as 'Obamacare' – a symbolic act given the impossibility of getting the same measure passed in the Democratically-controlled Senate and signed into law by the Democratic president. The Republicans also dangled the possibility of shutting down the government as an inducement to Democrats to cooperate with the Tea Party-inspired deep spending cuts. This partially worked. Since a government shutdown is quite disruptive, all involved desire to avoid it, and since the assent of both chambers of the legislature and separately the executive are required, the House Republicans do have a blackmail power in the divided government scenario. However, with the next election less than two years away, the Republicans proceeded carefully, lest they appear to be the party of 'no' instead of a governing partner.

Conclusion

The American journalist, Michael Goldfarb (2010), writing around the same time as the conservative commentators referred to in our introduction, concluded that the Republicans (whom he described as zealots fighting Obamacare and the culture wars, determined to cut welfare but spending a fortune on defense) and the Conservatives (pragmatists intent on preserving the NHS, content to live and let live, cutting defense spending and putting a stop to Labour's more authoritarian anti-terrorist measures), were 'like Gondwana and Pangaea', inexorably drifting apart. The metaphor is memorable but also misleading. The two parties, like the two nations in which they operate, have rarely walked in lockstep. Conversely, we can overstate the extent to which they are now sailing off in opposite directions.

There are some obvious differences, but even these have to be qualified a little. Goldfarb (who is well acquainted with both countries) is right to point in particular to defense and health care. Although it is too early to tell whether they will survive the convulsions in the Middle East, the deep spending cuts forced on all three armed services by the Cameron government were not made at the behest of the Liberal Democrats in the coalition but done off the Conservatives' own bat. Yet while defense reductions would be anathema to most in the Republican Party, it would be more than possible to find some conservatives who would be keen to reduce foreign aid and investment. As for health care, it is clear that as American conservatives continue to consider it their patriotic duty to do all they can to stymie the progress of what they see as socialized medicine, their British counterparts seem determined to preserve it. On the other hand, they have embarked on a radical (and, before the election, unannounced) shake-up of the NHS which will almost certainly introduce more private provision, albeit (at the moment anyway) paid for by the taxpayer rather than the individual. Nor can anyone be absolutely sure that the party's commitment to one of Britain's most popular institutions derives from a genuine belief in its ideals and its manifest efficiency or, instead, from fear of retribution by voters were they to appear to place it at risk. Moreover, there are many Tories (for whom 'going private' is routine in their own lives) who believe that in the end the electorate will not stand for the level of taxation required to keep the NHS going strong and will eventually come round to the idea, at the very least, of an insurance-based system.

On the other differences Goldfarb discerns, it is even easier to find common ground. Republicans may not advocate closing Guantánamo, but one would be hard pressed to find many who would have objected to the Conservatives' decision to abandon Labour's plans for ID cards and its insistence on long periods of detention of UK citizens without charge. Likewise, while it is undeniable that the majority of Republican politicians have to be seen to consider so-called alternative lifestyles and lifestyle choices as illegitimate, even immoral, a significant minority of them and their supporters (perhaps more so in private than in public) share the reluctance of British Conservatives to condemn. And some libertarians in America would probably go even further in their insistence that government has no right whatsoever to tell people what to do in their personal lives. On the other side of the ledger, there are plenty of Conservatives – politicians and voters – who are uneasy about what they think is the excessively liberal stance of their leaders on social issues, up to and (for some of them) including abortion. Certainly, one area in which the Cameron government has had to tread very carefully for fear of alienating its base is law and order, with suggestions that spending reductions may mean fewer prison places and concomitantly shorter, less punitive sentencing going down like the proverbial lead balloon. The other highly sensitive area is immigration: Cameron needs to be seen to deliver his promise to make major reductions in the numbers coming in, yet he cannot completely ignore the concerns of large and small businesses, and of the economically crucial higher education sector. Republicans are quite certain that hostile positions toward immigration work for them electorally – at least in the short run – but as long as they don't have to implement or enforce the policies they champion. This allows them to mollify their base of nationalistic supporters (the same ones who doubt that Obama is a native-born American despite the repeated release of his valid birth certificate) while still running a guest worker program for immigrants to take seasonal jobs that are not attractive to most American citizens.

More generally, it is clear that the response of the two parties to the budget deficits they face reflects their very similar instincts on public spending and the size of the state. True, there are differences of degree if not kind, but even these can be exaggerated. Cameron may not be a Tea Party Tory, but if his government sticks to its plans then – and this may come as a surprise to many – the British state is on course to consume a lesser proportion of GDP than its American counterpart for the first time that anyone can remember (see Taylor Gooby and Stoker, 2011). Meanwhile, there are obvious parallels between American practice and discourse and Cameron's stated determination to reduce the welfare roll by reducing the incentives to people seemingly content to live on the taxpayer's largesse – and his aspiration to shift some social provision from the state towards local providers and volunteers as part of his so-called 'Big Society'. In promoting the latter, and in attempting to use the crisis to undertake a serious reappraisal of the role and extent of government, Cameron seems to be betting that Britain is (or can be made to be) ultimately more American than European. Americans, on the other hand, consistently demand to bake, box, and eat their cake by choosing divided government. They give the message that the state should be smaller – but not too much, especially for retirees; American foreign policy should be isolationist – unless it is focused on eliminating terrorism or high energy prices; and that market rationality should prevail – unless people are forced out of their homes en masse in which case the government should help them. Indeed, both parties champion views more conservative than the electorate will generally choose. Therefore, they follow similar paths to reconcile their policy beliefs with their political viability.

Notes

1. This and the sections that follow on the Conservative Party draw on Bale (2011) and Bale and Webb (2010).
2. For details, see Thompson (1996).
3. For example, Christine O'Donnell, a Tea Party-backed candidate in Delaware, won the Republican nomination for the US Senate but lost handily in the general election. In Alaska, Republican incumbent Senator Lisa Murkowski was defeated in her primary by Tea Party-backed Joe Miller. However, Murkowski decided to run in the general election as an independent write-in candidate, defeating both Republican Miller and Democrat Scott McAdams.

Bibliography

Ashbee, Edward (2003) 'The US Republicans: Lessons for the Conservatives?', in Mark Garnett and Philip Lynch (eds), *The Conservatives in Crisis* (Manchester: Manchester University Press).

Bafumi, Joseph, Robert S. Erikson and Christopher Wlezien (2011) 'Postmortems of the 2010 Midterm Election Forecasts: Forecasting House Seats from Generic Congressional Polls: A Post-Mortem', *PS: Political Science & Politics*, 44(1), 2.

Bale, Tim (2009) 'The Conservatives: Trounced, Transfixed – and Transformed?', in Terrence Casey (ed.), *The Blair Legacy: Politics, Policy, Governance, and Foreign Affairs* (Basingstoke: Palgrave Macmillan).

Bale, Tim (2011)*The Conservative Party from Thatcher to Cameron* (Cambridge: Polity Press).

Bale, Tim, and Paul Webb (2010) 'The Conservative Party', in Nicholas Allen and John Bartle (eds), *Britain at the Polls* (London: Sage).

Buchanan, Patrick J. (2010) 'Tea Party Tory', *American Conservative*, 22 October, online edition.

Campbell, James E. (2010) 'The Midterm Landslide of 2010: A Triple Wave Election', *Forum*, 8(4), Article 3, www.bepress.com/forum/.

Chaddock, Gail Russell (2010) 'Six Big Achievements of a Surprisingly "Do Something" Congress', *Christian Science Monitor*, 23 December.

Connelly, Jr, William F., and John J. Pitney, Jr (1994) *Congress' Permanent Minority? Republicans in the U.S. House* (Lanham, MD: Rowman and Littlefield).

Courser, Zachary (2010) 'The Tea Party at the Election', *Forum*, 8(4), Article 5, www.bepress.com/forum/.

D'Ancona, Matthew (2010) 'The Tories Need to be More Michael Palin than Sarah', *Sunday Telegraph*, 7 November.

Dumbrell, John (2006)*A Special Relationship: Anglo-American Relations from the Cold War to Iraq.* (Basingstoke: Palgrave Macmillan).

Evans, Rowland, and Robert Novak (1981)*The Reagan Revolution: An Inside Look at the Transformation of the U.S. Government* (New York: E.P. Dutton).

Goldfarb, Michael (2010) 'Why Republicans and Tories No Longer See Eye-to-Eye', BBC, 16 November, online edition, www.bbc.co.uk/news/.

Jones, Charles O. (1970) *The Minority Party in Congress* (Boston: Little, Brown).

Jones, Peter (1997) *America and the British Labour Party: The Special Relationship at Work* (London: I.B. Tauris).

Rappoport, Ronald B., and Walter J. Stone, (2005) *Three's a Crowd: The Dynamic of Third Parties, Ross Perot, and Republican Resurgence* (Ann Arbor: University of Michigan Press).

Taylor Gooby, Peter, and Gerry Stoker (2011) 'The Coalition Programme: A New Vision for Britain or Politics as Usual?' *Political Quarterly*, 82(1), pp. 4–15.

Thompson, Helen (1996) *The British Conservative Government and the European Exchange Rate Mechanism, 1979–94* (London, Routledge).

7
The Crisis of Capitalism and the Downfall of the Left

Graham Wilson

The global financial crisis (GFC) that ended the first decade of the twenty-first century was the most severe crisis in the global financial and economic system since the Great Depression (Sorkin, 2009: Financial Crisis Inquiry Commission, 2010). Only extraordinary measures by central banks and governments prevented it from being a replay of the Great Depression. These extraordinary measures required politicians to renounce long-held beliefs to cope with the emergency; in the United States, for example, the administration of George W. Bush took into public ownership or took extensive stock holdings in failing banks and the giant insurance company, AIG. Soon after, his successor, President Obama, effectively nationalized one of the three major US auto companies (General Motors) and arranged the sale of another, Chrysler, to the Italian auto company, Fiat. These were extraordinary steps for any US president to take, and that they were taken initially by a determinedly conservative Republican president was all the more startling. These measures might also prompt some re-thinking in the academic world. For example, these policy responses were scarcely compatible with the popular 'Varieties of Capitalism' (VoC) school which asserted the dominance of liberal economic beliefs and practices in the US (and UK) (Hall and Soskice, 2001).

Although VoC approaches treat the US and UK as essentially the same in economic policy and practices, the UK had of course a much longer and extensive history of public ownership, and so at first glance the nationalization of failing banks by the Labour government was a less impressive policy change. However, the 'New Labour' project launched by Tony Blair and Gordon Brown in the 1990s had at its heart an acceptance of capitalist markets and resolve not to take back into public ownership any of the enterprises privatized by Mrs Thatcher (King, 1990; Blair, 2010). Indeed, the Blair government pressed ahead with further measures of privatization beyond those undertaken by the preceding Conservative governments, for example, in air traffic control. Labour also promoted the involvement of private finance in public projects such as the modernization of the London Underground through a public-private finance scheme (the Private Finance Initiative, or PFI) determinedly promoted by then Chancellor of the Exchequer Gordon Brown in the face of all obstacles and objections (Crewe and King, 2010).

Arguably the policy changes made by central banks, particularly the taking over of banks' worthless assets by the Fed or exchanging them for Treasury bonds and the adoption of 'quantitative easing' (loosely describable as printing extra money) by the Federal Reserve in the US, the Bank of England and others around the world were as dramatic as the steps taken by elected politicians. Pushing out money to inflate demand and providing credit for major companies – including in the case of the Fed, companies that were foreign-owned, such as Barclays – central banks accepted unprecedented responsibility for short-term management of the economy in contradiction of the monetarist nostrums that they should limit themselves to achieving a fixed and steady growth of the money supply.

If the shock of the crisis produced dramatic change in policies favored by the ruling elites, its impact on the general public could have been expected to be equally dramatic, not only as they observed the behavior of political elites, but because of the direct impact of the crisis on their lives. Millions of families lost their homes in mortgage foreclosures and unemployment reached disturbing heights. Long-term unemployment in the US as well as in Europe was particularly disturbingly high, while the cutbacks in the US's modest welfare state made in recent decades increased the degree of suffering the crash brought. Even those citizens – the vast majority of course – who had kept their homes and their jobs faced unpleasant consequences of a crisis they had done nothing to bring about. In both the UK and the US, risk has been privatized or more accurately personalized; fixed benefit retirement schemes have been replaced for most employees by schemes in which they and their employer invest money in stocks which can go up in value, but can equally well go down (Hacker, 2002, 2006). In consequence, those who retired or who planned to retire after 2008 found themselves dramatically poorer than those who retired in, for example, 2007 as the value of their pension funds collapsed. As the well-worn joke had it, 401K retirement accounts had become 201K in value. In contrast, the price of economic

failure for major economic institutions had been socializ
of every age group could contemplate the cost to them as
the bailouts of financial institutions or other enterprises st
companies regarded as 'too big to big to fail'. The leaders of man
firms saw no problem in paying themselves and their top officials in the
bonuses even as they begged for taxpayer support. In extreme cases such
as Iceland and Ireland, citizens were obliged to adopt massive financial
obligations because of the malfeasance of banks over which they had no
control and had no prior legal responsibility. The collapse of its recently
deregulated banks left Iceland's citizens accountable for their vast debts
equivalent to about $175,000 per citizen and in aggregate equal to over
75% of gross domestic product (GDP) (McKinsey Global Institute, 2010).
Thus the crisis witnessed the personalization of risk for citizens and the
socialization of not merely of risk but of the costs of failure for major
capitalist enterprises.

It was not unreasonable, therefore, to expect that a wave of anti-capitalist
anger would sweep the world. Voters could see their leaders abandoning
the almost unfettered commitment to neoliberal, market-oriented
policies that had characterized the previous three decades. They could
see ordinary people paying a price in numerous ways for the misdeeds
and miscalculations of major financial institutions. There was increasing
attention to the massive increase in inequality that had occurred in the
United States, the UK and, to some degree, in more or less all advanced
countries. Hacker and Pierson provide a compelling argument that, at
least in the US, this increase in inequality was the product of public
policies that advantaged the affluent, not merely economic trends (Hacker
and Pierson, 2010). The realization that social mobility had declined
sharply in the US and UK might have been confined to academic and
informed elites; however, the rising proportion of respondents telling
opinion pollsters that they expected that their children would not be as
well off as themselves suggests some recognition of the trend (Bradbury
and Katz, 2009; CBS Poll, 2009). The stage seemed set for a radical revival.

The political context

The historically minded might point out that the Great Depression
produced an interesting contrast between the politics of the UK and the
politics of the US. In the US, the great economic catastrophe of the 1930s
produced the pattern we might have expected; the Democrats established
a formidable hold on all the elected components of the US political system
and implemented the great reforms of the New Deal that continue to have

a profound effect on American life. In the UK in contrast, a Conservative-dominated Coalition government ruled throughout the 1930s and while its policy innovations were greater than is commonly appreciated, there was no British 'New Deal' and major period of radical reform came after the Second World War (Rodgers, 1998). The most obvious explanation for the contrast is the political context of the Depression: in the UK, the crisis overwhelmed and divided a Labour government, whereas in the US the Republicans were in power when the crisis struck and bore the ignominy of being unable to solve it. Arguably a similar dynamic occurred in the most recent crisis. The Republicans were once again in power in the US when the crisis struck and paid a political price for it. In the UK, Labour was in power and as its leader, Gordon Brown, had previously exulted in the success of his economic policies as Chancellor of the Exchequer in producing steady economic growth and an end to 'stop–go' (alternating periods of economic growth and stagnation), it found it hard to evade responsibility. The 2010 election result was one of the worst for Labour in modern times, rivaling the calamitous result in 1983 when Labour was led by Michael Foot into a near catastrophe (Wilson, 2011).

The apparently sharp contrast between UK and US politics was limited, however, by the 2010 midterm elections in the US and characteristics of the 2010 general election in the UK. As is well known, the Democrats suffered massive reverses, losing not only many seats in Congress but, because of that, control of the House of Representatives. In a massive reversal of fortunes, the Republicans were triumphant whereas two years previously they had been routed. The most energetic political force came from the far right (the Tea Party movement) whose success has been much exaggerated but certainly became a major force in internal Republican Party politics. Arguably the Republicans would have captured control of the Senate as well as the House had they not been stuck with unelectable candidates favored by the Tea Party in Delaware and Arizona, while in Alaska the establishment Republican, Lisa Murkowski, pulled off the almost unprecedented feat of triumphing as a write-in candidate over the Tea Party-backed candidate who had won the Republican nomination. In all events, the midterm election was seen as a triumph of conservatism. The obvious fact is that the Democrats lost on a massive scale; their midterm election losses were the heaviest a party has suffered numerically since 1938 and the heaviest in percentage terms since 1922 (Campbell et al., 2011).

While it is often suggested by journalists that all parties that control the White House lose seats in midterm elections, the fact is that there is considerable variation between midterm elections, and while some (for example, 1946, 1958, 1974, and now 2010) have hurt the president's party badly, in others, midterms losses have been modest. An amendment of the claim to say that the party controlling the White House does badly in midterm elections when the economy is bad makes more sense, although even here the record is mixed; the Republicans lost only 26 seats in 1982 and the Democrats actually gained seats in 1934. The objective economic record (if there is such a thing) has to be weighted by perceptions of whether the economy is improving or is sensed to be improving; both President Reagan and Prime Minister Thatcher were able to construct plausible stories (or 'frames') about how, given time, their policies would work and that it was therefore important to 'stay the course' until that happened. Contrary to conventional wisdom, therefore, there was nothing inevitable about the extent of Democratic losses in 2010; a more adroit performance by President Obama and the Democrats more generally in explaining that they had inherited a disastrous economic crisis and yet had a viable strategy for solving the crisis could have mitigated substantially the scale of their losses. Observers of British politics will know that Labour emphasized the Conservatives' economic failures of 1992 in the general election campaigns of 2001 and 2005 as well as 1997. It seemed reasonable to assume that in the United States the Democrats could make hay with the 'Republican Crash of 2008' for several elections to come.

Superficially, the 2010 election in the UK did seem to have a purely economic explanation; the incumbent party paid the price for the economic downturn. However, the election in the UK can be characterized as the election that everyone lost (Wilson, 2011). Clearly, Labour was crushed, but the Conservatives did not benefit from the poor state of the economy nearly as much as could have been expected, winning only 36 percent of the vote and falling short of having a majority in the House of Commons. The attempts by the Conservative leader, David Cameron, to modernize the party and to change its image had enjoyed only limited success. Only by forming a coalition with what had been perceived to be a left-of-center party, the Liberal Democrats, could Cameron gain power. The Conservative's failure to do better was all the more striking as the election campaign witnessed numerous disasters for Labour. Perhaps the most vivid was 'Duffygate' when Labour leader Gordon Brown, appearing to confirm all the worst stories about him, was caught off-camera insulting a long-time Labour supporter (Gillian Duffy) he had just embraced warmly on camera. Thus the Conservatives' failure to achieve a clear victory was striking given both the economic circumstances and the dynamics of the election campaign. In short, this was not a great result for Conservatives. Once again, economic determinism seems an inadequate explanation for the election. The crisis alone had not doomed the left (Wilson, 2011).

A deeper problem for the left

The instinct for Labour and the Democrats is to say that the only problem was that they were in the wrong place at the wrong time. Given the depths of the Republican humiliation in 2008, this story was never convincing for the Democrats in the US; we have argued that it was also unconvincing for Labour in the UK. Instead we shall argue that the center-left was locked into an unpopular obligation to prop up capitalism, was unable to articulate a compelling account of its policies and that public opinion had not reacted with the hostility to financial institutions that might have been expected. We start with the last point: whom did the public blame?

Whom did the public blame?

In the 1936 election campaign, Franklin Roosevelt famously attacked business interests:

> We had to struggle with the old enemies of peace – business and financial monopoly, speculation, reckless banking, class antagonism, sectionalism, war profiteering … They had begun to consider the Government of the United States as a mere appendage to their own affairs. We know now that Government by organized money is just as dangerous as Government by organized mob … Never before in all our history have these forces been so united against one candidate as they stand today. They are unanimous in their hate for me – and I welcome their hatred.

It is hard to imagine Barack Obama giving a similar speech. If he had, would it have worked politically? Opinion polls suggest that while the American public saw many to blame for the crisis, its hostility was not focused on business alone. While opinion polls differ in the actual questions asked and how they are structured, a reasonable summary is that while bankers are blamed more than most, blame is widely distributed and the proportion of the public blaming government is surprisingly close to the proportion blaming bankers. A few examples make the point. In an opinion poll in late September 2008, only 20 percent blamed 'greedy executives' for the crisis and large numbers also blamed government regulators, Congress, the Bush administration or, most commonly, all of the above (Fox News/Opinion Dynamics). A contemporaneous Associated Press/Gfk Roper poll found that two-thirds of Americans blamed the federal government 'a lot or quite a bit' for the crisis because it had failed to regulate the banks adequately. This was almost as high as the percentage of people (78 percent) who blamed bankers for the crisis by making risky loans. An October 2008 *Wall Street Journal*/NBC poll asked 'Which of the following do you think is most to blame for the current financial crisis? If you do not know enough about this to have an opinion, just say so ... Banks who made loans to people with bad credit, the Bush administration, which did not provide enough oversight of banks and investment companies, homeowners who took out loans they could not afford, investment firms who sold bad loans as investments, Congress, which did not provide enough oversight of banks and investment companies?' (NBC News/*Wall Street Journal* Poll, October 2008). Eighteen percent blamed banks making loans to people with bad credit; 14 percent, the Bush administration for not overseeing financial institutions adequately; 13 percent, homeowners taking out loans they could not afford; 11 percent, investment firms who sold bad loans as investments; 11 percent, Congress for not providing enough oversight; 24 percent blamed all of the above, and 8 percent did not know or were unsure.

In short, the public was likely to blame government officials and politicians for the crash rather than focusing the blame on the failings of financial institutions and their executives. This did not mean that financial institutions were out of the political woods; the opinion polls could be read as supporting a return to more stringent regulation. However, in the absence of a clear political lead, public opinion was inclined to see the crisis as everyone's fault, not just the bankers. Interestingly the Commission appointed by Congress to inquire into the causes of the crash also subsequently failed to reach unanimity on its causes in its January 2011 report (Financial Crisis Inquiry Commission, 2010). Instead it produced three contending reports: one by the Democratic nominees to the Commission, one by a majority of the Republican nominees and one by a sole Republican who wished to place the blame on government because it had pressured bankers to provide mortgages to low income and racial minority Americans. Thus at the end of the day there was neither popular nor elite consensus on the causes of the crash.

British public opinion seemed also ambivalent with less than enthusiastic support for left-wing policies. The proportion of Britons supporting an increase in welfare payments – 27 percent – was much lower than during the Thatcher years when around 60 percent supported such a policy. The proportion saying that government should redistribute incomes had also fallen from about 45 percent to about 35 percent (British Social Attitudes 27th Report). The Report also concluded that there was less support for 'Big Government' in Britain today than at any time since the late 1970s. Alison Park, one of the co-authors of the Report, concluded that although the crisis had made people feel less secure financially, 'The sight of governments rescuing banks and the stories of bankers' bonuses does not seem to have made them question their views about the role that government should play in the market place. There certainly has been no renewal of enthusiasm for more active government' (Curtice and Park, 2010).

The market as prison

Charles Lindblom famously argued that markets constrain political choice (Lindblom, 1977). Politicians do not need to be pressured, coerced or bribed into acting in a manner welcome to business because failure to do so would result in economic failure, job losses and harm to society more generally. The ultimate 'privileged position' of business is that politicians are forced against their instincts and values to bow to business's wants (ibid.). This is what center-left leaders such as Obama and Brown were obliged to do. President Obama expressed his frustration at the costs of the bank rescue in a 13 December 2009 interview for CBS's program, *Sixty Minutes*:

> I did not run for office to be helping out a bunch of fat cat bankers on Wall Street. Nothing has been more frustrating to me this year than to salvage a financial system at great expense to taxpayers that was precipitated, that was caused in part by completely irresponsible action on Wall Street.

Similarly, in his 2010 State of the Union address, Obama explained why he had taken action to rescue banks that he and others found distasteful.

> Our most urgent task upon taking office was to shore up the same banks that helped cause this crisis. It was not easy to do. And if there's one thing that has unified Democrats and Republicans, it's that we all hated the bank bailout. I hated it. You hated it. It was about as popular as a root canal … But when I ran for President, I promised I wouldn't just do what was popular – I would do what was necessary. And if we had allowed the meltdown of the financial system, unemployment

might be double what it is today. More businesses would certainly have closed. More homes would have surely been lost ... So I supported the last administration's efforts to create the financial rescue program. And when we took the program over, we made it more transparent and accountable. As a result, the markets are now stabilized, and we have recovered most of the money we spent on the banks.

Gordon Brown faced similar pressures. Announcing a scheme that involved government providing aid to the banks equivalent to £2,000 per person living in the UK, the then prime minister argued that 'for every family in the country, the stability of the banking system matters' (*Daily Telegraph*, 8 October 2008). Brown argued that his rescue of the banks was undertaken 'not to save the bankers but to ensure that ordinary people's savings, jobs and mortgages and the businesses on which jobs depend were secure' (*Hansard House of Commons Debates*, Volume 497, Column 910).

The inevitable consequence of these policies was, as Obama hinted, unpopularity. Obliged to bail out the bankers whose recklessness had caused the crisis and who continued to reward themselves with massive bonuses, the center-left incurred opprobrium for helping those who were its natural opponents politically. An admittedly somewhat oddly phrased question asked by Democracy Corps in November 2010 found 85 percent of Americans agreeing with the idea that 'middle class families and small businesses' played by the rules while big banks, CEOs and Wall Street did not, but received a bailout denied ordinary Americans. Sixty percent agreed with these comments strongly. The Troubled Asset Relief Program (TARP) that Obama had inherited from President Bush was seen by more Americans (43 percent) as having hurt the economy; 36 percent thought it would help (*Allstate/National Journal Heartland Monitor* Poll, 3–7 January 2010.) By July 2010, a clear majority (58 percent) thought TARP was an 'un-needed bailout' while only 28 percent agreed that TARP 'was necessary to prevent the financial industry from failing and drastically hurting the US economy' (Bloomberg Poll, 9–12 July 2010) Ironically, TARP was never fully implemented and was quietly restructured into a different plan which instead of buying 'toxic assets' put capital into the banks directly. TARP was therefore both provocative to public opinion and technically misconceived. Unfortunately for Obama, many more Americans believed erroneously that TARP was one of his policies rather than correctly identifying it as one of Bush's. Meanwhile, the administration was chastised by business groups for any rhetoric critical of business on the grounds that it not only evinced evidence of Obama's 'socialism' but also damaged the prospects for economic recovery. Thus center-left politicians suffered from the economic crisis twice over: first, simply because economic conditions were bad; second, because structurally imperative policies needed to rescue the banks and forestall a depression brought added unpopularity. In the aftermath of the midterm election, Obama moved sharply to the right. Remarkably, after the crisis had shown the weakness of financial regulations, the administration launched a drive for deregulation in January 2011, accepting business arguments that corporations were beset by torrents of unnecessary and costly regulations. A new White House Chief of Staff with a business background, William Daley, was appointed in part to prove that the administration was not 'anti-business'.

Was this determined?

The discussion so far suggests that the center-left was a victim of circumstances, and that had the center-right been in power it would have suffered the same fate. The combination of a poor economy and the pressing need to save the economy form total collapse made its losses inevitable. Was this the case?

As we noted above, the historical record indicates that it has been possible to do well politically when times are bad; models predicting the outcome of midterm elections are not based on economic variables alone but include crucially variables such as evaluations of a president's performance. If a political leader or party can make a plausible case for its policies, it may receive at least a temporary stay of execution even though economic times are bad. Unfortunately for the center-left it has failed to do so in the US and UK. Although counterfactuals cannot be proved, it is reasonable to suggest that this failure contributed to their problems.

One of the central puzzles of the Obama administration's early record is why a supposedly great communicator during the election campaign proved so incapable of putting across his case in office. The most likely explanation was that, trapped by campaign promises of being a 'post-partisan' president, he felt obliged to pursue deals and compromise with Republicans even though they were intent on total, uncompromising opposition to all his policies. From the early days of the 2008 campaign he was saying he could work across party lines.

I think that there are a whole host of Republicans, and certainly independents, who have lost trust in their government, who don't believe anybody is listening to them, who are staggering under rising costs of health care, college education, don't believe what politicians say. And we can draw those independents and some Republicans into a working coalition, a working majority for change. (*Washington Post*, 7 January 2008)

Of course all politicians make comparable statements, but for Obama this promise to change Washington by bringing people together was more than the usual rhetoric. It was a means of signaling a key difference between himself and his principal rival for the nomination, Hillary Clinton, beloved by many Democrats and disliked as intensely by Republicans. It resonated with the appeal of crossing racial divides by voting for the first ever African-American president. It might even have reflected Obama's personality and beliefs. In short, this promise to be a bridge builder not a partisan was central to Obama's message, style and possibly personality rather than being mere rhetoric. It was therefore a major constraint on his strategy in his first years in office. Had this constraint been absent, Obama could have followed the playbook so frequently used in British politics in which a leader inheriting an economic mess places the blame for it over and over again on the party that was in power when it occurred. It is true that as the scale of the midterm disaster became apparent, Obama switched styles, warning against allowing the driver who had driven the car into the ditch to re-take control after it had been hauled out. However, it was a little late to blame the Republicans after many months of eschewing partisan criticism.

A not altogether different problem faced the Labour government in the UK. Gordon Brown, as incumbent prime minister in a Westminster model political system that concentrates power, could scarcely blame the Conservatives for the GFC. He could have blamed and excoriated the bankers. The limits on Brown following this strategy were that it was scarcely compatible with either the New Labour project in general (which he had helped create) or Labour's support for the City of London and financial institutions in particular. The economic basis on which the entire New Labour strategy rested was the achievement of greater economic growth so that public sector services could be drastically improved without noticeably raising taxes. This strategy required fostering a pro-business environment and promoting sectors such as finance that generated not only employment but very large revenue streams for the Exchequer. It would have been totally unconvincing for Brown or Labour in general to attack in Rooseveltian language 'the malefactors of great wealth'.

If one political alternative for the Democrats in the US could have been to emphasize Republican responsibility for the crash, another move could have been to emulate Bill Clinton's use of policy initiatives with limited impact but great symbolic value; his endorsement of school uniforms was one such example derided by Obama. This also cut against the administration's instincts not simply because it was associated with the Clintons but because it conflicted with the President's commitment to focusing on serious policy issues. According to one inside account (Alter, 2010, p. 399), Obama said at one tense meeting as they fought for health care, 'I wasn't sent here to do school uniforms.' This was a derogatory reference to President Clinton's knack for seizing on a small-scale issue that had much wider meaning to the public; in this case, advocating school uniforms meant restoring discipline to American schools. Admirable though that sentiment might be, surely there was some room for 'school uniforms' or at least similar initiatives of limited cost and high symbolic value in the context of the bailouts.

One of the sources of public anger over the bailout was a feeling that it had received nothing in return for its money. Again, we might question why so little was done to assuage this sentiment. The recovery of the banks and the General Motors would surely not have been undermined if in return for the money, they had been required to make a series of politically popular commitments on job training, the environment and working with schools in the areas in which they operate. Except in the most altruistic actions, guarantees carry with them some implication that the rescuer gets to influence the future behavior of the rescued. The bailouts in the UK and the US provided a considerable opportunity to extract from rescued companies commitments to social responsibility. That opportunity was not taken, leaving both Democrats and Labour with certain businesses understanding that being 'too big to fail' confers on them significant commercials advantages. For example, a 'too big to fail' business being less risky than one that is not 'too big to fail' can borrow more cheaply because its bonds or debts have less risk attached to them. It would therefore be entirely reasonable to expect those businesses to make some sort of additional contribution to society. This opportunity was not developed. In consequence, governments were left looking as though they merely cared about the bankers who had triggered the crisis. Ironically it was the Conservative Chancellor of the Exchequer, George Osborne, who made the point well that little was received from the banks in return for being rescued:

It would have been better if, when we were bailing the banks out, we had secured something from the banks in return. Unfortunately I was not chancellor at the time. (BBC News Online, 8 February 2010)

Osborne himself, however, in the Merlin Project, an agreement between the government and the major banks, secured only modest commitments from the banks to invest more and restrain the magnitude of bonuses for executives. Meanwhile, in both the UK and the US, policy changes in reaction to the crisis were muted. In a quite extraordinary speech for a Governor of the Bank of England (normally expected to be a voice for financial interests), Mervyn King attacked the behavior of the banks and suggested that nothing had been done that would prevent a recurrence of the GFC. In the US, a massive law, the Wall Street Reform and Consumer Protection Act (sponsored by Senator Christopher Dodd and Representative Barney Frank) was passed whose long-term significance was unclear but which neither tackled the deeper causes of the crisis nor obtained commitments from the banks to act in a manner that furthered public policy goals. Crucially, the Act left untouched the high degree of concentration in the financial sector. Indeed, the demise of Lehman Brothers and the takeover of Merrill Lynch by Bank of America meant that the degree of concentration in the US financial sector since the onset of the GFC had in fact intensified. Fewer institutions were even too bigger to fail. Meanwhile, the agencies supposedly able to regulate and restrain the excesses of the financial industry remained numerous and in important respects in competition with each other. Financial institutions can in effect choose which agency will regulate them and receive the fees levied on them. This has created powerful incentives for regulators to be adaptive to the needs of the institutions and has also left each of them without adequate resources to consider the systemic effects of their behavior (Financial Crisis Inquiry Commission, 2010). Moreover, the Dodd-Frank Act was more the beginning than the end of a political process and it requires the promulgation of hundreds of regulations to give it effect. The hordes of lobbyists employed by financial institutions vigorously contested any regulation – for example, limiting the percentage of a payment that a credit card company could take in fees – that they disliked. The process of promulgating regulations was therefore likely to see the modest provisions of Dodd-Frank diluted further.

Move on?

It is of course not difficult to imagine circumstances in which the center-left bounces back. Current opinion polls in the UK indicate that

Labour has a clear lead over the Conservatives and that their coalition partners, the Liberal Democrats, have lost half their support. It is likely that President Obama will be re-elected and that if the Republicans allow themselves to be dominated by the Tea Party, the Democrats might yet retain a majority in the Senate and even recapture the House. The Republicans' failure to win Senate seats in Delaware and Nevada points to the dangers, even though the Democrats have many more Senate seats at risk in 2012 than the Republicans. The full implications of the coalition's cuts (and the Republicans' proposed cuts in the US) may yet destroy their prospects in the UK. An implosion of Liberal Democratic support leaves Labour as the only alternative to unpopular Conservatives.

Yet this rosy scenario for the center-left is at best a scenario that produces a recovery by the center-left, a modest outcome for the part of the political spectrum that had seemed to be the natural beneficiary of the worst crisis of capitalism since the Depression. Moreover, the recovery of the center-left may well be a return to being in office but not in power. There would seem to be neither the appetite nor, to continue the analogy, the menu available for a return to the nostrums of the left. We have noted earlier the findings of the British Social Attitudes Report that the crash did not in fact result in an increased appetite for an activist role for government in the economy. The failure of the Obama health reforms to find majority support is a striking testimony to the American public's lack of enthusiasm for an extension of the New Deal and Great Society programs, even if most of them would be beneficiaries of such an extension. While some of the unpopularity of health care reform might have been influenced by the messy congressional maneuvering that was required to secure its passage, Obama's signature domestic program failed to gain additional support as time passed. Except in almost endearingly anachronistic parts of British society, such as unions such as Unite, the collectivist moment may have passed. One suspects that for many Americans, the response to the crash reinforced individualist tendencies by appearing to show that Big Government and Big Business were in cahoots at their expense and with precious few immediate benefits for the ordinary citizen except, of course, for preventing things from being even worse! The Tea Party reflects this Jacksonian tradition in which big is always bad and likely to hurt the interests of the ordinary citizen. The now much-derided New Labour approach provided a linked response to the problems of the center-left in an age of globalization. The economy would be operated in a manner that increased growth even if this meant accepting lower taxes on the wealthy and reduced power for labor unions. Increased growth would generate increased tax revenues that could be used to improve public services. The aspirations of most Labour supporters as well as of the rest of the population for a materially better life (homeownership, a new car, and so on) would be respected. 'Mondeo Man' was welcome in the Labour Party. (The Mondeo was an automobile popular with aspirational suburbanites who had moved out from the city.) So far the Labour Party has based its policies on cutting government expenditure less and more slowly than the coalition plans. This may well be popular but is scarcely a platform for achieving much in government. As for the Democrats, the most likely scenario is that they will retain enough power to prevent a substantial rollback of existing policies. New initiatives on topics such as climate change can be forgotten. If the Supreme Court displays enough of an appetite to make law from the bench and in a fit of judicial activism invalidates the health reform law, the Democratic achievement will look modest.

It would be unfair to suggest that the American and British center-lefts are alone in seeking a new way forward. The German SDP and Swedish Social Democrats are both currently (2011) trying to analyze the reasons for the past failures and clues to an effective strategy in the future. While there might be disagreement on their relative importance, there is probably widespread agreement on what the factors involved are. First, the base of the left, the traditional working class and unions, have both declined. Left-of-center parties have even less hope of winning today relying on working-class and union support than in the past simply because the proportion of the population in those categories is too small. Second, to make matters worse for the left, 'class decomposition' has resulted in reduced loyalty to the left even among the traditional working class that remains. Third, a more individualistic materialist culture makes the public less likely to support traditional center-left policies such as extending the welfare state, as the failure of President Obama's reform of health care illustrates. Fourth, globalization creates important constraints on policy choice; even after the GFC, banks, for example, have been able to resist strict regulation, successfully threatening to relocate to another country, and corporation tax rates in all advanced democracies have shrunk in recent decades as countries compete for investment.

These challenges to the center-left have resulted in a variety of responses. The first exemplified by Old Labour and its friends in the labor unions is to deny the need to change, usually by denying the degree to which social class has changed and that globalization constrains policy choice. This approach avoids the need for possibly painful rethinking of policies but has the consequences of leaving the left seemingly irrelevant to current concerns of most voters. A second alternative approach is to recalibrate the focus of the left to a concern with the rights and problems of minorities defined on the basis of race, gender, ethnicity or sexual preference. While having the virtue of attracting new constituencies for the left, this strategy runs the risk of alienating even further some of the left's traditional supporters. The third approach, often called the Third Way, was that of the New Democrats and New Labour to embrace capitalism and aim to boost spending on public goods and the welfare state through reserving a portion of the resulting growth for the state without increasing tax rates. This approach worked well for a time but was dependent on the continued growth and success of capitalism itself. If, as in the GFC, capitalism stumbled or seemed to have inherent problems such as contradictions between the interests of finance capitalism, on the one hand, and other sectors of the economy, on the other, the strategy faltered.

How a politician creates support for and implements policies aimed at improving the condition of the least well off and tackling challenges to collective interests such as climate change is hard to see. It has been suggested above that one strategy might be to take seriously the notion that responses to the GFC embodied a contract between corporations and society which, in return for the stabilization of the economy and individual businesses by the state, created social obligations on corporations. These obligations could be met through extensions of corporate social responsibility and by commitments extensions of civil regulation in which business voluntarily commits to higher performance, for example, on environmental issues. While civil regulation (like government regulation) is open to criticism, it can also be a means to the pursuit of social and collective goods. Finally, recent history suggests that perhaps the most effective approach for the center-left is to win an election on competence grounds (Clarke et al., 2009) – or rather on the incompetence of opponents – and implement useful incremental changes once in power; Clinton's increase in the provision of health care for uninsured children would be a case in point. This strategy has the disadvantage of being incremental, and yet incremental gains can be important. However, in a contest based on competence it is all the more important that the left be seen to be confronting honestly developments such as globalization rather than wishing them away.

The question of what might be a successful strategy for the left in the future is inevitably highly speculative; we will know what works for the left only after it has succeeded. One point, however, is clear and obvious: the GFC seemed to provide the center-left with an unexpected opportunity for dominance but that has proved to be an illusory promise.

References

Alter, Jonathan (2010) *The Promise; President Obama Year One* (New York: Simon and Schuster).

Blair, Tony (2010) *A Journey: My Political Life* (New York: Alfred Knopf).

Bradbury, Katherine, and Jane Katz (2009) 'Trends In US Family Income Mobility 1967–2004', Federal Reserve Bank of Boston Working Papers 09–7.

Campbell, James E., et al. (2011) 'Postmortems of the 2010 Midterm Election Forecasts', *PS: Political Science and Politics*, 44, 1–6.

CBS News Poll (2009) May, www.cbsnews.com/.

Clarke, Harold, David Sanders, Marianne C. Stewart and Paul F. Whitely (2009) *Performance, Politics and the British Voter* (Cambridge; Cambridge University Press).

Crewe, Ivor, and Anthony S. King (2010) 'On the Causes of Domestic Policy Failure in UK Government'. Paper presented to the Annual Convention of the American Political Science Association, Washington, DC, September 2010.

Curtice, John, and Alison Park (2011) 'A Tale of Two Crises: Banks, M.P.s' Expenses and Public Opinion', in *British Social Attitudes 27th Report* (London: Sage).

Financial Crisis Inquiry Commission (2010) *The Financial Crisis Inquiry Report: Final Report of the National Commission on the Causes of the Financial and Economic Crisis in the United States* (Washington, DC: GPO).

Hacker, Jacob S. (2002) *The Divided Welfare State: The Struggle Over Public and Private Social Benefits in the United States* (Cambridge: Cambridge University Press).

Hacker, Jacob (2006) *The Great Risk Shift: The Assault on American Families, Jobs, Health Care and Retirement and How You Can Fight Back* (Oxford: Oxford University Press).

Hacker, Jacob S., and Paul Pierson (2010) *Winner Take All Politics: How Washington Made the Rich Richer and Turned its Back on the Middle Class* (New York: Simon and Schuster).

Hall, Peter, and David Soskice (eds) (2001) *Varieties of Capitalism; The Institutional Foundations of Comparative Advantage* (Oxford: Oxford University Press).

King, Anthony S. (ed.) (1998) *New Labour Triumphs: Britain at the Polls* (Chatham, NJ: Chatham House).

Lindblom Charles E. (1977) *Politics and Markets: The World's Political and Economic Systems* (New York: Basic).

McKinsey Global Institute (2010) *Debt and Deleveraging; The Global Credit Bubble and Its Economic Consequences* (McKinsey).

Rodgers, Daniel T. (1998) *Atlantic Crossings: Social Politics in a Progressive Age* (Cambridge, MA: Harvard University Press).

Sorkin, Andrew Ross (2010) *Too Big To Fail: The Inside Story of How Wall Street and Washington Fought to Save the Financial System – And Themselves* (New York: Viking).

Washington Post (2008) 'GOP Doubts, Fears "Post Partisan" Obama', 7 January.

Wilson, Graham K. (2011) 'The British General Election of 2010', *Forum*, 8, Article 1, Berkeley Electronic Press.

8
Third Parties and Political Dynamics in the UK and the US

Arthur I. Cyr

Two countries, two systems

The differences between politics in the United Kingdom and in the United States are both obvious and subtle, providing a relatively wide range of opportunities for comparative analysis. The quip that Britain and America contain two populations separated by a common language is popular because the observation is not only insightful but also readily applicable to a range of experiences, from daily life to more complex encounters. Because cultural differences are relatively subtle, comparative research can become particularly challenging.

Following the Second World War, the established tradition of praising Britain's political system for effectiveness and party responsibility continued for a time, but was challenged relatively quickly. A new, more negative attitude was a function of both the drastically weakened economic condition of the nation, and the replacement by the US as principal maritime and military power with great global reach. The established party system seemed unable to initiate public policy departures effectively to arrest long-term decline, either internationally in perceived power and influence, or domestically in deteriorating standards of living and industrial production. A corollary trend involved renewed emphasis on perceived strengths and advantages of political dynamics in the United States, reflected with persuasive though differing insights in the work of Leon Epstein, Samuel P. Huntington, Kenneth Waltz and others (Epstein, 1980; Huntington, 1957; Waltz, 1967, especially chapter 3).

This chapter evaluates the respective fates in the 2010 elections of the Liberal Democrats in the UK and the Tea Party in the US. Both political movements gained extraordinary attention in the mass media. The Liberal Democrats did not significantly increase their vote, but nonetheless held the balance of power in the House of Commons, and joined the Conservatives in the first Coalition government in Britain since the Second World War. More Tea Party candidates lost than won election, but the movement emerged as a significant faction of the Republican Party, especially in the House of Representatives. On the surface, support for a party or informal association distinctive from the major parties does not appear to be a logical or rational choice, at least on the most obvious level of participating in political formations closest to or most engaged with the power to govern. Surely for a vote to count it should be cast for one or the other of the two major parties. That at least is the argument used in both countries by major-party partisans to dissuade unconventional voting. Political activism, however, encompasses a variety of drives and incentives. Emotional and moral, as well as more dispassionate and pragmatic, sentiments define political participation in total by activists and voters. Whether or not a particular party is likely to secure actual governing power may be a principal consideration for large sections of the electorate, but not necessarily the only one, even for voters who are attempting to make a rational calculation of how their individual votes can be translated into influencing the outcome. Voters demonstrate significant incentives running from dispassionate evaluation of which party's policies are most in line with their own views, to being drawn to the charisma of a particular candidate and how that individual articulates a message more in personal than substantive terms. That helps to explain the appeal of third parties relatively far removed from power. For example, Professor Bryan Caplan, in his economist's study of electoral options, quotes Lewis Carroll's classic *Through the Looking Glass* to explain the complexity of human drives: "'I can't believe that!' said Alice. "Can't you?" the Queen said in a pitying tone. "Try again: draw a long breath, and shut your eyes."' (Caplan, 2007, p. 115).

Third parties in the US historically have pursued distinctive policy initiatives, which in turn often have been adopted by one or the other of the two major parties. Walter Dean Burnham, in a now classic work, persuasively analyzed the proposition that third parties can be indicators of strategic party realignment in the US (Burnham, 1971). A variety of other scholars and more informal observers have developed these points. A principal argument developed herein is that both the Liberal Democrats and the Tea Party currently are performing this function in Britain and the US, though so far with contrasting consequences which reflect the different party structures and political cultures involved. Additionally, the inability of either the Conservatives or Labour to win a clear House of Commons majority in the 2010 general election reflects very broad growth of third party movements in Britain, including but reaching well beyond the Liberal Democrats per se (Kavanagh and Cowley, 2010, pp. 385–9). By contrast, the Tea Party has operated within the context of the Republican Party, at least so far.

Arguably, third parties historically have been more prominent in the US than in Britain. In the US, the twentieth century witnessed Theodore Roosevelt's Bull Moose Party, the independent Progressive Party presidential candidacy of Robert LaFollette, the Dixiecrat nomination of Stom Thurmond in 1948, and Ross Perot's presidential candidacy in 1992 and 1996. The last major party realignment in Britain occurred with the rise of the Labour Party early in the twentieth century. However, Britain has been experiencing significant expansion in number and support for small parties beyond the established major parties.

Liberal Democrats and Conservative 'Tea Party'

There are very obvious differences in history and structure between the two political organizations which are the focus of this study. The Liberal Democrats are heirs to an impressive political history of major party role and rule in the nineteenth century, along with the long-term frustrations experienced by the Liberal Party in the twentieth century and the short-term spiral from political birth to extinction of the Social Democratic Party. However much frustrated over the years in efforts to achieve governing power, especially in general elections, the Liberal Democrats are a clearly defined and well established party, with a national organization and membership. The party also has established procedures for leadership and candidate selection. While arguably not as rigorous or disciplined as the Conservative and Labour Parties, they are nonetheless a competitor roughly on a par with these two dominant political organizations (Cyr, 1977, pp. 24–5, 188–9).

The Liberal Democrats fought the 2010 general election following relatively dramatic leadership turnover and some turmoil. Leader Charles Kennedy had been overthrown from within following the 2005 general election because of growing concern, even among his inner circle of strongest supporters, that he was not effective as a leader. Some argued that, beyond a publicized weakness for alcohol, his leadership style was inherently relatively disengaged, more chairman than chief executive. Reflecting the power of the modern media, simmering discontent became a major internal leadership crisis when at the start of 2006 the Liberal

Democrats learned that the Independent Television Network (ITN) was about to run an exposé on the internal controversy over Kennedy, with very specific quotes from unnamed party members. After several days of internal party strife, centered on revolt among Liberal Democrats in Parliament, Kennedy was out. His successor, Sir Menzies 'Ming' Campbell, provided a study in contrasts with Kennedy, who had personified youth and, to his critics, immaturity as well. Campbell was senior and sober by whatever definitions one chooses. He also shrewdly emphasized teamwork in his campaign for the top post, underscoring the vital mission for any seasoned executive of bringing along younger talent and encouraging potential successors. He secured support from a majority of the Liberal Democratic MPs, and in the leadership election among party members was victorious by a comfortable margin. However, two of his competitors were forced to withdraw in the wake of public revelations regarding their personal behavior. Dennis Kavanagh and Philip Cowley note that in combination with publicity about Kennedy's problem with alcohol, that meant 'Many within the party were worried that these revelations … were beginning to turn the Liberal Democrats into a laughing stock' (Kavanagh and Cowley, 2010, p. 99). This was more than an immediate concern. During decades in the wilderness as a small party, the Liberal Party had to battle constantly against an image of eccentricity and a reputation for erratic behavior. Former party leader Jeremy Thorpe had been involved in a particularly disturbing personal scandal and trial in the 1970s (Cyr, 1988, p. 122).[1]

Campbell soon ran into problems of his own in maintaining leadership. In the ruling Labour Party, Gordon Brown succeeded Tony Blair as prime minister. The new prime minister quickly made moves to sound out Liberal Democrats about participating in a possible Coalition government. Campbell, apparently following the advice of his very close adviser Lord Kirkwood, seemed to encourage the possibility. Prime Minister Brown briefly publicized his desire for 'a government of all the talents', specifically offering a cabinet post to former Liberal Democrat leader Paddy Ashdown and advisory posts to other individuals (Kavanagh and Cowley, 2010, p. 102). When this became known within Liberal Democratic ranks, the reaction was highly negative. Throughout the years since the Second World War, party leadership has explored possibilities for coalition with one or the other of the major parties, usually Labour. Very substantial elements of the membership have generally been opposed to such pragmatic efforts. The principal exception is the Liberal–Social Democratic Alliance of the 1980s, which evolved in the following decade into the Liberal Democrats. In the case at hand, when Brown decided against holding a general election in 2007, this effectively isolated Campbell, who stepped down. Among other additional considerations, he would be nearly 70 years old when the next general election likely would be held (Kavanagh and Cowley, 2010, pp. 103–4).

Sir Menzies' successor was Nicholas Clegg, a favorite of the relatively traditional Liberal Democratic establishment, and notably younger than Campbell. Clegg had a reputation for pragmatism and a stated desire to broaden the party's base beyond the strongly committed and declared individual membership. This proved a challenge in his leadership contest with Chris Huhne, who had earlier run for leader and was the more doctrinaire of the two, reflected in his role as Environment Spokesperson, a portfolio congruent with the dedicated activism of some of the most committed Liberal Democrats. Clegg's more flexible style, however, was doubtless well suited to the Coalition government negotiations which occupied the Conservative, Labour and Liberal Democratic parties following the 2010 election. Moreover, in the ultimate contest each of the leaders of the three main parties was in the top party post for the first time in a general election.

By contrast with the relatively well-established if often frustrated Liberal Democrats in Britain, the Tea Party in the US is a very recent phenomenon, at least in terms of historic continuity of organization. According to accepted party gospel, the founding moment was 19 February 2009. Rick Santelli, a financial commentator for CNBC, was on the floor of the Chicago Mercantile Exchange. Apparently spontaneously, he declared that the Obama administration's economic bailout policies were misguided, to say the least. Specifically, he denounced a mortgage assistance plan. He was specific in complaining about 'losers' who look to government subsidies, in contrast to honest hardworking citizens who had 'played by the rules'. An enthusiastic, robust crowd of commodities traders cheered him on. Mr Santelli went on to talk about a possible reenactment of the Boston Tea Party, which had helped spark the American Revolution, to be held on the shores of Lake Michigan in July. He declared there would be 'a Chicago Tea Party'. According to the widely circulated story, this led to enormous, spontaneous grassroots eruptions of popular support, and masses of television viewers responded to the message (Zernike, 2010, p. 13).

Unfortunately for the promoters of this legend, as for those who purvey other legends, the real story is different, or at least not as dramatic. Three days earlier, the first of the contemporary Tea Party rallies had been held in Seattle, Washington. The prime initiator of this protest was Keli Carender, whose main job was teaching mathematics to adults receiving public aid, supplemented by acting in an improvisational theatre company on weekends. She did not have a history of political activism, and had become energized by specific unhappiness with the rapidly escalating federal spending and deficits under President George W. Bush, and the unconventional, at least quasi-liberal leanings of Senator John McCain, the Republican Party presidential nominee in 2008 (Zernike, 2010, pp. 8–9, 13–17).

The election of clearly liberal President Barack Obama, especially given the by then dominance of the Democratic Party as well in both houses of Congress, seemed to foreclose likely attractive policy alternatives in both major parties. While some moderate and conservative Democrats were part of the new Senate and House majorities elected in 2006, the congressional party was rightly perceived to be predominantly liberal. Hence, there developed the apparently independent radical conservative statements and initiatives of Carender, Santelli, and a growing population of other disaffected citizens. A common theme which quickly emerged to unify these apparently disparate groups and individuals is that Washington and associated policy and interest group elites are distant from average, struggling American taxpayers, who in turn are systematically being disenfranchised. These events sparked a number of others, such that the Tea Party movement was a national force as candidates and party organizations were gearing up for the 2010 elections for Congress, governorships, and state legislatures. Prominent Tea Party activists are fairly consistent in stating that they are conservatives and not inherently Republican partisans or naturally aligned with that party.

Critics of the Tea Party, especially those given to conspiratorial interpretations of events, were quick to accuse established conservative activists and groups of engineering the movement.

FreedomWorks, a powerful ideological lobby for conservative causes, which is well funded and also based in Washington, is frequently mentioned as an instigator, along with popular commentator Glenn Beck of FOX News, and even the FOX network itself. Australian media executive Rupert Murdoch, with worldwide commercial holdings, great wealth, and a very private operating style, makes an ideal devil for devil theories of politics.

Kate Zernike, author of the superb book *Boiling Mad – Inside Tea Party America*, argues persuasively that FreedomWorks and other established national organizations, at least some of them well connected to the national Republican Party establishment, did not spark the Tea Party movement but did move expeditiously and efficiently to provide organizational as well as financial support. Glenn Beck is also credited for charisma as well as support in mobilizing supporters. He organized a mass rally in Washington, DC, in the summer of 2010 which not surprisingly drew extensive media attention, although by 2011 his television program was cancelled by the FOX Network. The movement remains, however, essentially a grassroots phenomenon. While supporters regularly deny formal affiliation with either major party, polls show that in fact they are heavily Republican in partisan orientation. Their efforts to influence elections have been concentrated on Republican nomination processes (Zernike, 2010, pp. 4, 221).

American history scholar Walter Russell Mead has written a persuasive essay placing the story-in-motion of the Tea Party within the web and roots of American populist history. He emphasizes the initial intense and highly divisive contest between the Federalists and their Whig successors, who gave high priority to banking and commerce, and the agrarians suspicious of those interests from the start of the Republic. If the patrician Thomas Jefferson was restrained in expressing, and even more in implementing, his philosophical convictions, radical Democrat Andrew Jackson was not. As president, he destroyed the Bank of the United States established by the Federalists led by Alexander Hamilton, emphasized and symbolized his personal commitment to the common people of the country, and – by the way – also paid off the federal debt of his time. Later in the nineteenth century, Democratic Party populism was personified notably by William Jennings Bryan, who was nominated three times for the presidency and remained throughout a strident critic of banking interests in general, and the gold standard in particular. Early in the twentieth century, Republican populism emerged to pursue a range of corporate, social services and public safety reforms, personified by Theodore Roosevelt, Robert LaFollette and others. Professor Mead echoes Ms Zernike in describing the Tea Party as a disorderly political stew, with many different ingredients. He describes an 'amorphous collection of individuals and groups that range from center right to the far fringes of American political life'. A key characteristic is what is not present: 'a central hierarchy that can direct the movement or even declare who belongs to it' (Mead, 2011, p. 29). Such characterizations can be applied to much of the history of American populism.

Individual elections and associated publicity are important for third-force candidates in both Britain and the US. The sustained attention devoted by the Liberal Democrats and their predecessors to parliamentary by-elections provides particularly persuasive evidence for this point. National media can be attracted to highlight a locality, limited financial and also human resources can be concentrated on the district, and a victory for the third party can resonate across the country.

For the Tea Party, all this symbolism and more were provided by the special U.S. Senate election in Massachusetts on 19 January 2010. The winner, Scott Brown, had spent his career in the Republican Party, including service in the state legislature. Although relatively conservative in a liberal (blue) state, he captured the seat which had been held for nearly half a century by enormously influential Senator Edward M. Kennedy, and he fully welcomed Tea Party endorsement. A savvy phrasemaker, the new Massachusetts Senator declared he had won 'the people's seat', simultaneously appealing to populism, which included but reached well beyond the Tea Party, and providing satisfaction to those who resented a perceived sense of entitlement and privilege in the Kennedy family. Until one month before the election, Democratic nominee Martha Coakley was far ahead in the opinion polls. The publicity resulting from this surprising election upset resonated forcefully across the nation for weeks, and the timing was perfect for boosting Republican Party prospects in the November elections, and Tea Party prospects in the numerous nominating primaries earlier in that year (Zernike, 2010, p. 82).

Election realities

Both the Liberal Democrats and the Tea Party supporters began their respective national election seasons in a state of justified optimism. Both parties had secured extensive publicity. Liberal Democratic leader Nick Clegg briefly became a media superstar thanks to a highly effective performance in the three-party televised debates during the general election campaign. Sarah Palin, the Republican vice-presidential nominee in 2008, became a prominent fixture on the political landscape as she crisscrossed the country, giving emphasis to Tea Party candidates.

Yet the actual elections were disappointing for both groups. For Liberal Democrats, the 2010 election provided a roller coaster, with apparent movement of public sentiment in their direction so profound that a substantial gain in parliamentary representation seemed possible. Opinion polls in the second half of April for a time placed the Liberal Democrats ahead of the Labour Party, a direct result of Leader Clegg's outstanding debate performance on television. In the US, 37 percent of respondents to a nationwide public opinion poll in March 2010 expressed support for the Tea Party movement. Had that plurality been translated directly into votes, Tea Party-supported Republicans could have captured both houses of Congress, and at a minimum would have enjoyed substantial minority representation (Kavanagh and Cowley, 2010, p. 250; Mead, 2011, p. 30).

In electoral fact, the Liberal Democrats increased their vote over 2005 but ended with fewer members of the House of Commons. The nationwide vote increased from 22 percent to 23 percent, the best level of public support since the Liberal–Social Democratic Alliance in the general election of 1983, but the calculus of vote distribution in 2010 actually reduced seats in the House of Commons from 62 to 57. After the extremely optimistic, indeed heady, political atmosphere encouraged by opinion polls, and resulting media attention, this was a major disappointment. Nick Clegg spent a grim night following the election returns at his home in Sheffield. He was blunt in stating that the night had been 'disappointing', a term used only after internal party consultations, and that 'We simply haven't achieved what we hoped.' Nevertheless, dawn provided clear evidence that the Liberal Democrats would hold the balance of power in the newly elected 'hung Parliament', where no party held a majority of House of Commons seats. Clegg conferred with other senior party representatives on a morning train ride into London (Kavanagh and Cowley, 2010, p. 201).

Ultimately, a coalition arrangement was reached with David Cameron and the Conservative Party. The Liberal Democrats had developed a carefully-prepared negotiating strategy in December 2009, well before the general election, which facilitated a disciplined focus on pragmatic considerations. During the course of the complex three-way negotiations, with Labour Party as well as the Conservative Party representatives, Liberal Democrats eventually concluded that the Conservatives were more likely than Labour to be able to deliver their MPs on any coalition agreement reached. The Conservative and Liberal Democrat parties together would have a clear House of Commons majority; Labour and Liberal Democrats in combination would still fall short of the 326 seats need for a majority. Liberal Democrats made major policy compromises, notably regarding immigration, tuition fees, and public expenditure, where £6 billion in spending cuts over the next fiscal year was agreed to, at least in principle. The coalition accord reflected pragmatic conclusions by experienced successful politicians that the Conservative–Liberal Democratic possibilities for cooperation in day-to-day parliamentary governance were greater than those of any Labour–Liberal Democratic accord. Personality dynamics were inescapably part of the process, but there was also a strong feeling among Liberal Democrats that the Conservatives would be more likely to deliver later on any commitments made, thanks to the sheer arithmetic involved.

Psychologically as well as philosophically, the modern Liberal Democratic Party arguably has more in common with the Labour Party than with the Conservatives, but many contemporary Liberal Democrats do not agree with this assumption. None of the team of negotiators with the two larger parties had been in Parliament before 1997, and they tended to see Labour as old-fashioned, tied to outdated notions of class and collectivism. Moreover, Prime Minister Brown appeared to be indecisive, in line with his reputation, and they found his and other older Labour politicians' habit of referring to the Liberal Democrats as 'the Liberals' to be annoying and grating. Liberal Democrat negotiators testified that they were put off by Brown's style and personality, reinforcing other alienating factors. Moreover, the 'New Labour' strategy which brought election successes under Tony Blair created distance from activists on the political left drawn to the Liberal Democrats. Ironically, Labour government support for the US invasion and occupation of Iraq, and dilution of traditional commitments to the ideological left in economic and social dimensions, alienated Liberal Democrats as well as Labour Party stalwarts (Laws, 2010). A less attractive Labour Party, in policy and other terms, made the Conservative Party a more plausible partner.

Practical political calculations also reportedly were extremely important. There was concern that Prime Minister Brown had been greatly weakened by the election returns, and in consequence that he would likely not survive long even if the formal coalition were put in place. There could be no guarantees that his successor as leader of the Labour Party would feel bound by the predecessor's commitments to the minority party. In less personal terms, even if a Labour–Liberal Democratic coalition survived, there was significant danger that divisions within Labour would paralyze government effectiveness. While both Conservative and Labour Party leaders were reportedly willing to consider electoral reform, a key to expansion of Liberal Democratic representation in the House of Commons, the former were more credible in their case to Liberal Democratic negotiators. Commentators also have noted that David Cameron and Nick Clegg had more in common with one another in social and educational terms than either had with Gordon Brown, but this dimension probably reinforced other considerations and reactions, rather than being decisive alone (Kavanagh and Cowley, 2010, pp. 210, 221–5).

The fact that any Coalition government had been achieved was a major benchmark event. This is the first Coalition government in Britain since the national unity coalition which fought the Second World War, which had been a time of truly monumental national crisis. Moreover, Prime Minister Winston Churchill's controversial personality and highly atypical, uneven political career reinforced incentives to assemble the strongest possible political coalition around him to address a military challenge involving national survival. Nick Clegg became deputy prime minister, with Conservative Party Leader David Cameron as prime minister. The Liberal Democrats also secured four other cabinet seats: Danny Alexander, Chief Secretary to the Treasury;[2] Vince Cable, Secretary of State for Business, Innovation and Skills; Chris Huhne, Secretary of State for Energy and Climate Change; and Michael Moore, Secretary of State for Scotland.

The fate of the Tea Party in the November 2010 US election was broadly disappointing, in that extensive media attention and often dramatically optimistic rhetoric from movement representatives translated into relatively limited gains. In Senate races, the Tea Party captured five of the ten seats where a Republican candidate was explicitly endorsed by the movement, a noteworthy but not overwhelming performance. The actual impacts of Tea Party support tended to be blurred by the fact that candidates endorsed often would have clearly won with or without the backing of this particular faction. In several states, Tea Party intervention damaged Republican prospects. US Senate majority leader Harry Reid was considered in serious trouble for re-election but prevailed narrowly over Republican Tea Party challenger Sharron Angle, even though she led in Rasmussen and other polls narrowly up until the election. Controversial Delaware Tea Party candidate and media commentator Christine O'Donnell upset popular relatively moderate Mike Castle in the Republican Senate primary, opening the door for the November victory of Democrat Christopher Coons. In Arkansas, Tea Party-endorsed Republican John Boozman defeated incumbent Senator Blanche Lincoln. Tea Party-backed candidates Rand Paul and Marco Rubio won in Kentucky and Florida, after defeating Establishment Republican primary election rivals. Popular West Virginia Democratic Governor Joe Manchin prevailed narrowly over Tea Party-backed John Raese. Manchin emphasized his own conservative credentials and kept a clear distance from the Obama administration. Arguably, these victories do not reflect decisive Tea Party impact. Southern Senate representation, once solidly Democratic, has been shifting to the Republican Party over the long term, beginning with the election of John Tower from Texas in 1962 and the dramatic party shift in 1964 by Senator Strom Thurmond of South Carolina. In Wisconsin, previously unknown conservative Ron Johnson defeated popular liberal Democratic incumbent Senator Russ Feingold, but then refused to join the Tea Party Caucus in the Senate, emphasizing instead Republican Party unity.

In races for the US House of Representatives, candidates backed by the Tea Party won only approximately a third of the seats they contested. In total, the Tea Party backed 130 candidates running for seats in the House. Only 43 of them were victorious with the voters. The winners are not concentrated in regional terms, which can be construed as good news for the Tea Party in indicating they are not regionally limited. By comparison, the Dixiecrat Party led by Senator Strom Thurmond of South Carolina in 1948 and the American Independent Party led by Governor George Wallace of Alabama in 1968 received some votes in all parts of the nation, but remained concentrated in the South in terms of core support (Moe, 2010, pp. 1–4).

House Speaker Republican John Boehner has so far been successful in orchestrating reductions from proposed spending, including an accord in April 2011 for $39 billion in cuts, while keeping the Tea Party within his wider coalition (Taylor, 2011, p. 1). Republican defections were held to approximately 25 percent of the party's House members, while Democrats split much more evenly on the bipartisan initiative. A respected pragmatic negotiator, the requirement to deal with this far-right faction within his party caucus may actually have facilitated reaching agreement with Democrats, by indirectly encouraging them to be more flexible. Moreover, the need to raise the national debt ceiling by the end of the summer 2011 has given fiscal conservatives considerable leverage. Boehner has (through May 2011) skillfully, effectively exploited this leverage, stating in a well-covered spring public address on Wall Street and elsewhere that any such change must be tied to comparable significant reductions in future spending.

Alienation and party politics

The Liberal Democrats in Britain, both currently and historically, represent a magnet for those alienated from the established two-party system. This population grew slowly but surely after the Liberal Party nearly became extinct during the early years following the Second World War, reaching a plateau of approximately 20 percent of the national vote during the decade of the 1980s. In 2010 as in previous elections, opinion polls showed evidence that the electorate was not strongly committed to the third party in any substantial proportions, and was very fluid. This also is congruent with party history.

Liberal Democratic Party Leader Nick Clegg's impressive debate performance attracted massive media attention to both him and his party, reflected in the apparent surge in support noted above. This complemented the overall strategy of the Liberal Democrats' leadership, which was to work hard to minimize Conservative gains, while concentrating aggressive efforts in seats held by Labour which appeared vulnerable. However, Clegg's appeal was clearly personal, and did not readily or directly translate into reliable in-depth support for the Liberal Democratic Party. Polling evidence is that public support was strongly associated with his image and projection over the media, not to a more comprehensive attraction to his party. Voters who indicated increased support for Clegg did not similarly show significant backing for Liberal Democrat policies, which in various ways contrasted with major established themes in both the Conservative and Labour parties. Moreover, party canvassers did not find similar evidence of broad movement to the Liberal Democrats. This apparent support may have been more an effort to give Clegg credit and recognition for notable skill in debate over television, with no actual intention of shifting one's vote to his party (Kavanagh and Cowley, 2010, pp. 144–5, 253). A review by the *Guardian* newspaper of detailed opinion surveys collected by the National Centre for Social Research indicated the public supported the Liberal Democrat approach in only two policy areas: support for families over the institution of marriage, and maintenance of existing levels of taxation and public spending. On other policies, including expanding social welfare benefits, liberalizing immigration, and electoral reform, the public was opposed to Liberal Democrat positions (Young, 2010, pp. 1–2).

A separate, distinctive factor in Liberal Democratic success is local community engagement. Candidates who were dedicated to very specific local services, especially helping residents limited by age, income or both in dealing with government bureaucracy and rigidities, profited significantly at the polls. This local community service dimension of the Liberal Democrats and predecessor Liberals has become strongly established in party culture, and is highly congruent with traditional Liberal philosophy. While community service may rightly be viewed in positive terms, motivation for this sort of dedicated effort also implies at least some alienation from more established mainstream agencies of government and party representation (Cyr, 1988, p. 165). At the same time, as the research of John Curtice demonstrates persuasively, there has been a marked decline in the number of marginal constituencies in Britain. This makes dramatic Liberal Democratic gains in future general elections less likely, and at least indirectly created pressure for Coalition government in 2010 (Kavanagh and Cowley, 2010, p. 223). As Vernon Bogdanor emphasizes, there has also been a growing geographic concentration of the Liberal Democrat vote over the past three decades.

For example, the Liberal–Social Democratic Party Alliance achieved 25 percent of the vote in the 1983 general election and 23 House of Commons seats, compared with a Liberal Democrat 2010 vote of 23 percent and 57 seats (Bogdanor, 2011, p. 124).

The tone of Tea Party partisans, including leaders, in these terms is strikingly and stridently different, with a very active hostility to established institutions and policies of government which is apparent and can easily dominate evaluation of the genesis of this highly visible new movement. In April 2010, a comprehensive and methodologically reliable survey of voters across the US was conducted by the *New York Times*/CBS News. What emerges from the data is strong alienation from government, including politicians as well as policies, on the part of Tea Party supporters in comparison with all respondents. Only 2 percent of respondents but 11 percent of Tea Party partisans felt the US is becoming a 'socialist' country. A total of 46 percent of all respondents but 91 percent of Tea Party supporters disapproved of President Barack Obama's handling of the economy. Percentages regarding other policy matters were similar, with 51 percent and 93 percent respectively disapproving his handling of health care, and 53 percent and 91 percent disapproving his handling of the federal deficit. Congress was unpopular with both sample populations. Significantly, foreign policy was generally not considered a priority by either group (Zernike, 2010, pp. 195–227).

Parties, public policies and governance

Examining and reflecting on the recent experiences of the Liberal Democrats and the Tea Party movement, in the respective contexts of their wider political systems, provides largely contrasting insights concerning their roles and prospects. Both political organizations reflect incentives reaching well beyond conventional calculations geared to achieving power within the status quo. Both have benefitted significantly from the capacity of modern media to bypass party organizations, facilitating direct communication between activists and candidates and the wider public. Yet arguably neither, despite extreme alienation by some Tea Partiers, is represented by the complete departure from reality personified by the Queen who challenged Alice in Wonderland.

As indicated at the start, historically the British parliamentary system was regularly praised by American political scientists and others. Often, these observers have been individuals giving high priority to commitment to the rule of law, sympathetic to Britain's historic accomplishments, and impressed by perceived pragmatism which contrasted with Continental practices. In more recent times, the weakness of the British economy and often acrimonious nature of party-political debate has encouraged more critical views.

Yet in the current discussion, the British political system is demonstrating notable collective effectiveness in channeling fundamental political disagreements in directions of effective compromise and, so far, governance. The unusual Conservative–Liberal Democratic coalition so far has survived and carried out legislative initiatives to address the exceptionally serious fiscal and financial challenges facing the nation. Conservatives have been committed to drastic expenditure cuts, while Liberal Democrats strongly support education and social services spending, yet the parties' partnership continues. This tension will also continue. Former prime minister Tony Blair sums up the situation in his memoirs, stating briefly and perhaps too bluntly that the 'challenge for the coalition' is that the two parties involved 'don't really agree' (Blair, 2010, p. 673). Blair, however, also personifies exceptionally pragmatic leadership which transformed his party into 'New Labour', abandoning socialist ideology and other policies unpopular with the contemporary electorate. Ultimately, pragmatic considerations were dominant in reaching the Conservative–Liberal Democratic Coalition government. Ironically, Blair had been instrumental in moving the Labour Party away from traditional policies and attitudes in ways which ultimately, combined with other considerations, made the Conservatives relatively more attractive as partners for Liberal Democratic leaders.

The two parties have based their alliance on policy understandings which include in particular a commitment to a referendum on reforming the electoral system from the existing traditional first-past-the-post approach, in which a voter marks the ballot for only one candidate per office, with the winner based on a majority or at least plurality of votes cast, to one of Alternative Vote (AV), a system in which voters indicate support for a pool of candidates for office, in order of preference. If no candidate has a majority after first preferences are counted, the one with the fewest votes is eliminated and those ballots reallocated to voters' second choice on the list. Liberal Democrats had opposed this structural change, preferring instead the Single Transferable Vote (STV), a variation in proportional representation in which voters' ballots are cast for their preferred candidates. After a candidate has been elected or eliminated, the remaining ballots are cast in order of preference for remaining candidates. Liberal Democrats compromised on form of representation on the reasonable perception that they could not do any better, and the proposed system if implemented will almost certainly result in more

Liberal Democrat MPs. The Conservatives were successful in creating the Coalition government at least in part because they were willing to open the door to electoral reform, to be decided by a popular referendum in May 2011, and were seen by the Liberal Democrats as more likely than Labour actually to deliver on this promise.

The issue of changing the national voting system was settled for the lifetime of the Conservative–Liberal Democrat coalition, and perhaps many years to come, by the 5 May 2011 referendum, which coincided with local and regional elections. The Liberal Democrats suffered devastating losses on all fronts. The major victor was the Scottish National Party, which won 69 of the 129 seats in the Scottish Parliament, capturing a majority for the first time. The British electorate rejected the AV system by a margin of more than two to one. Liberal Democrats were also decimated in local councils, losing nearly 700 seats, a third of their total; a massive strategic defeat, especially given the traditional and broadly recognized commitment of the party to success through community service. To some extent, the party suffered from becoming a target for public resentment of the extensive austerity and spending cuts introduced by the government to address the economic crisis and fiscal deficit. Beyond that, Conservative Party leaders decided in January to shift to a stance of active hostility to electoral reform.

This stance rankled the Liberal Democrats, who accused the Conservatives and others in the 'No to AV' camp of using misinformation, untruths, and outright lies in their campaign. Liberal Democrat Minister Chris Huhne even confronted Prime Minister Cameron in cabinet over the issue shortly before the vote, demanding that he disavow the tactics of the referendum's opponents. Protests aside, there were no silver linings from the May 2011 elections results for the Lib Dems. Respected analyst John Curtice of the University of Strathclyde adds that policy does matter, and dramatic Liberal Democrat shifts on public spending, student fees and other matters to accommodate the Conservative Party were strongly resented in particular by strongly committed Liberal Democrats. Nevertheless, there was no significant move to abandon the Conservative–Liberal Democrat governing coalition (interview, John Curtice, 11 May 2011; Cowell, 2011; Vinograd, 2011).

While foreign policy was not a highlight of the election campaigning, marked differences between substantial anti-European Union (EU) pressures within the Conservative Party, and historic Liberal support for the EU, conceivably could mean political trouble down the road. Over approximately the past one and one-half decades, anti-EU sentiment has grown markedly among Conservative MPs. A substantial number of

MPs who had been pro-Europe retired from politics at the time of the 1997 general election, and many of their successors are characterized by skepticism or outright hostility to the long-term movement toward European economic and administrative integration. The research of Mark Garnett and Philip Lynch has confirmed that general hostility to Europe and support for British nationalism, often with strongly emotional overtones, has grown over the years in the Conservative Parliamentary Party, but they also indicate the subject became less divisive and central to internal party discussion and debate after the decade of the 1990s (Garnett and Lynch, 2003, pp. 155–8). In this context, public attitudes generally appear to be moving in negative directions regarding the EU. A March 2011 ComRes opinion poll showed that 63 percent of Conservative supporters and 66 percent of Liberal Democratic supporters want a referendum regarding continued membership in the EU. Only 38 percent of Labour supporters felt this way. Only 29 percent of the entire sample felt that Britain 'gets a good deal' from membership of the EU, while 55 percent disagreed with the statement.[3]

The political system overall is undergoing major transition in the steady long-term loss of support for both major parties, in favor of the Liberal Democrats and a wide range of other party formations. When Samuel H. Beer and R.T. McKenzie published classic studies of British party politics in the 1950s and 1960s, both authors devoted almost exclusive attention to the Conservative and Labour parties, and largely ignored the Liberal Party and others (McKenzie relegated the Liberals to three pages in an appendix). Beginning in the 1960s, third parties have become steadily if unevenly stronger. In the elections in June 2009 for representatives to the EU, fully 40 percent of the vote went to parties other than the Conservatives, Labour and Liberal Democrats. In the 2010 general election, the Conservatives and Labour together received only 66.6 percent of the votes, the lowest for the two parties together since Labour replaced the Liberal Party in popular support. The current governing coalition in Westminster therefore reflects long-term structural change in British politics (Kavanagh and Cowley, 2010, pp. 115–26, 385).

The Tea Party faces a much more uncertain present and future, with no history of survival and long-term revival comparable to the Liberals and Liberal Democrats. Rather, by definition a highly innovative new phenomenon in organizational terms has no well-defined political road. In this regard, extensive media coverage during the 2010 political campaigns, only to end in some significant election defeats, gives pause to any prediction of long-term survival and influence. Rigidly inflexible adherence to ideological prescriptions among members of the faction in the House of Representatives may stymie effective policy implementation, including reductions in federal spending. House Speaker John Boehner so far has proven adept, however, at maintaining the Tea Party within the Republican coalition.

Foreign policy also contains challenges for extreme conservatives on the US side of the Atlantic. Walter Russell Mead contrasts the neo-isolationism of Patrick Buchanan, Texas Congressman Ron Paul and (his son) newly elected Kentucky Senator Rand Paul with support for interventionism, and emphasis on backing Israel, personified by Sarah Palin and various neoconservatives in and around the administration of President George W. Bush (Mead, 2011, pp. 31–2). In the case of Britain, renewed controversy over EU membership could sunder the Conservative–Liberal Democratic coalition. In the US, if the Republican Party in 2012 recaptures the White House, or even the Senate, these serious foreign policy concerns which characterize the political right could feed a central, intense policy debate.

In recent years, American political analysts have not usually looked to Britain for inspiration. Yet Karl Marx developed his definitions of alienation as well as class conflict through direct experience in Britain, the country which launched the world's first Industrial Revolution. In both countries, third parties have served to channel activists and voters alienated from the mainstream of politics and the two major political parties. So far, the British system is proving more effective in translating current populist pressures in manageable political directions (Cannadine, 1999, chapter 5; Cyr, 1988, chapter 6). Liberal Democratic participation in government represents pragmatic channeling of increasingly diffuse British voter preferences. By contrast, the Tea Party has reinforced and underscored strongly felt ideological drives and divisions within the US body politic.

Notes

1. Party leader Jeremy Thorpe was first caught up in financial problems connected with the failure of a bank with which he was associated. This was soon overshadowed by the accusation that he allegedly was involved in a murder conspiracy involving a man with whom he had a personal relationship. His reluctance to give up the party leadership post caused great anxiety in party ranks.
2. The position originally went to David Laws, who was forced to resign after revelations of illegal parliamentary expenses.
3. ComRes data available at www.comres.co.uk/.

References

Beer, Samuel H. (1967) *British Politics in the Collectivist Age* (New York: Alfred A. Knopf).

Blair, Tony (2010) *A Journey – My Political Life* (New York and Toronto: Alfred A. Knopf).

Bogdanor, Vernon (2011) *The Coalition and the Constitution* (Oxford and Portland, OR: Hart Publishing).

Burnham, Walter Dean (1971) *Critical Elections and the Mainsprings of American Politics* (New York: W.W. Norton & Company).

Butler, David, and Dennis Kavanagh (1994) *The British General Election of 1992* (Basingstoke, London and New York: Macmillan and St. Martin's Press).

Cannadine, David (1999) *The Rise and Fall of Class in Britain* (New York: Columbia University Press).

Caplan, Bryan (2007) *The Myth of the Rational Voter – Why Democracies Choose Bad Policies* (Princeton and Oxford: Princeton University Press).

Cowell, Alan (2011) 'Liberal Democrats Dealt Huge Blow in Britain Votes', *New York Times*, 6 May 2011.

Crewe, Ivor, and Anthony King (1995) *SDP – The Birth, Life and Death of the Social Democratic Party* (Oxford and New York: Oxford University Press).

Cyr, Arthur I. (1977) *Liberal Party Politics in Britain* (London and New Brunswick: John Calder Ltd And Transaction Books, Inc.).

Cyr, Arthur I. (1988) *Liberal Politics in Britain* (New Brunswick and Oxford: Transaction Books, Inc.).

Duverger, Maurice (translated by Barbara and Robert North) (1963) *Political Parties – Their Organization and Activity in the Modern State* (New York: John Wiley & Sons, Inc.).

Epstein, Leon (1980) 'Whatever Happened to the British Party Model?', *American Political Science Review*, 14, 9–22.

Garnett, Mark, and Philip Lynch (2003) *The Conservatives in Crisis: The Tories After 1997* (Manchester and New York: Manchester University Press and Palgrave Macmillan).

Huntington, Samuel P. (1957) *The Soldier and the State – The Theory and Politics of Civil-Military Relations* (Cambridge, MA: The Belknap Press of Harvard University Press).

Hurst, Greg (ed.), et al. (various years) *The Times Guide to the House of Commons* (London: Times Books, HarperCollins Publishers).

Kavanagh, Dennis, and David Butler (2006) *The British General Election of 2005* (Basingstoke: Palgrave Macmillan).

Kavanagh, Dennis, and Philip Cowley (2010) *The British General Election of 2010* (Basingstoke: Palgrave Macmillan).

Laws, David (2010) 'Why the Lib Dems Rejected Labour', *New Statesmen*, www.newstatesman.com/2010/12/labour-lib-andrew-coalition.

Mead, Walter Russell (2011) 'The Tea Party and American Foreign Policy – What Populism Means for Globalism', *Foreign Affairs*, 90(2), 28–44.

Moe, Alexandra (2010) 'Just 32% of Tea Party Candidates Win', *MSNBC*, 3 November, http://firstread.msnbc.msn.com.

Phillips, Kevin (1993) *Boiling Point – Democrats, Republicans, and the Decline of Middle-Class Prosperity* (New York: Random House).

Rasmussen, Scott, and Douglas Schoen (2010) *Mad as Hell – How the Tea Party Movement is Fundamentally Remaking Our Two-Party System* (New York: HarperCollins Publishers).

Taylor, Andrew (2011) 'Budget Pact Barely Touches Current Year Deficit', Associated Press, 13 April, www.ap.org.

Vinograd, Cassandra (2011) 'UK Coalition Government Will Endure, Politicians Stress', *Globe and Mail*, 7 May.

Waltz, Kenneth (1967) *Foreign Policy and Democratic Politics – The American and British Experience* (Boston: Little, Brown and Company).

Young, Penny (2010) 'What Voters Really Think of Lib Dem Policies', *Guardian*, 23 April, www.guardian.co.uk.

Zernike, Kate (2010) *Boiling Mad – Inside Tea Party America* (New York: Times Books/ Henry Holt and Company).

9

Party Polarization and Ideology: Diverging Trends in Britain and the US

Nicol C. Rae and Juan S. Gil

Major political parties in the US have traditionally been regarded as organizationally weak, highly decentralized, and ideologically incoherent by comparison with the highly disciplined, ideological, class-based parties of the UK. Indeed, for a period after the Second World War American parties' scholarship tended to look approvingly at the UK as an alternative model of a well-functioning party system for modern advanced industrial democracies (Schattscheider, 1942; Ranney, 1962; Beer, 1965). British scholar David Butler and others had challenged this interpretation as early as the 1950s (Butler, 1955), but it was the late Leon Epstein (1980) in his 1979 American Political Science Association (APSA) presidential address 'What Happened to the British Party Model?' who convincingly argued that the UK party system was no longer – if it ever had been – an appropriate model for American political parties.

Epstein may have ended the debate over whether British-style 'responsible party government' had any relevance as a prescription for America's weak, non-ideological, political parties and separated governmental system, yet since he wrote it appears that in several aspects American and British parties have become more similar. American political parties are now more ideologically polarized, more disciplined and united in Congress, and more centralized in their operations than they were in the post-war decades, when the APSA's famous report *Toward a More Responsible Two Party System* (1950), bemoaned the US parties' lack of those very characteristics. In the UK, by contrast, social change has eroded the dominance of the class-based political parties of mid century, promoted ideological convergence between the Labour and Conservative parties, and assisted the increasing fragmentation of the British party system in the post-Thatcher era.

Here we argue that contemporary American and British parties remain fundamentally different – particularly in their organizational aspect – and the apparent convergence is due more to changes in the respective societies as British society has become somewhat less polarized while American society has become more so since the 1960s.

The evolution of the mass party in the UK

The landslide victory of the Labour Party under Clement Attlee in the 1945 election concretized the shift to modern mass political parties in the UK (Garnett and Lynch, 2007). According to Maurice Duverger (1964) – building on the earlier work of Robert Michels (1962) – the centralized, disciplined, and ideologically-based 'mass' party was the essential twentieth-century political organization. The socialist (and later communist) parties that evolved to represent the newly enfranchised working class in rapidly industrializing late nineteenth-century Europe pioneered the form, which became so electorally successful that it was replicated successfully by ideological movements of the far right (Fascism and Nazism) and the center right (British conservatism, post-1945 Christian democracy): a process described by Duverger as 'contagion from the Left'.

The evolution of mass parties in the UK in the late nineteenth and early twentieth centuries stemmed from the electoral reforms of 1832, 1867, and 1884. These reforms – combined with rapid industrialization, urbanization and the increasing dissemination of socialist ideas – ignited a perfect storm amongst the newly enfranchised and rapidly growing working class (Epstein, 1967; Strayer, 2009). Trade unions emerged to voice their concerns but found inadequate room for the representation of working-class interests within the Liberal and Conservative parties, which were dominated by landed and business interests respectively. The Trades Union Congress (TUC) thus became the propelling force behind the creation in 1900 of the Labour Representation Committee (LRC) that laid the groundwork for the Labour Party (Beer, 1982; McKenzie, 1963).

In the 1918 election another extension of the franchise to all men aged over 21 and all women aged over 30, combined with the social unrest generated by the First World War, led to a dramatic surge in support for Labour. As working-class voters rallied increasingly behind the burgeoning mass party, the existing major parties were forced to either adapt or be overtaken. In the inter-war years the Conservatives successfully evolved organizationally and ideologically to the new mass party politics while the divided Liberals floundered and were reduced to clear minority party status by the 1930s. The Tory adaptation had been in progress since the 1860s when Benjamin Disraeli had the foresight to create the National Union of Conservative Associations in an effort to mobilize Tory support among the middle and working classes. After 1918, while Labour relied on the trade unions, the National Union served as a recruitment and organizational tool for the Conservatives (Blake, 1970; Pugh, 1982).

Whereas nineteenth-century British party politics was characterized by loosely organized coalitions in Parliament (Duverger's 'cadre parties'), twentieth-century politics became characterized by majoritarian mass party government. In the nineteenth century religion played a key role in determining the British vote, but by 1945, Labour had succeeded in making social class the predominant basis for division in British politics. The political conversation now revolved around the level of unemployment, the social conditions of the working class, and the nationalization of industries. This was buttressed by the social fabric of twentieth-century British society where nearly half of the population consisted of manual laborers. Although there was always a significant working-class electoral 'defection' to the Conservatives, by mid century manual workers constituted a formidable electoral base for the Labour Party (Halsey, 1986; Beer, 1982).

In the post-Second World War era each major party, Conservative and Labour, would be characterized by a mass, dues' paying membership and a highly structured national organization that wielded tight control over its local branches (McKenzie, 1963). The freedom of MPs was also severely limited by the threat of expulsion from the party. Beer termed this the end of the individualistic structure of representation and the dawn of a collectivist era that gave greater power to the mass membership of the parties (Beer, 1982). McKenzie gave some caution to this characterization by observing the inevitability of bureaucratic top-down governance in any large social organization invoking Michels' 'iron law of oligarchy' (McKenzie, 1963). Nevertheless, compared to the mid nineteenth century, power had decisively seeped away from the individual MP toward the party leader, the party whips, and the national party organization.

The period 1945–70 constituted the apogee of two-party politics in Britain. The two major parties regularly captured over 95 percent of the two-party popular vote and almost 100 percent of the seats in the House of Commons. Both parties had developed hierarchical national organizations that held MPs accountable for enacting the party's program.

In the post-war years the UK's mass parties came closest to exemplifying the 'responsible party government' that so impressed American political scientists dissatisfied with the current state of the American major parties. The foundation of the British system was the two-tiered structure of British society: essentially a class dichotomy that persisted from the end of the First World War into the 1960s (Butler and Stokes, 1974). While there were clear ideological differences between the major parties, a rough consensus persisted between them on an interventionist economic policy, the maintenance of the welfare state, the Atlantic Alliance, and the supremacy of the House of Commons in Britain's liberal democratic political system. All of these would come under challenge, as would the two-party system itself and the nature of mass party politics, in Britain after 1970.

America's anomalous party system

The American party system has long been regarded as an oddity by comparison with the post-Second World War party systems of the other major industrial democracies (Duverger, 1964). The most conspicuous difference has been the absence of the mass party form and the mass socialist or communist parties of the left that spawned it in the European context (Michels, 1962). Numerous explanations have been proffered for this aspect of 'American Exceptionalism'. The most commonly accepted versions have held that America's individualistic, 'Lockean Liberal' political culture precluded socialism from even emerging as a substantial political force (Hartz, 1955; Lipset and Marks, 2000). Others focused on the additional factor of historical timing and the enfranchisement of a mass electorate in the US by 1830, prior to the onset of the cataclysmic social forces – rapid industrialization, urbanization and political democratization – that would help to unleash socialism in Europe in the last decades of the nineteenth century (Epstein, 1967). Other versions explained the limited appeal of socialism to the American masses in terms of a weakened working-class consciousness due to mass immigration in the late nineteenth century, higher working-class living standards, and political repression, or a combination of the three (Kolko, 1967).

Universal adult, white, male enfranchisement by the 1820s gave rise to America's first seriously organized and durable national political party in the form of the Jacksonian Democrats (Wilentz, 2005). Jackson's various opponents had similarly organized themselves into the Whig Party by the time of the 1836 election. The Jacksonian parties were highly decentralized with real authority lying with largely autonomous state and local party leaders and the national party only really having an existence in presidential election years (Silbey, 1994). By the 1840s many of these local organizations had morphed into 'political machines' with local bosses controlling party nominations and blocs of voters and rewarding their supporters with the spoils of office – patronage and favors. By the last quarter of the nineteenth century the most powerful state and local machine bosses essentially determined the choice of the party's presidential nominees at the quadrennial national party convention.

These party machines were highly organized and disciplined in their own locale but they were definitely not mass membership organizations on the lines of the emerging European model. To say the nineteenth- and early twentieth-century American parties were not ideological would be an exaggeration except in a very strict Marxist sense of the term. Their differences on policy issues were real and they clearly represented differences in approaches to government and society to the voters of their day (Gerring, 1998). The differences with European – and particularly British – parties became more pronounced when the latter adopted a clearly mass party form in the early twentieth century (Michels, 1962; Duverger, 1964) while the American parties retained their very loose definition of party membership, and their other decentralized, relatively non-ideological, characteristics. Indeed, the American parties were organizationally weakened by the reforms of the Progressive Era (1900–17) which were specifically designed to reduce the influence of party bosses and machines over American politics (Hofstadter, 1955).

How then were the clearly aberrant American parties to be explained? For Duverger (1964) the only answer was that the American parties were pre-modern 'cadre parties' based on local cliques of notables that would hopefully eventually evolve along European mass party lines. The American political scientists who authored the 1950 APSA report and the other admirers of the post-war UK parties shared this hope, although in general they were fairly pessimistic that America's apparently ramshackle and nebulous major parties could be so transformed (Committee on Political Parties, 1950; White and Mileur, 2002). The post-New Deal Democratic Party with its reactionary southern segregationist wing that dominated the US Congress in the post-war years seemed like a very poor analogue for Clement Attlee's Labour Party. Neither of the American parties made much sense in European ideological terms.

Leon Epstein (1967) was very much the exception among scholars of political parties on both sides of the Atlantic in taking the American parties seriously on their own terms. He did not see them as retrograde forms of a predominant and desirable European mass party model but as adaptations by American parties to specifically American conditions: to the 'American Mold', as he put it in his later textbook on US parties (Epstein, 1986). He also did not view the mass party European model as necessarily enduring. Social change in European societies prior to the Second World War has given rise to the mass party, but Epstein anticipated that continuing social change in post-war Europe might well begin to erode the predominance of class-based mass parties. Since the mid 1960s this is exactly what has happened in the UK, as we shall see in the next section. On the other side of the Atlantic, American parties have also undergone an adaptation to a changed social and political universe that has brought them somewhat closer in form to their European counterparts. Yet there remain specifically American social features that explain persistent differences in the nature of party cleavages in the two countries.

British parties since 1970

By comparison with the mid twentieth century, the dominance of the UK's major parties has significantly attenuated. Party membership, which had peaked in the 1950s at 3 million for the Conservative Party and 1 million for Labour, had fallen by 2009 to a meager 250,000 and 166,000 respectively (Marshall, 2009). Additionally, although both major parties have maintained a top-down hierarchical structure, recent decades have witnessed several rebellions of parliamentary backbenchers, and even cabinet ministers, who were nevertheless able to survive politically with little disciplining from the party leadership. Furthermore, the political conversation between the parties had changed from the ideologically polarized class politics of the immediate post-war decades. New Labour's triumph in 1997 did not promise any new nationalization of industries or an expansion of redistributive economics. Instead the 1997 party manifesto focused on the stabilization of the economy, improvement of government services and constitutional reforms (Seyd, 1998). Finally, one need look no further than the resurgence of the Liberal Party since the mid 1960s and the emergence of the nationalist parties as a major political force in Scotland and Wales (and the divorce of electoral politics in Northern Ireland from UK party politics following the onset of civic unrest in the province in the late 1960s) to recognize that significant electoral gains can now be made without appeal to class antagonism. Thus, in all significant respects, the UK has witnessed a significant erosion of the two-party system and the mass party model (Webb, 2000; Lynch, 2007).

Several alternative theories of political parties and party systems have risen to fill the explanatory vacuum. The 'catch-all party' model emphasizes the declining role of ideology after the 1960s and presents the major parties as opportunistic marketing organizations, willing to highlight party personalities in order to have a centrist appeal (Kirchheimer, 1966). The 'cartel party' model depicts the major UK parties as aiming for control of state resources in order to deny the minor parties the ability to achieve power. Like the 'catch-all party' this theory de-emphasizes ideology in favor of a more hardnosed thirst for electoral spoils (Katz and Mair, 1995). Perhaps the most accurate alternative model (and one that also has relevance for political parties in the contemporary US) is Panebianco's (1988) 'electoral professional party', which correlates recent social and technological developments with changes in the campaign practices of political parties as the latter, by electoral necessity, respond to these changes. The UK parties now rely more on big donations from wealthy businessmen than on dues from a dwindling mass membership to run their campaigns. As technology and political media have evolved (for example, television and the internet) the perceived relational distance between the voter and the candidate has decreased. These developments have allowed political party campaigns to become increasingly more professional and technocratic, employing a specialized array of opinion pollsters, speech writers, political consultants, and spin-doctors. The marketing of candidates now emphasizes personality rather than party ideology and relies on a scientific understanding of the electorate to 'target' specific categories of voters. Whatever the theoretical advantages or disadvantages of either of the preceding theories, their similarities reveal a definite waning in the appeal of the mass party model as a function of the decline of party ideology, the rising emphasis of candidate personality over party policy, and the decline in party membership.

The erosion of the mass party model has been in large part a consequence of the breakdown of the socio-economic realities that legitimatized it as a workable theory. Britain came out of the Second World War as a battered and bruised second-tier power that still experienced high economic growth and rising living standards during the 1950s and 1960s. The rapid changes that struck British society had also transformed the occupational division of labor. Manual laborers in 1900 comprised close to three-quarters of the British workforce. By 1950, this number had dropped to below two-thirds, and by the time of New Labour's victory in 1997 to below a third. Replacing the decrease in the traditional working class was a robustly growing sector of white-collar, professional, and technical workers (Halsey, 1986). In their classic work on the British electorate, Butler and Stokes (1974) found some evidence of what they have termed a class 'de-alignment' as Labour's traditional working-class base appeared less likely to vote loyally for the party. Heath et al. (1985) observed that the core class-based electoral constituencies of the Conservative and Labour parties had in fact largely adhered to their traditional party allegiances, but the relative sizes of the traditional Labour and Tory bases had decreased within the overall electorate. This development offered an opportunity for the Liberal Party and the Nationalists in Scotland and Wales to make gains amongst the growing sector of white-collar professionals.

Ronald Inglehart (1977) has proposed that in times of political peace and relative economic growth, the priorities of voters change from basic material needs to more value-laden and lifestyle-oriented concerns. If correct, the post-materialist theory could afford us an explanation as to the new consensus and cleavages in British party politics. The Labour victories following the Conservative Thatcher–Major era (1979–97) did not see the repeal of the relatively popular planks of Tory policy – privatization, lower taxes, and restrictions on trade union power. Thus, as it concerns the economy, there has developed a degree of consensus (not without marginal differences) between the parties on fiscal policy and economic management. Tony Blair's 1997 victory was to a great extent due to an increase in voters' confidence that the Labour Party could manage the economy as well as the Conservatives (not to mention his decision to jettison the cherished Clause IV of the Labour Party constitution that committed the party to state ownership of industry). New Labour's promise not to raise taxes nor extend nationalization of industries seemed to leave no substantive differences between the Labour and Conservative parties on the economy (Seyd, 1998). The greater differences between the parties now concerned constitutional reforms, improvement of government services, devolution, and the UK's degree of integration with the European Union (EU).

This shift has been accompanied by a fragmentation of politics at the regional level – most particularly in Scotland and Wales – and a lack of party cohesion in European policy. As already mentioned, John Major in the early 1990s could not bring the Conservatives together under a common European policy, but neither did Blair succeed in doing so with Labour after 1997. Tony Blair's pro-European integration policies and speeches were commonly met by opposition from his Chancellor of the Exchequer Gordon Brown, who wielded great influence amongst Labour MPs (McKay, 2006).

In conjunction with determining its future in Europe, Britain is also treading new political territory at home by experimenting with its own version of federalism. During the heyday of the two party system in the 1950s, there was relatively little regional deviation from national electoral results in terms of the performance of Labour and the Conservatives. Since the 1960s stark regional variations in support for the major and minor parties have appeared leading commentators to talk of a so-called 'North–South divide' with a dramatic decline in support for the Conservatives in northern England, Wales and Scotland, and for Labour in the South and South East of England. In large tracts of Britain, either the Liberal Democrats or Nationalists are the greatest electoral threat to Labour or the Conservatives. Scotland, Wales, and Northern Ireland's politics are now characterized by multiparty electoral systems and Coalition governments encouraged by the proportional electoral systems used to elect the devolved Parliaments in Edinburgh, Cardiff and Belfast (Webb, 2000; Lynch, 2007). Indeed, after four years of leading a minority government the Scottish Nationalists secured an outright majority in the Scottish Parliament as a result of their stunning success in the May 2011 elections, perhaps portending a shift toward a 'dominant party' model within a multiparty system in Scotland.

With Blair's establishment of devolved governments and Parliaments in Scotland, Wales, and Northern Ireland and the new directly elected Mayor in London, government in the UK has splintered in hitherto unforeseen ways. Coupled with the growing power of the EU over British government policy, we can see that the supremacy of Parliament itself has come under challenge from above and below. Thus, despite having reached a relative consensus on the economy the new political cleavages in Britain seem to be fragmenting its politics and presenting new difficulties for deliberation on post-materialistic issues.

Ideological 'sorting', culture war, and US parties since 1980

In the decades following the 1950 APSA report, the evidence seemed to indicate that the major American parties were slipping further into decline and irrelevance. Traditional party machines continued to erode as civil service reform and state and federal welfare dried up their traditional sources of rewards to their adherents (Burnham, 1981). The advent of television further personalized politics and placed an onus on individual candidates and personalities rather than party programs (Ranney, 1978). Evidence from voting behavior studies during the 1960s and 1970s seemed to demonstrate a move away from both political parties toward independence as the party identities forged in the New Deal era eroded with the passage of time (Nie et al., 1979; Ladd and Hadley, 1978). US presidents after Franklin D. Roosevelt largely abandoned attempting to govern with their parties and turned to personal appeals and coalitions of support on an issue by issue basis (Milkis, 1993). In Congress the party leadership remained weak in the face of powerful congressional committees in the 1960s and 1970s, and reforms that eroded the power of committee chairs in the early 1970s appeared only to have diffused power further to subcommittees and individual members (Patterson, 1978). Post-Second World War American parties remained stuck in a peculiarly American mold: decentralized, undisciplined, and, by comparison with the European mass parties, ideologically incoherent.

Yet while parties' scholars were proclaiming the final demise of the American political parties as anything more than ballot labels for 'structuring the vote' (Ranney, 1978), during the late 1970s and 1980s they missed signs of a dramatic transformation of America's major political parties and the emergence of a new era of partisan polarization in American politics. These changes occurred in all aspects of party activity: organization, governing institutions, and electoral support.

After the 1968 election debacle, the Democratic Party's McGovern-Fraser Commission, established to propose reforms in the party's rules for presidential delegate selection, more or less created the new primary system of presidential candidate selection through the imposition of national party rules on the Democratic state parties (Shafer, 1983). This was an unprecedented development (later upheld by the federal courts) in American party history since state parties had hitherto been sovereign over national parties. By contrast the Republican Party – starting in the mid 1960s under the national chairmanship of Ray Bliss – led the way (the Democrats had caught up by the 1990s) in the development of the national party committees as fundraising machines and providers of services such as candidate recruitment, polling, and candidate and campaign consultant training (Cotter and Bibby, 1980; Bibby, 1980). This transformed the role of the national committees from doing little beyond organizing the quadrennial national party conventions to regularly coordinating national party campaigns. The evolution of what John Aldrich (1995) has described as 'the party in service' (a concept somewhat similar to Panebianco's 'electoral professional party') has led to far more visible and effective national party organizations in American politics than was the case at the time of the APSA report.

The rise of partisanship in the electorate and in government since 1970 has been driven by the long-term fallout from the civil rights revolution of the 1960s (Abramowitz, 2010). For the generally progressively-inclined political scientists writing about US parties in the 1940s and 1950s, the presence of the white segregationist South in the Democratic Party was the single greatest barrier to an American party alignment along the class lines more familiar in other advanced democracies (Key, 1949). Once the Democrats adopted the cause of black civil rights in the 1960s and enforced desegregation and equal voting rights on the recalcitrant South in the mid 1960s, the barrier was removed as newly enfranchised Southern black Democrats enrolled overwhelmingly as Democrats and the more economically conservative elements in the White South moved towards the increasingly conservative national Republican Party after the 1964 Goldwater campaign (Rae, 1994). Lower-status white Southerners were initially homeless in the post-civil rights Southern political system, many gravitating toward the former Alabama governor and segregationist George Wallace in 1968 and Southern Democrat Jimmy Carter in 1976. Since 1980 they have generally aligned with the Republican Party largely due to their conservatism on cultural-religious issues (Layman, 2001).

Following the civil rights revolution Southern white conservative Democrats in Congress were largely replaced either by African-Americans or Republicans, depending on the racial composition of the district. Those who survived compiled a voting record much closer to the liberal mainstream of the national Democratic Party than their white segregationist predecessors (Rohde, 1991). The result in Washington and in many state legislatures has been two more ideologically homogeneous parties with members keen to implement liberal and conservative goals in legislation. To do that these members have strengthened the party leadership in both chambers of Congress at the expense of committees and committee chairs. In turn the leadership is expected to manipulate the procedures of the House and Senate to achieve partisan objectives (Sinclair, 1995; Aldrich and Rohde, 2000). The upshot since 1980 has been a degree of partisan unity and partisan voting unprecedented since the last decades of the nineteenth century, and a much more polarized relationship between the parties on Capitol Hill and between the White House and Congress when they happen to be controlled by different parties: witness the government shutdown of 1995, the 1998 impeachment of President Clinton, and the battles over continued funding of the Iraq War and the 'War on Terrorism' between President George W. Bush and the Democratic Congress in the last two years of Bush's presidency.

Polarization in Washington has been reinforced by growing electoral and societal polarization – particularly on economic and cultural issues.

The civil rights revolution led to more ideologically homogeneous liberal (Democrat) and conservative (Republican) parties in Washington, DC, and as this persisted over time perceptions of party ideology filtered down to the electorate as voters took their cues from political elites (Hetherington, 2001). Political Scientists have also noted that: (1) voters increasingly perceive the ideological distinctions between the parties; and (2) the number of ideologically attuned partisans in the electorate has increased (Abramowitz, 2010). These voters of course are those most likely to be involved in political campaigns at all levels and to turn out in disproportionate numbers for the low turnout primary elections that select party candidates. As congressional and legislative redistricting has become a more exact science through the utilization of computer technology, so the majority of congressional districts are now drawn in such a manner as to guarantee the election of one party or the other, and this being the case more ideological candidates reflecting the activist base of the predominant party in the district are more likely to be elected (Fiorina et al., 2005). Redistricting cannot be the whole story; however, as party polarization has also risen in the US Senate, and it has been demonstrated that competitive districts have also been selecting ideologically polarized major party candidates (Oppenheimer, 2005; Abramowitz, 2010).

It thus seems that polarization in the American electorate goes deeper than mere gerrymandering of Congressional districts to produce specific partisan outcomes. And while critics such as Fiorina (2005) have pointed out that the degree of issue polarization among party elites is not really replicated at the mass level, this may be largely irrelevant as voters appear to be increasingly taking their voting cues from those ideologically polarized elites (Hetherington, 2001). Another aspect of the increasing polarization is the so-called 'culture war', where the strongest divisions between the parties have occurred on issues with a religious-cultural dimension, such as abortion and gay rights (Layman, 2001). The more religiously observant voters and areas of the country have gravitated toward the Republican Party while the more secular regions on the coasts have become increasingly Democratic. In the 2004 election it was estimated from exit polls that the degree of religious observance had been the single greatest determinant of electoral choice (Jacobson, 2007). The strong role played by cultural-religious issues in electoral politics is almost unique to the contemporary US with its much higher level of religious observance, and has hardly been apparent in the more secular UK.

In sum, American party politics has become markedly more polarized over the past 40 years, and the major American political parties far more homogeneous. In terms of organization the mass party model remains as remote as ever, however. Traditional state and local-based party machines have virtually disappeared, but the parties at the national level have become far more important players in electoral politics through their control of party rules and the development of the 'party in service'. The driving forces behind polarization have been the various material and cultural interests associated with either party whose endorsements are eagerly sought by party candidates in low-turnout primary elections, and whose adherents account for most of the activist base of both parties. The expectation by the interests and the candidates they help elect that the party should 'deliver' for them in terms of policy once in power, accounts for the greatly enhanced power of party leaders on Capitol Hill. All of this does not amount to the evolution of a mass party but an adaptation of the American party system to a more ideologically charged and polarized national cultural climate than was the case half a century ago. And while something approaching 'responsible party government' has become more feasible in Washington than in the 1950s, the American constitutional system still places formidable barriers – the separation of powers, the short election cycle, and the supermajority requirements for most legislation in the Senate – in its path.

Recession and the party system

The onset of economic recession in the UK and the US in 2008 and the subsequent near collapse of the US and British banking systems certainly had major short-term electoral impact in each country.

In the US the recession and the banking crash helped refocus the political debate on issues of size of government and competence in economic management, and guaranteed a comfortable if not overwhelming victory for Democrat Barack Obama, with a Democratic Congress in the November 2008 general election. In the wake of the election there was a great deal of speculation that the outcome foreshadowed the sublimation of the culture war by a new era of interventionist government. But almost all of the interventionist measures implemented by the new Democratic administration – the 2009 economic stimulus package, the bailout of General Motors and Chrysler, and the massive expansion of the federal role in health care envisaged in the Obama heath care plan passed in March 2010 – proved to be not only unpopular with Republican and independent voters but inspired a conservative revival via a new conservative popular movement – the Tea Party (Rasmussen and Schoen, 2010). The January 2010 victory of Republican Scott Brown in the Massachusetts special US Senate election for the seat of legendary liberal

Democrat Edward Kennedy was an early demonstration of the potency of the Tea Party. The latter also played a critical role in the 2010 midterm elections which witnessed the return of the US House to Republican control with the largest House gains (63 seats) since 1938, and a net gain of six US Senate seats (Pew Research Center, 2010; Rasmussen and Schoen, 2010). Yet the culture war and its Red/Blue regional divisions were still evident in the 2010 electoral results. The Republicans made their greatest gains in areas of existing strength – the culturally conservative South and Midwest – and the Republican wave met its greatest resistance in New England and the Pacific Coast. The Democrats held on to four critical US Senate seats in Nevada, Colorado, Connecticut and Delaware and control of the chamber due to a reaction against Republican candidates who were too culturally conservative for these states. The partisan polarization that had characterized US politics since the 1970s rose to even higher levels in the first two years of the Obama administration with unprecedented levels of party voting in Congress and increasingly exaggerated partisan rhetoric on cable television, internet blogs and social networks (Brownstein, 2011). So while size of government issues definitely seemed to have gained ascendance over religious cultural matters relative to the pre-2006 situation, it seemed likely that the onset of economic recovery would see a return to the cultural-religious and lifestyle cleavages that had dominated US politics over the previous two decades.

In the fall of 2008 the UK experienced its own banking crisis and bailout with the government essentially taking over several major UK banks – such as the Royal Bank of Scotland. The recession also hit hard in Britain with rising unemployment and growing public concern about the UK's escalating budget deficit. From a balanced budget, when Labour came to power under Tony Blair in 1997, the deficit had escalated to £170 billion by early 2010. With a general election imminent, the need for drastic reductions in public spending to deal with the deficit resuscitated the traditional economic cleavage between Labour and the Conservatives. The latter emphasized the need for public spending reductions, while Labour, under Blair's successor as prime minister, Gordon Brown, advocated combining spending reductions with tax increases and sparing the social services.

The economic meltdown certainly was the major contributory factor to Labour's dismal showing in the May 2010 UK election, when its popular vote total fell below 30 percent (Wilson, 2010). This led to big gains by the Conservatives under David Cameron, but the Tories' popular vote total increased only by 3.8 percent and they failed to secure an overall majority in the House of Commons. To do so they had to form an unlikely coalition with the Liberal Democrats who did not make the major advance expected of them during the campaign but whose vote held up well enough to deny the Tories an overall majority and simultaneously seal Labour's doom. The 2010 election was characterized by the increasing importance of party leader personalities (as exemplified by the UK's first televised debates between party leaders), the micro-targeting of voters, and the funding of the parties by large donations from outside interests rather than membership dues. The 'party in service' thus continued its ascendancy in UK electoral politics.

The advent of a full Coalition government for the first time since the Second World War was another indication of the UK's move to multiparty politics. In return for joining the Conservatives in government, the Liberal Democrats were given five cabinet seats including the position of deputy prime minister for their leader, Nick Clegg. They also extracted a promise from Cameron that a referendum would be held on the use of the Alternative Vote (AV) system for Westminster elections. The advent of Britain's first Coalition government since the Second World War has consolidated the development of multiparty politics – already commonplace in Scotland, Wales, and Northern Ireland and in local government throughout the UK – at the national level. This is likely to be the case even given the continuance of the plurality voting system for Westminster elections following the defeat of the proposal to introduce AV by a more than two to one margin in the May 2011 poll.

Conclusion: convergence and divergence

The fundamentals of the American political system have not changed since Epstein (1980) wrote, but the US parties have undoubtedly become more polarized and ideological, while Britain's – as we have seen in the preceding section – have become somewhat less so and the mass party organizational form of the major parties has come under considerable strain. From this it would appear that party polarization is not a product of strong party organization but deeper societal forces. In the US the mass party never developed and US parties remain organizationally weak (although their national organizations are currently more vigorous than at any previous point in US history). Yet the existence of increasingly strong cultural cleavages in American society has polarized the party system as party activity at all levels has become dominated by single-issue activists and interest groups on either side of the cultural-religious divide. The end result has been a party system that more closely matches the prescriptions of the 1951 APSA report, although whether this has had the desired positive effect on the quality of American democracy and government is highly debatable.

In the UK, new models such as Panebianco's 'professional party' and Aldrich's 'party in service' seem to more accurately describe much of current political party activity than the mass party model. The mass party organizational structure of the Conservative and Labour parties remains fundamentally the same, but membership in both parties has drastically reduced and private financing of parties has come to play a much greater role. As the British political universe has changed due to societal and technological change so the old socio-economic class basis of British politics has attenuated, regional electoral cleavages have become much more salient, and a new set of post-materialist issues has appeared on the political spectrum although none of these is as strong as the religious-cultural cleavage in the US. The multiparty system has become prevalent in the new devolved politics of Northern Ireland, Scotland and Wales, and is becoming increasingly evident at the national level as well with the major parties now regularly securing less than 70 per cent of the national popular vote and the formation of the first Coalition government since the 1940s after the 2010 general election. In the devolved Parliaments the multiparty system has been further encouraged by the adoption of more proportional electoral systems.

In short, the changes noted by Epstein (1980) in the traditional British party model so venerated by post-war American party scholars have been accelerated and reinforced since he delivered his APSA presidential address in 1979. The UK has continued to move toward a multiparty system and the prevalence of the old mass parties – Labour and Conservative – has eroded in favor of newer party formations more reflective of a less class-based British society. Given this situation it seems less likely than ever that the British parties and party system could ever again serve as a model for the US. Conversely it appears that the influence has recently been more in the other direction, as the British parties – both old and new – have taken on more attributes of the contemporary American party in service in terms of organization, financing, and campaigning, and reduced emphasis on traditional class-based ideologies. To this extent there is now probably greater convergence in the nature of party politics between Britain and the US than at any time since the cadre party era of the early nineteenth century.

This convergence toward the American 'party in service model' is not unique to Britain, of course, as trends in party organization and competition in the other major democracies since the Second World War have been in the same direction: the decline of class based parties, more post-materialist politics and parties, and the development of sub-national party systems. The separation of powers in the US as opposed to the European parliamentary systems probably continues to be the most significant factor in structuring the essential differences between American parties and those of Britain and the other European democracies. In parliamentary systems a concentration of power at the center of the party is necessary to gain power and form a government. The separated US system encourages a deconcentration of power that will keep American parties relatively decentralized and undisciplined relevant to the UK. Comparison between the two party systems will remain relevant in so far as we can use this comparison to assess changes in the nature of political parties and party politics in contemporary democracies. Yet the time when the party systems of Britain and the US might serve as models for each other has truly passed.

References

Abramowitz, Alan I. (2010) *The Disappearing Center: Engaged Citizens, Polarization and American Democracy* (New Haven: Yale University Press).

Aldrich, John H. (1995) *Why Parties: The Origin and Transformation of Political Parties in America* (Chicago: University of Chicago Press).

Aldrich, John H., and David W. Rohde (2000) 'The Consequences of Party Organization in the House: The Role of the Majority and Minority Parties in Conditional Party Government', in J.R. Bond and R. Fleisher (eds), *Polarized Politics: Congress and the President in a Partisan Era* (Washington, DC: CQ Press), pp. 31–72.

Beer, Samuel H. (1965) *British Politics in the Collectivist Age* (New York: Random House).

Beer, Samuel H. (1967) *Modern British Politics* (London: Faber and Faber).

Bibby, John F. (1980) 'Party Renewal in the Republican Party', in Gerald M. Pomper (ed.), *Party Renewal in America: Theory and Practice* (New York: Praeger), pp. 102–15.

Blake, Robert (1970) *The Conservative Party from Peel to Churchill* (London: Eyre & Spottiswoode).

Brownstein, Ronald (2011) 'Pulling Apart', *National Journal*, 24 February.

Burden, Barry C. (2001) 'The Polarizing Effect of Congressional Primaries', in Peter F. Galderesi, Ezra Marni and Michael Lyons (eds), *Congressional Primaries and the Politics of Representation* (Lanham, MD: Rowman & Littlefield), pp. 95–115.

Burnham, Walter D. (1981) *The Current Crisis in American Politics* (New York: Oxford University Press).

Butler, David (1955) 'American Myths about British Parties', *Virginia Quarterly Review* 31, 46–56.

Butler, David, and Donald Stokes (1974) *Political Change in Britain: The Evolution of Electoral Choice* (London: Macmillan).

Committee on Political Parties, American Political Science Association (1950) *Toward a More Responsible Two-Party System* (New York: Rinehart & Company, Inc.).

Cotter, Cornelius P., and John F. Bibby (1980) 'Institutional Development and the Thesis of Party Decline', *Political Science Quarterly*, 95, 1–27.

Duverger, Maurice (1964) *Political Parties: Their Origin and Activity in the Modern State* (London: Methuen).

Epstein, Leon D. (1967) *Political Parties in Western Democracies* (New York: Praeger).

Epstein, Leon D. (1980) 'Whatever Happened to the British Party Model?', *American Political Science Review*, 74, 9–22.

Epstein, Leon D. (1986) *Political Parties in the American Mold* (Madison: University of Wisconsin Press).

Fiorina, Morris P., Samuel J. Abrams and Jeremy C. Pope. (2005) *Culture War? The Myth of a Polarized America* (New York: Pearson-Longman).

Garnett, Mark, and Philip Lynch (2007) *Exploring British Politics* (Harlow: Pearson Longman).

Gerring, John (1998) *Party Ideologies in America: 1828–1996* (New York: Cambridge University Press).

Hartz, Louis (1955) *The Liberal Tradition in America: An Interpretation of American Political Thought since the Revolution* (New York: Harcourt, Brace).

Hasley, A.H. (1986) *Change in British Society* (Oxford: Oxford University Press).

Heath, Anthony, Roger Jowell and John Curtice (1985) *How Britain Votes* (Oxford: Pergamon Press).

Hetherington, Marc J. (2001) 'Resurgent Mass Partisanship: the Role of Elite Polarization', *American Political Science Review*, 95, 619–31.

Hofstadter, Richard A. (1955) *The Age of Reform: From Bryan to FDR* (New York: Knopf).

Inglehart, Ronald (1997) *Modernization and Postmaterialism: Cultural, Economic, and Political Change in 43 Societies* (Princeton: Princeton University Press).

Jacobson, Gary C. (2000) 'Party Polarization in National Politics: The Electoral Connection', in Jon R. Bond and Richard Fleisher (eds), *Polarized Politics: Congress and the President in a Partisan Era* (Washington, DC: CQ Press), pp. 9–30.

Jacobson, Gary C. (2007) *A Divider, Not a Uniter: George W. Bush and the American People* (New York: Pearson Longman).

Katz, Richard S., and Peter Mair (1995) 'Party Organization, Party Democracy, and the Emergence of the Cartel Party', *Party Politics*, 1, 5–28.

Key, V.O., Jr (1949) *Southern Politics in State and Nation* (New York: Knopf).

Kirchheimer, Otto (1966) 'The Transformation of West European Party Systems', in Joseph LaPalombara and Myron Weiner (eds), *Political Parties and Political Development* (Princeton: Princeton University Press), pp. 177–99.

Kolko, Gabriel (1967) *The Triumph of Conservatism: A Reinterpretation of American History, 1900–1916* (Chicago: Quadrangle).

Ladd, Everett C., and Charles D. Hadley (1978) *Transformations of the American Party System: Political Coalitions from the New Deal to the 1970s*, 2nd edn (New York: Norton).

Layman, Geoffrey (2001) *The Great Divide: Religious and Cultural Conflict in American Party Politics* (New York: Columbia University Press).

Lipset, Seymour M., and Gary Marks (2000) *It Didn't Happen Here: Why Socialism Failed in the United States* (New York: Norton).

Lynch, Philip (2007) 'Party System Change in Britain: Multi-Party Politics in a Multi-Level Polity', *British Politics*, 2, pp. 323–46.

Marshall, John (2009) 'Membership of UK Political Parties', House of Commons Library, Standard Note SN/SG/5125, 17 August.

McKay, David (2006) 'The Reluctant European: Europe as an Issue in British Politics', in John Bartle and Anthony King (eds), *Britain at the Polls 2005* (Washington, DC: CQ Press), pp. 78–96.

McLean, Iain (2006) 'The Politics of Fractured Federalism', in John Bartle and Anthony King (eds), *Britain at the Polls 2005* (Washington, DC: CQ Press), pp. 97–124.

McKenzie, Robert T. (1955) *British Political Parties* (London: Heinemann).

Michels, Robert (1962) *Political Parties: A Sociological Study of the Oligarchical Tendencies of Modern Democracy* (New York: Free Press).

Milkis, Sidney M. (1993) *The President and the Parties: The Transformation of the American Party System Since the New Deal* (New York: Oxford University Press).

Nie, Norman S., Verba, Verba and John R. Petrocik (1979) *The Changing American Voter*, 2nd edn (Cambridge, MA: Harvard University Press).

Oppenheimer, Bruce I. (2005) 'Deep Red and Blue Congressional Districts: the Causes and Consequences of Declining Party Competitiveness', in Lawrence C. Dodd and Bruce I. Oppenheimer (eds), *Congress Reconsidered*, 8th edn (Washington, DC: CQ Press), pp. 135–57.

Panebianco, Angelo (1988) *Political Parties Organization and Power* (Cambridge: Cambridge University Press).

Patterson, Samuel E. (1978) 'The Semi-Sovereign Congress', in Anthony King (ed.), *The New American Political System* (Washington, DC: American Enterprise Institute), pp. 125–77.

Pew Research Center (2010). 'A Clear Rejection of the Status Quo, No Consensus about Future Policies: GOP Wins Big Despite Party's Low Favorability', 17 November, http://pewresearch.org.

Polsby, Nelson W. (1983) *Consequences of Party Reform* (New York: Oxford University Press).

Pugh, Martin (1982) *The Making of Modern British Politics: 1867–1939* (Oxford: Blackwell).

Rae, Nicol C. (1994) *Southern Democrats* (New York: Oxford University Press).

Ranney, Austin (1962) *The Doctrine of Responsible Party Government: Its Origins and Present State* (Urbana: University of Illinois Press).

Ranney Austin (1978) 'The Political Parties: Reform and Decline', in Anthony King (ed.), *The New American Political System* (Washington, DC: American Enterprise Institute), pp. 213–47.

Rasmussen, Scott, and Douglas Schoen (2010) *Mad as Hell: How the Tea Party Movement is Fundamentally Remaking Out Two-Party System* (New York: HarperCollins).

Rohde, David W. (1991) *Parties and Leaders in the US House* (Chicago: University of Chicago Press).

Schattschneider, E.E. (1942) *Party Government: American Government in Action* (New York: Farrar and Rinehart).

Seyd, Patrick (1998) 'Tony Blair and New Labour', in Anthony King et al., *New Labour Triumphs: Britain at the Polls* (Chatham, NJ: Chatham House Publishers), pp. 49–74.

Shafer, Byron E. (1983) *Quiet Revolution: The Struggle for the Democratic Party and the Shaping of Post-Reform Politics* (New York: Russell Sage Foundation).

Silbey, Joel (1994) *The American Political Nation: 1838–1893* (Stanford: Stanford University Press).

Sinclair, Barbara (1995) *Legislators, Leaders, and Lawmaking: The US House of Representatives in the Postreform Era* (Baltimore: Johns Hopkins University Press).

Sinclair, Barbara (2005) 'The New World of US Senators', in Lawrence C. Dodd and Bruce I. Oppenheimer (eds), *Congress Reconsidered*, 8th edn (Washington, DC: CQ Press), pp. 1–22.

Strayer, Robert W. (2009) *Ways of the World* (Boston: Bedford-St. Martin's).

Webb, Paul D. (2000) *The Modern British Party System* (London: Sage Publications).

White, John K., and Jerome M. Mileur (2002) 'In the Spirit of Their Times: "Toward a More Responsible Two-Party System" and Party Politics', in John C. Green and Paul S. Herrnson (eds), *Responsible Partisanship: The Evolution of American Political Parties since 1950* (Lawrence: University Press of Kansas), pp. 13–35.

Wilentz, Sean (2005) *The Rise of American Democracy: Jefferson to Lincoln* (New York: Norton).

Wilson, Graham K. (2010) 'The British General Election of 2010', *Forum*, 8(2), Article 1, hwww.bepress.com/forum/vol8/iss2/art1.

10
Economics, Partisanship and Elections: Economic Voting in the 2010 UK Parliamentary and US Congressional Elections

Michael J. Brogan[1]

Introduction

The outcome of the 2010 UK general election and the US midterm elections provided an unequivocal reminder of the impact of economic downturns on electoral politics. A vast literature on economic voting confirms that voters typically respond to economic fluctuations; they tend to reward incumbents for a good economy and punish them for a poor one (Lewis-Beck and Stegmeir, 2007). Though the reward–punish hypothesis is a common theme in the economic voting literature, there are limits to its application. It is unable to fully capture the dynamic in which voters select their party's candidate regardless of economic performance (Campbell et al., 1960; Evans and Anderson, 2006; Gerber and Huber, 2009).

This raises intriguing questions about what really motivated voters' decisions as to the polls in both the US and UK elections. Were the Obama administration and Brown government effective in recasting the elections not as a referendum on their parties' performances, but rather on which party's economic platform would best steer each country out of the current economic downturn? Or did voters simply reject these claims and punish the incumbent parties as a result of the economic downturn?

Though evidence points to the latter, the results of the 2010 election in both countries, nevertheless, provide a puzzle for researchers. Though the 2010 UK general election and the US midterm elections resulted in a change of power, the outcome of each contest does not fully conform to the reward-punish hypothesis. The UK general election resulted in a Coalition government between the Conservatives and Liberal Democrats. Though the Conservative Party gained 97 seats, the increase was not enough to secure an outright majority. In the US, power was divided among the Democratic and Republican parties between the two chambers in Congress. The Republican Party secured majority status in the House of Representatives with an historic gain of 63 seats, but fell short of taking control of the Senate, even though the party gained seven seats. The outcome of both elections leads us to ask if voters truly engaged in economic voting or if their political partisanship biased their economic perceptions, thus limiting the impact of the economic vote (Evans and Anderson, 2006; Lewis-Beck and Nadeau, 2001; Lewis-Beck, 2006).

Electoral results in both countries provide fertile ground in which to test the economic vote comparatively. The two dominant sentiments that defined voters' perceptions of the 2010 elections, economic pessimism and anti-incumbency, are essential characteristics for understanding economic voting in both countries. For instance, in the US, an average of 85 percent of voters felt the economy had gotten worse over the past year,[2] and in the US, an average of 45 percent of Americans felt economic conditions had deteriorated. In terms of assessments of Prime Minister Brown and President Obama, both leaders had low approval ratings among the public. For Prime Minister Brown, an average of 26 percent of the electorate[3] were satisfied with his performance and, for President Obama, he had an average of 46 percent approval for 2010, which was a decline of 6.5 percentage points from his first year in office.

Though both anti-incumbency and economic pessimism typically cause economic voting, the primary reason why this process did not trigger a complete rejection of the incumbent parties (Labour and the Democrats) in either or both nations, or the embrace of the major opposition parties (Conservatives and Republicans), is due to the interactive relationship between voters' partisanship and their perceptions of the overall performance of the economy. The conditioning process between these two factors in voting behavior influences voters' decisions at the polls. This relationship points to a limit within economic voting theory – namely that economic fluctuations do not necessarily provide an efficient form of democratic accountability as suggested by the reward–punish hypothesis (Anderson, 2007).

The interaction between voters' partisanship and their economic perceptions helps explain the reason that not all voters engaged in economic voting during the 2010 elections and how some voters chose to vote against their economic interests. How did this occur? Among voters who did vote against their economic interest, these individuals nevertheless perceived the economy was a problem but did not hold the incumbent party accountable because of it. Partisanship plays a dominant role in voters' decisions at the polls, and in the case of the 2010 elections, it helps explain why UK and US voters engaged in a form of limited economic voting, which can be characterized as a decision-making process of aggrieved acquiescence. Though voters were angry with the Labour and Democratic parties over their management of the economy, this did not mean they were ready to embrace the Conservatives and Republicans as viable alternatives.

Overall, this chapter provides a comparative analysis of economic voting in the 2010 UK general election and US Congressional House of Representatives election.[4] The chapter is organized into four parts. After a brief review of the economic voting literature to date, the second section defines the economic-minded partisan model. The third section offers an analysis of individual level voting behavior before and after the campaigns in each country. The chapter concludes with a brief discussion of the model's findings and what we can expect in the near term for the Obama administration and Cameron government.

Economic conditioning and partisan conditioning of economic voting

A substantial body of research has found that voters' economic perceptions influence their voting choice (Kramer, 1971; Kinder and Kiewiet, 1978; Nadeau and Lewis-Beck, 2001; Lewis-Beck et al., 2008; Dolan et al., 2009). Within the literature, significant research also finds that voters' partisanship influences their economic perceptions in voting decisions (Campbell et al., 1960; Key, 1966; Hibbs, 1977; Fiorina, 1978; Kiewiet, 1981; Evans and Anderson, 2006; Lander and Wlezien, , 2007; Gerber and Huber, 2009). Below is a brief summary of how Partisan Conditioning (PC) and Economic Conditioning (EC) proponents explain the economic voting process.

The primary argument among PC proponents is that voters' partisanship acts as a filter for their economic perceptions. Voters who are ill-informed about political and economic issues tend to respond more to cues provided to them by political parties than more informed voters (Keech, 1995; Gerber and Huber, 2009). Political parties, in turn, help shape the perceptions of voters who are unable or unwilling to sift through and process the political and economic information available

(Zaller, 1992; Nelson and Kinder, 1996). Voters welcome information from their political parties that share their values and belief systems.

EC scholars, in contrast, argue that economic forces condition voters' economic impressions (MacKuen et al., 1992). When voters observe the economy, they form assessments that reflect current conditions (Nadeau and Lewis-Beck, 2001; Lewis-Beck, 2006; Lewis-Beck et al., 2008). Their personal well-being and how they perceive the overall performance of the economy then define their perception of the economy (Kinder and Kiewet, 1978).

A critical review of the literature illuminates some of the limitations of the PC and EC arguments on the economic voting process. Namely, the literature on the conditioning of voters' economic perceptions does not offer a comprehensive argument on how economic forces inform voters' decisions. PC scholars say that voters make choices at the polls primarily on partisanship, which in turn influences their economic evaluations. This point of view ignores outside forces that influence voters, suggesting that political parties can simply prime them on to how perceive the economy and lead them to particular voting decisions. The limit of this rationale is that it presumes that voters have already made up their minds going into an election, because their partisanship has determined this, and that partisan cues determine the level of consideration voters give to these arguments when making their voting decisions (Just et al., 1996). A more persuasive argument is that voters make their considerations about the economy the moment that changes in economic conditions are significant enough to resonate with them (Zaller, 1992).

Further, PC and EC scholars do not fully explain the process by which electoral outcomes shape voters' economic perceptions. PC scholars contend that if the opposition party wins, then voters are likely to form positive economic assessments. In this case causality is defined by winning the election, which, in effect, changes partisan supporters' view of the economy. In addition, an implicit claim in EC scholars' research is that voters make selections based on the economy to protect their own economic interests. The limitation of this claim is that electoral forces can at times moderate voters' economic evaluations. Voters may make a political decision based not only on their economic interests, but also on their political preferences. What ensues from this process is that electoral outcomes cause voters' economic assessments to change. Partisan supporters of the party that has just lost the election develop more negative economic perceptions. From their vantage point, the major opposition party that is now in power will have policies that will likely make the economy worse.

Defining economic-minded partisans

What I call the 'economic-minded partisan model' is based on how voters' economic perceptions and partisanship *in combination* condition their voting behavior. In this model, partisanship influences voters to make decisions reflecting their main political beliefs and values. Economic perceptions simultaneously influence voters as they assess the incumbent government's past competence in handling the economy and evaluate its prospects for managing it in the future. This model reflects the reality that partisanship and economic perceptions are sometimes difficult to separate.

Economic-minded partisans engage in limited economic voting. Voters' partisanship dampens their economic perceptions in the voting process. Economic-minded partisans make their voting decisions when changes in the economy are distinct enough for them to take notice. Voters then decide if they will reward or punish the incumbent party based on these changes. At the same time, voters' partisanship moderates their evaluations of the economy as a means to cope with its uncertainty. Partisanship, therefore, not only mitigates whether individuals approve or disapprove of the incumbent government's management of the economy, but also determines if voters will choose a party that differs from their existing partisan preferences. As a result, the presumption that partisan voters uniformly engage in economic voting is unlikely. The level of support for a political party tends to be a strong and reliable factor in explaining voting behavior.

This model does not assume a high level of political sophistication among voters. Rather, it assumes the following: First, individuals pay varying levels of attention to politics. Second, voters' reactions to issues and events are limited by their knowledge of particular phenomena. Third, voters' perceptions of the economy are not constant, but reflect immediate reactions that result from changes in the political and economic environments. Fourth, voters use existing partisan attitudes to process new economic information, as well as to assist them in considering previous information on the economy when voting (Fiske and Linville, 1980; Conover et al., 1986). Fifth, voters' economic perceptions are more likely to be based on sociotropic assessments – defined as voters' evaluation of the broader economy – of the economy that can either be retrospective or prospective (Kinder and Kiewiet, 1978). Lastly, voters' perceptions of the economy and their partisan intensity are based upon the information that is most salient to them (Zaller, 1992).

The intent of the model is to demonstrate how the economic vote works when it is conditioned by partisanship and economic perceptions. In addition, the economic-minded partisan model argues that non-partisan voters, like partisan voters, are susceptible to partisan conditioning and economic conditioning when voting. The theory postulates that non-partisans, when compared to partisans, are more sensitive to differences between the parties in their evaluations of how well each party has managed economic and political conditions during an election cycle. Since non-partisan voters are not bound by pre-existing attachments to a political party when voting, they actively look for differences between the parties and their candidates in competence in managing economic and political conditions (Popkin, 1992). In addition non-partisans, like partisans, are receptive to partisan and economic conditioning because they make their voting decisions based upon some combination of the following factors: issue preferences, candidate evaluations, knowledge of politics, ideology, assessment of the economy, and information provided to them during the campaign (Basinger and Levine, 2005).

Analyzing the 2010 British general election

Table 10.1 summarizes the two-stage probit estimates from the 2010 UK general election taken during the pre-election period – June 2008 through March 2010 – and during the actual campaign – from 12 April 2010 to polling day on 6 May 2010. Overall, the model meets the critical threshold, and all of its coefficients are statistically significant.

Of particular interest to this research is the economic-minded partisan variable. A one-unit change in this variable, other things being equal, yields a –0.17 drop in the likelihood of voting for the incumbent party during the campaign. During the pre-election period, a one-unit change on this variable resulted in a –0.37 drop in the probability of voting for Labour, other things being equal.[5]

The results also uncover the impact economic voting had on the campaign. To start, the effect size of the model's coefficients diminish in the campaign period, compared to voters' prior preferences in the pre-election period. More specifically, when comparing the pre-campaign with the campaign period, there was a drop in the direct effects of voters' partisanship and voters' positive economic perceptions by roughly –22 percent and –46 percent respectively. This trend suggests that as UK voters began to make up their minds on the party they would support, the campaign's effects may not have helped either party gain traction. Rather, the campaign period provided voters with enough information to guide their voting decisions and gave them an opportunity to determine how intensely they would punish the Labour Party, either by voting for another party, or by voting at all, due to an overall pessimism among voters as a result of the economic downturn (Gelman and King, 1992).

Table 10.1   Two-stage probit estimates 2010 UK general election (cross-sectional data)

Variables	Campaign Two-stage probit			Pre-election Two-stage probit		
	Probit estimate	Standard error	t	Probit estimate	Standard error	t
Partisanship	1.1	0.0	29.4	1.4	0.0	76.0
Economic-minded partisans	–0.2	0.0	–3.9	–0.4	0.0	–6.5
Sociotropic retrospective (good economy or stayed the same)	1.0	0.2	4.8	1.8	0.3	7.1
Liberal Democrat	–0.5	0.1	–3.9	-0.9	0.0	–16.2
Constant	–4.8	0.1	–35.1	–6.4	0.0	–74.4
Overall Model Fit						
Chi-square		2,927.6		7,080.9		
Classification correctly		88.5%		86.9%		
N		6,962		15,832		
Hierarchical model test of interactions						
χ^2 with interactions		2,927.7		7,080.9		
χ^2 without interactions		2,914.9		6,941.9		
χ^2 difference		12.8		139		
Difference in d.f.		1		1		
Significance level		0.00		0.00		

Source: British Election Survey (2010).

The economic-minded partisan variable indicates that not all voters uniformly engaged in economic voting. This is due to both the conditioning process of voters' partisanship and voters' economic perceptions in explaining voting behavior. To illustrate the conditioning process between these two variables, Figure 10.1 shows average changes in voting for the Labour Party based on voters' partisanship. It compares changes in economic perceptions between those who felt the economy had gotten better or stayed the same and those who felt the economy had gotten worse.

Voters who were most likely to engage in economic voting in the election were leaning partisans who supported Labour and the Conservative parties. For instance, during the campaign there was a drop of 12 percentage points in the probability of voting for Labour, based on changes from positive to negative economic perceptions. Prior to the campaign, there was a decrease of 26 percentage points in voting for Labour among leaning Labour supporters. This type of behavior also occurred among leaning partisans who supported the Conservatives. During the campaign, the change from positive to negative economic perceptions resulted in a nine percentage point drop and during the pre-election period, an 18-point decrease, in voting for the Labour party. As one moves toward each end of the scale, changes in voting for the incumbent party based on the economic vote decline. This finding suggests stronger partisans did not engage in economic voting, compared to nominally partisan voters. Both weak and strong partisans who supported Labour were not likely to change their initial decisions to vote for their parties' candidates as a result of their economic perceptions; the same was true among strong and weak Conservative voters.

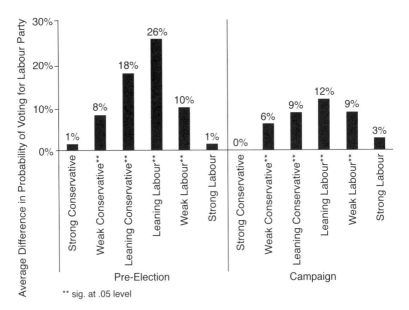

Figure 10.1   Average difference in probability of voting for the Labour Party based on economic vote (economy has 'stayed the same or better' from economy has gotten 'worse')

Source: British Election Survey (2010).

Campaign effects appeared to cause a drop in swings among individual British voters. Forced to make a choice between the two parties' platforms the closer they got to election day, voters were not as likely to solely cast an economic vote. This may have been a problem for the Conservative Party; despite voting swings in its favor reflecting the economic vote, the size of these swings decreased when the official campaign was underway. This may have been a result of many Labour and Liberal Democrat voters finding it difficult to vote for the Conservative Party because their partisanship would not let them do so.

Analyzing the 2010 US congressional vote

Table 10.2 presents estimates from the 2010 US congressional vote model in February and September 2010. The data provide a point of comparison that shows voters' behavior before major campaigning began and during the middle of the campaign. This approach allows the analysis to evaluate the degree to which campaign effects changed voting behavior. It controls for voters' partisanship, their economic perceptions, and the interaction between these two variables.

The two-stage probit results indicate that all of the variables included in the model exceed its critical threshold and that all of its variables are significant. Prior to the campaign, the variable that specifies economic-minded partisans yields a –0.58 decrease in the probability of voting for the Democratic Party. In September 2010, the effect size of this variable increased to –0.32 units, other things being equal.[6]

As was the case in the UK, there was also a decline in the effect size of the model's parameters during the campaign (September 2010) when compared to the period before the campaign (February 2010). The findings indicate a significant drop of –11 percent in the effect size of voters' partisanship and a –46 percent drop in voters' positive economic perceptions. The impact for the latter parameter was on par with the UK results. As was the case in the British election, the American results point to the asymmetric impact of the economic downturn on a drop in overall intensity levels among incumbent party supporters the closer to election day. Voters were, therefore, more likely to use the campaign as a means to reinforce their negative assessments of the economy and political environment in general, thus causing them to punish the Democratic Party, rather than embrace the Republican Party as the more desirable outcome. This may have resulted in an overall decline in the likelihood of turnout for the Democratic Party among its own supporters on election day. However, this possibility was not directly tested in this model. At the same time, these factors may have contributed to an overall boost in the propensity of individuals who were motivated to punish the incumbent party for poor economic conditions to turn out to vote.

Table 10.2   Two-stage probit estimates 2010 US congressional elections

Variables	September 2010 Two-stage probit			February 2010 Two-stage probit		
	Probit estimate	*Standard error*	*t*	*Probit estimate*	*Standard error*	*t*
Partisanship	0.9	0.0	27.7	1.0	0.0	13.8
Economic-minded partisans	–0.3	0.0	–4.4	–0.6	0.1	–3.6
Sociotropic retrospective (good economy or stayed the same)	1.2	0.3	3.6	2.2	0.6	3.3
Constant	–3.6	0.1	–27.3	–3.8	0.3	–11.9
Overall model fit						
Chi-square	204.9			204.9		
Classification correctly	86.8%			88.4%		
N	3,431			1,332		
Hierarchical model test of interactions						
χ^2 with interactions	862.8			204.7		
χ^2 without interactions	851.2			198.3		
χ^2 difference	11.5			12.8		
Difference in degrees of freedom	1			1		
Significance level	0.00			0.00		

Source: Pew Research Center for the People and the Press (2010).

Last, Figure 10.2 plots changes in the probability of voting for the incumbent party, based on differences between voters' negative and positive economic perceptions by voters' partisan level. The US findings indicate a similar distribution among voters as in the UK. Namely, less partisan voters were more likely to engage in economic voting than strong partisans. These individuals appear to be swing voters who left the Democratic Party and voted for the Republican Party during the 2010 election. Among these less partisan voters, a change from positive to negative economic perceptions resulted in a 32 percent drop in the probability of voting for the party in February 2010 and a 38 percent decrease by September 2010. By comparison, Democratic voters had a 10 percent drop in February 2010 and a 17 percent decrease in voting for the Democratic Party in September 2010. The differences between February 2010 and September 2010 indicated that over the course of the campaign, voters were more likely to engage in economic voting. At first blush, these effects appear to have hurt the Democratic Party, diminishing the impact of campaigning efforts undertaken by President Obama. Clearly, these results suggest that American voters engaged in retrospective voting, treating the 2010 midterm election as a referendum on the President rather than a choice over the two party's platforms.

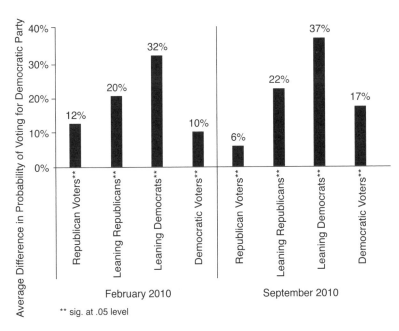

Figure 10.2 Average difference in probability of voting for the Democratic Party based on the economic vote (economy has 'stayed the same or better' from economy has gotten 'worse')

Source: Pew Research Center for the People and the Press (2010).

The politics of aggrieved acquiescence

The results indicate that in the last election both British and American voters engaged in economic voting. Yet the data also reveal that not all voters did so equally. Strong partisan voters proved less likely to be economic voters, compared to leaning and weak partisans, as well as independent voters. This heterogeneity among voters' voting decisions leads us to ask: Did voters *truly* vote based on the economy, or did voters use the economy to *reinforce* their pre-existing partisan bias?

This research suggests an answer to this question. Voters used their partisanship as the baseline for updating their political assessments. Thus, individuals were likely to make judgments about the economy the moment that changes in economic conditions were significant enough to resonate with them. In the case of the 2010 elections, partisanship among major opposition party supporters served as the conduit by which voters punished the Labour and Democratic parties.

The results also imply that the electoral strategies employed by the Obama administration and Brown government did not persuade voters that the elections would be a choice over which parties' economic platforms would best steer each country out of the current economic downturn. A more plausible explanation was that campaigning by the incumbent president and prime minister reminded voters that they wanted to punish their party for the poor economy. Voters who were less partisan, non-partisan, or strong partisans who supported the major opposition party tended to reject the claims made by both the Obama administration and Brown government about the state of the economy, their ability to manage it, and how their party's policies would lead to economic growth in the near future. Yet less partisan and non-partisan voters who engaged in rejecting the incumbent party in each country were not likely to wholeheartedly embrace the alternative parties' platforms. Frustration with the status quo and acceptance of the economic policy choices offered by the Republican and Conservative parties are not necessarily part of the same decision-making process among voters. Thus, the 2010 elections in the UK and US can be understood as a feeling of *aggrieved acquiescence* among voters. When presented with two choices, individuals tend to be reluctant to accept the alternative choice when this decision is based primarily on their dissatisfaction with the other option. Voters' emotional reaction to the recent economic downturn triggered an immediate political response to punish the incumbent party. This process is likely to continue in the near term if the economy does not improve, thus, threatening the stability of the recently elected incumbent parties in upcoming elections.[7]

This outcome may be part of the reason that Britain's Conservative Party has struggled to secure a majority of parliamentary seats in the House of Commons and that the Republican Party has not won control of both chambers in Congress. Even though British voters saw the economy, as was also the case among American voters, as the most important issue during the campaign, and voters sought to punish the incumbent Labour Party for it, not all voters were ready to swing to the Tories in their voting decisions.

Two popular arguments have emerged as to why this happened in the UK. First, voters were acting strategically in their voting decisions. Therefore weak and strong Labour partisan supporters were left with supporting their party or the Liberal Democrats but not the Conservatives. Second, systemic problems caused this outcome; the first past the post electoral system limited the ability of large swings in voting behavior. Though the national mood was pessimistic, and voters were not happy with Labour's economic performance, people across all districts didn't share these feelings equally. Conservatives were unable to swing enough Labour districts to their side because many voters in these districts either stayed with their party or went with the Liberal Democrats as a safe ideological alternative to the Tories.

In the US this was also a problem for the Republicans in taking control of both the House of Representatives and the Senate. Typically, midterm elections primarily bring out strong partisans. This limits economic voting compared to presidential elections. High incumbency rates within the House further downplayed the effectiveness of the economic vote. What occurred is that within the 2010 midterm election, turnout and enthusiasm levels were critical variables. Prior to the election, Gallup found a 22 percent gap between Republicans and Democrats in plans to vote.[8] The economic-minded partisan model's results suggest that the economic vote mobilized the opposition party and depressed voting among incumbent party supporters. A major difference between the American case and the British one is that in more competitive districts, these Democratic-leaning supporters did not have a realistic third choice, as Labour supporters had with choosing to vote for Liberal Democrat candidates. Therefore, in the US, it actually took effect in only a handful of the 435 districts in the House of Representatives (the 63 districts in the House that went to the Republicans). Chamber and constituency differences in the US Congress also dampened the impact of the economic vote.

The rise of the Tea Party in the US also contributed to the difficulty of voters in fully engaging in economic voting. It was an additional reason that the Republican Party failed to win control of the Senate,[9] though this faction of voters within the Republican Party was successful in motivating individuals to vote and for getting its candidates onto general election ballots throughout the country. In many instances, moderate voters saw Tea Party candidates as being too extreme in their ideology.[10] This was a likely reason why voters did not fully embrace them, and as a result, made it difficult for voters in certain parts of the country to base their voting decisions solely on the state of the economy. Voters used their partisanship in order to balance their partisan preferences against candidates they felt were too far outside of mainstream politics. While the Tea Party did win major upsets in Senate races in Wisconsin, Kentucky and Florida, the group also contributed to losses in Nevada and Delaware, where Republicans were favored to win early in the campaign. In sum, the results indicate that individual voters' political partisanship remained a constant factor in their voting decisions and thus biased their economic perceptions; this process limited the impact of the economic vote.

The 2010 election results also point to another limitation of the economic voting hypothesis. The final election tallies make it difficult to assess whether individual voting decisions of leaning Democrats and Independent voters caused these voters to stay home on election day, or, if they did vote, whether they were willing to vote for an alternative party. From the results, coupled with an overall enthusiasm gap among Republican voters, the odds were in favor of leaning Democrats and Independent voters choosing the Republicans over the Democrats.

Finally, past electoral patterns have indicated that it is more likely that voters engage in partisan voting, rather than in economic voting, in midterm congressional elections. Voters' economic perceptions therefore become an extension of their partisan preferences. An earlier study using American National Election Study (ANES) data from 1980 to 2008, found that voters are less likely to engage in economic voting in House elections when compared to presidential elections (Brogan, 2009). For instance, the effects of partisanship on voting for a House incumbent within a particular district is six times the size as voters' national economic retrospective assessments. For presidential elections, the differential between partisanship and economic perceptions is roughly two to one. As a result, partisanship remains a primary factor in voters' decisions at the polls in congressional contests. The conditioning process (voters' economic perceptions by their partisanship) results in changes to the probability of voting for the incumbent party by less than 1 percentage point (Brogan, 2009). Even though leaning Democrats and Independents are less likely to support the Democratic Party, this does not mean economic voting is an efficient form of democratic accountability. As was the case in the UK general election, the efficacy of the economic vote would be dampened by voters' partisanship. Such an outcome made it difficult for the Republican Party to win a majority of seats in both chambers.

To conclude, the economic-minded partisan model indicates a significant interactive relationship between voters' partisanship and their economic perceptions in explaining vote choice in both the UK and US. The results suggest that the economic vote works in both systems. However the process of economic voting is limited by the conditioning of voters' economic perceptions by their partisanship, as well as by the difficulties of using national level factors to help explain local political outcomes.

In the near term, the Cameron government and Obama administration are going to continue to face economic-minded partisan voters. They will likely be forced to focus on policies and positions that attempt to shift voters' focus away from the negative aspects of the economy and to push supporters (this includes leaning, weak, and strong partisans) to stick with their own parties' candidates during the next election. For this governing strategy to be effective, incumbent party supporters must continue to perceive that their party's policy positions will improve the economy, regardless, even if most individuals continue to have negative economic perceptions. Economic voting in the near term will likely continue in both the US and UK; however, the impact of this process would be blunted by the effects of voters' partisanship, thus making it difficult for incumbents in both countries to stay in power. Thus, the new norm for the Obama administration and Cameron government is more electoral volatility, and less political stability, as a result of economic fluctuations.

Appendix

The data used to test the model on the UK election comes from the 2010 British Election Study (British Election Survey, 2010). Data used for the American case come from the Pew Foundation's Political Survey (Pew Research Center for the People and the Press, 2010) conducted in February 2010 and September 2010. The economic-minded partisan model estimates incumbent party vote choice – Labour in the UK, the Democrats in the US. Two-stage probit estimations are used to calculate the model. Because of endogeneity concerns in the model, voters' partisanship is considered an instrumental variable. Dependent and independent variables used in the model are defined as shown in Table 10.3.

Table 10.3   Defining the variables for the economic-minded partisan model

Dependent variable	Comments
Incumbent vote choice	The dependent variable is specified as a dichotomous variable that provides two choices; '0' for those voters who did not vote for the incumbent party and '1' for those voters who voted for the incumbent party.

Independent variables	Comments
Partisanship	The variable has been coded on a six-point scale (a five-point scale in the US; the Pew Survey does not include a question for weak partisans only for leaning partisans) to capture differences of partisan supporters from both the incumbent and opposition parties. Lower values on this variable indicate partisans who support the opposition party, while higher values specify incumbent partisan supporters. Third party and independent supporters are coded as '4' in the American case. Third party supporters and independent voters and coded as '0' in the British case.
Sociotropic retrospective economic perceptions	These evaluations are based on voters' perceptions of changes in the economy over the 12 months prior to the election. The variable is coded as '1' equals 'the economy has gotten better, or the economy has stayed the same,' and '0' equals 'the economy has gotten worse.'
Economic-minded partisans	This variable specifies the cross-product interaction between voters' partisanship and their sociotropic economic retrospective assessments. The variable ranges from a minimum of zero to a maximum of six (five in the American case, due to the coding of the Pew Survey), with higher values representing strong partisan supporters of the incumbent party who felt the economy has 'gotten better or stayed the same' over the past year, and lower values representing voters who felt the economy had 'gotten worse' over the past year.
Previous incumbent party vote choice	This variable is binary and is coded as '1' for voters who voted for the incumbent party during the last election and '0' for those voters who did not vote for the incumbent party during the last general election. This variable is not included in the American estimates because the Pew Survey did not ask this question of voters.
Liberal Democrats	This variable is binary, with '1' equaling voters who identify themselves as Liberal Democrats, and '0' corresponding to all other voters.
Ideology	The American model uses a five-point index of ideology. Scores above '3' are for liberal voters, while scores under 3 are for conservative voters. Moderates are coded as '3.' This variable is used as to calculate the partisan instrumental variable.

Notes

1. I would like to thank Lorraine Sova, Charles Tien, David R. Jones, John Bowman, Jeff Freyman, Jonathan Mendilow, Frank Rusciano, Robin Fiske-Rusciano, Barbara Franz, Lucien Frary, Jonathan Millen and Elaine Pofeldt for their helpful comments and criticisms.

2. For the UK, this estimate comes from the monthly Continuous Monitoring Survey (CMS) from June 2008 until April 2010, which was part of the 2009–10 British Election Study (http://bes.utdallas.edu/2009/cms-data.php). For the US, this figure comes from the average (January 2010 to October 2010) of the Gallup's Economic Confidence Index of respondents who said economic conditions were 'fair or poor' (www.gallup.com/poll/110821/Gallup-Daily-US-Economic-Conditions.aspx).

3. Ibid.

4. The data used for the UK election comes from the 2010 BES. Data used for the American case comes from the Pew Foundation's Political Survey conducted in February 2010 and September 2010.

5. A test of equality of coefficients for the two time periods indicates significant differences in all of the model's parameters.

6. In addition to the UK case, a test of equality of coefficients for the two election time periods in the US indicates significant differences in all of the model's parameters.

7. In the British case, as of January 2011 the Labour Party began to beat the Tories among British voters in their vote intention if general election were to be held tomorrow (http://ukpollingreport.co.uk/voting-intention). This has held true to the time of this writing (May 2011). In the US, at the height of the campaign, the Democratic and Republican parties had equal favorability ratings, even though the Republican Party consistently beat the Democrats on the generic ballot measure throughout the campaign (www.gallup.com/poll/143213/Republican-Democratic-Party-Favorability-Identical.aspxz).

8. http://2010central.gallup.com/2010/04/conservative-enthusiasm-surging.html.

9. This was the case in senate races in Nevada and Delaware, where Republican candidates were seen as too ideologically extreme, even though most voters felt the economy was the most important election issue. In the Nevada Senate race, approximately 66 percent of all voters said the economy was the most important issue in the election but a majority of these voters (51 percent) chose the incumbent candidate over the opposition candidate. A reason for this was due to voters feeling (45 percent) the Republican candidate was 'too conservative'. In Delaware 86 percent of voters were worried about the economy and from this group 53 percent supported the Democratic candidate. Overall within the Delaware electorate, a plurality of voters (45 percent) had a negative opinion of the Tea Party and of these individuals, 93 percent voted Democrat.

10. An example of this was conservative candidate Christine O'Donnell who ran for Senate in Delaware. Ms O'Donnell was the Tea Party-backed candidate in the Republican primary. She ended up beating Republican incumbent Mike Castle to win the nomination to run in the general election.

References

Anderson, Christopher J. (2007) 'The End of Economic Voting? Contingency Dilemmas and the Limits of Democratic Accountability', *Annual Review of Political Science*, 10, 271–96.

Basinger, Scott J., and Howard Lavine (2005) 'Ambivalence, Information, and Electoral Choice', American *Political Science Review*, 99(2), 169–83.

British Election Survey (2010) 'The British Election Study-2009-10', www. bes2009-10.org.

Brogan, Michael J. (2009) 'Economic-Minded Partisans: Understanding How Economic Perceptions and Political Partisanship Condition Voting Behavior'. Dissertation, The Graduate Center, The City University of New York.

Campell, Angus, Phillip E. Converse, Warren E. Miller and Donald E. Stokes (1960) *The American Voter* (New York: Wiley and Sons Inc.).

Conover, Pamela Johnston, Stanley Feldman and Kathleen Knight (1987) 'The Personal and Political Underpinnings of Economic Forecasts', *American Journal of Political Science*, 31(3), 559–83.

Dolan, Chris J., John Frendreis and Raymond Tatalovich (2009) 'A Presidential Economic Scorecard: Performance and Perception', *PS: Political Science & Politics*, 42(4), 689–94.

Evans, Geoffrey, and Robert Andersen (2006) 'The Political Conditioning of Economic Perceptions', *Journal of Politics*, 68(1), 149–207.

Fiorina, Morris P. (1978) 'Economic Retrospective Voting in American National Elections: A Micro- Analysis', *American Journal of Political Science*, 22(2), 426–43.

Fiske, Susan T., and Patricia W. Linville (1980) 'What Does the Schema Concept Buy Us?', *Personality and Social Psychology Bulletin*, 6(4), 543–57.

Gallup Poll (2010) 'Conservative Enthusiasm Surging Compared to Previous Midterms', Gallup Poll, 23 April 2010.

Gelman, Andrew and Gary King (1993) 'Why Are American Presidential Election Campaign Polls so Variable when Votes are so Predictable?', *British Journal of Political Science*, 23(4), 409–51.

Gerber, Alan S., and Gregory A. Huber (2009) 'Partisanship and Economic Behavior: Do Partisan Differences in Economic Forecasts Predict Real Economic Behavior?', *American Political Science Review*, 103(3), 407–26.

Greene, William H. (2003) *Econometric Analysis*, 5th edn (New Jersey: Prentice Hall)

Hibbs, Douglas A. (1977) 'Political Parties and Macroeconomic Policy', *American Political Science Review*, 71(4), 1467–87.

Just, Marion R., Ann N. Crigler, Dean E. Alger, Timothy E. Cook, Montague Kern and Darrell West (1996) *Crosstalk: Citizens, Candidates, and the Media in a Presidential Campaign* (Chicago: University of Chicago Press).

Keech, William R. (1995) *Economic Politics: The Costs of Democracy* (Cambridge: Cambridge University Press).

Key, V.O., Jr (1966) *The Responsible Electorate: Rationality in Presidential Voting 1936-1960* (Cambridge, MA: Harvard University Press).

Kiewiet, D. Roderick, and Douglas Rivers (1983) 'A Retrospective on Retrospective Voting', *Political Behavior*, 6(4), 369–93.

Kinder, Donald R., and D. Roderick Kiewiet (1981) 'Sociotropic Politics: The American Case', *British Journal of Political Science*, 11(2), 129–61.

Kramer, Gerald H. (1971) 'Short-Term Fluctuations in U.S. Voting Behavior, 1896–1964', *American Political Science Review*, 65(1), 131–43.

Ladner, Matthew, and Chris Wlezien (2007) 'Partisan Preferences, Electoral Prospects, and Economic Expectations', *Comparative Politics*, 40(5), 571–95.

Lewis-Beck, Michael S. (2006) 'Does Economics Still Matter? Econometrics and the Vote', *Journal of Politics*, 68(1), 208–12.

Lewis-Beck, Michael S., and Mary Stegmeier (2007) 'Economic Models of Voting', in Russell J. Dalton and Hans-Dieter Klingemann (eds), *The Oxford Handbook of Political Behaviour* (Oxford: Oxford University Press).

Lewis-Beck, Michael S., Richard Nadeau and Angelo Elias (2008) 'Economics, Party, and the Vote: Causality Issues and Panel Data', *American Journal of Political Science*, 52(1), 84–95.

MacKuen, Michael B., Robert S. Erikson and James A. Stimson (1992) 'Peasants or Bankers: The American Electorate and the U.S. Economy', *American Political Science Review*, 86, 597–611.

Nadeau, Richard, and Michael S. Lewis-Beck (2001) 'National Economic Voting in U.S. Presidential Election', *Journal of Politics*, 63(1), 159–81.

National Election Pool (2010) 'Exit Polls: 2010 U.S. Midterm Election', http://abcnews.go.com.

Nelson, Thomas E., and Donald R. Kinder (1996) 'Issue Frames and Group-Centrism in American Public Opinion', *Journal of Politics*, 58(4), 1055–78.

Pew Research Center for the People and the Press (2010) 'February and September Public Opinion Polls', http://people-press.org.

Popkin, Samuel L. (1994) *The Reasoning Voters: Communications and Persuasion in Presidential Campaigns* (Chicago: Chicago University Press).

Soroka, Stuart N. (2006) 'Good News and Bad News: Asymmetric Responses to Economic Information', *Journal of Politics*, 68(2), 372–85.

Tufte, Edward R. (1978) *Political Control of the Economy* (Princeton: Princeton University Press).

Zaller, John R. (1992) *The Nature and Origins of Mass Opinion.* (New York: Cambridge University Press).

Part III

The Shifting Ground
of Public Policy

11
The Politics and Changing Political Economy of Health Care in the US and the UK

Alex Waddan

In the US, health care provision and potential reform of that provision has been a source of consistent controversy since at least the 1930s. There have been a series of set-piece political battles as different presidents have, with mixed success, attempted to reshape existing arrangements (Blumethal and Morone, 2010). In the UK, on the other hand, following the establishment of the National Health Service (NHS) in 1948, there was a period of relative policy stability. There were debates about how best to achieve the NHS's goals but there was a period of 'consolidation' if not exactly fulfillment of the initial expectations for the service. That era of relative consensus ended in the late 1980s (Klein, 2006), and since then arguments over health care have continued in British political life. And in both the US and UK these ongoing arguments over health policy quickly took center stage with the changing of the partisan guard in Washington in 2009 and Westminster in 2010. This chapter, therefore, explores the problems faced by the incoming Obama and Cameron administrations with regard to health care policy and examines how, and how radically, they proposed to change existing arrangements in the US and UK respectively.

The dilemma facing health policy-makers across industrialized nations is broadly similar. What is the best way to reconcile the potentially contradictory goals of providing individuals access to care at a reasonable aggregate cost with optimal system efficiency? In answering that question the US and UK have arrived at quite different policy settlements. The US, if slightly misleadingly, is perceived as a market-based system in contrast to the state-dominated health care landscape in the UK. That divergence in health care policy is especially notable given how the two countries are often grouped together in typologies that consider overall welfare state policy frameworks (Esping-Andersen, 1990). Yet, manifestly a country's health care system is central to its welfare state arrangements and, moreover, central to the distributional organization of the state itself: 'Health care institutions are large-scale concentrations, and means of allocating society's resources' (Moran, 1999, p. 4). Consequently health care reform has significant implications not just for the provision of health care but also for the wider distributional organization of the state. In turn this helps explain why the political battle over health care reform has been so intense in the US and UK, especially the former.

In the US the bitter political fight over health care reform that was initiated when Obama took office was resolved in legislative terms with the passage of the Affordable Care Act (ACA) in March 2010, but the partisan conflict continued through the 2010 midterm elections while legal challenges to the constitutionality of the ACA were also mounted (Saldin, 2010). In the UK general election of 2010, the future of the NHS was not a first-order issue, but shortly after the election Secretary of State for Health, Andrew Lansley, revealed plans for a major shakeup of the role of doctors and hospitals in the service (Secretary of State for Health, 2010). Opponents derided the plans as a threat to the integrity of the NHS, and health care quickly became a primary political battleground between the Coalition government and the Labour opposition (Ramesh and Williams, 2010). Before moving on to look at the controversies surrounding these reform proposals it is important to clarify what was being reformed and why reform was felt to be necessary.

Health care states

In 1987 the Organization for Economic Co-operation and Development (OECD)'s study of comparative health systems distinguished between system types based on the sources of funding for care and the degree to which arrangements prioritized 'consumer sovereignty' or 'social equity' with the 'former being characterized by incentives, the latter by control'. Using these criteria the OECD described the US and UK as 'prototypical country examples' of different system types (OECD, 1987, p. 24). And the distinction between the UK, with its state-dominated system emphasizing equal access and government funding from general tax revenues, and the US, with its reliance on private sources of funding with individuals responsible for accessing their own care and government providing a safety net, was clear. Twenty years on, this model retained considerable interpretive value. The state remained the dominant payer in UK health care. In 2008, 82.6 percent of health care spending in the UK was public expenditure, making the UK the second highest ranking of OECD countries in that category after Iceland (OECD, 2010). Through this spending the NHS provides free care, at the point of use, by both General Practitioners (GPs) and hospitals for everyone who is 'ordinarily resident' in the UK. Of aggregate NHS spending, 90.3 percent came from general tax revenues, 8.4 percent from National Insurance contributions and 1.3 percent from patient charges, mostly arising from prescription charges and payments for dental services (Delamothe, 2008a).

In contrast, in 2008 the US was the only OECD country where public expenditure accounted for less than half of aggregate health care spending (OECD, 2010), and most Americans accessed health care through private insurance coverage. Nevertheless, the idea that the US has a free market in terms of health care is misleading. First, even in the US the consumption of health care is mostly collectively organized. Only the very rich could afford to enjoy the full range of health care services on a pay as you go basis (Moran, 2000, p. 141). The market solution for this is insurance, but it is questionable whether health insurance is quite the same as most other types of insurance. Given the consumer's imperfect knowledge, then consumers who are insured, and who thus have the security of a third-party payer, are likely to over-consume health products, especially since it may be in the interests of the expert provider for this to be the case (Barr, 2004, pp. 258–63). Also, since the risk of illness and injury generally increases over the lifecycle, consumers will become increasingly unattractive to insurers just as the consumer is most likely to call upon the insurance. Further, while, from a commercial perspective it makes sense for insurers to exclude a pre-existing illness from insurance coverage, this seems medically unethical. If, however, as stipulated by the ACA, insurers are forced to offer insurance coverage to all, then the commercial autonomy of insurers is being infringed.

Second, the US government is a major payer in US health care. Established in the mid 1960s, Medicare and Medicaid provide health insurance for the elderly and the poor, respectively (Marmor, 2000). By 2008 the costs of these two programs meant that US government spending accounted for 46.5 percent of total health care expenditure (OECD, 2010). In addition to this direct spending the government effectively subsidizes employer-based insurance, which provided cover to 52.3 percent of the population in 2008 (Kaiser Family Foundation, 2010), by granting tax relief to employers who provide health insurance coverage to their employees. In 2005 the tax relief amounted to approximately $75 billion (Howard, 2007, p. 52).

Overall, the OECD's typology helps initial understanding about the relative roles of the state and market in helping people access health care, but it needs significant qualification in practice. Furthermore, there are aspects of the health care state that the typology does not adequately address. In particular, it does not take into account the degree to which the state organizes health care providers. To what extent are doctors and hospitals under the control of the state? That is, while the rules governing access to health care are obviously critical, so too are the rules that govern the behavior of providers of care (Moran, 1999, 2000). Expanding on the categorization of health care states, Moran labels the original NHS a model of 'command and control' while the US had evolved into a 'supply state' (Moran, 2000, pp. 147–54).

The concept of the 'supply state' adds significant dimensions to discussion of the US system. In particular it brings more attention to the independent power of providers, notably hospitals and physicians, rather than just to the position of consumers of care. It also makes sense of the fact that public funding has been given to further American medicine to fund medical research and hospital building through measures such as the Hospital Survey and Construction Act of 1946 (Jacobs, 1995). In contrast, the NHS was initially notable not only for government funding but also for effective government ownership of hospitals and hospital employees. That command and control was always more restricted with regard to the position of GPs or primary health care providers in the UK. Unlike doctors who work in hospitals as salaried employees, most GPs have contracts with, rather than salaries from, the NHS. As will be explained below, the semi-autonomous position of GPs is critical in understanding why Lansley's reform proposals proved so contentious.

The cry of 'crisis'

Whatever the different norms and procedures both systems have seen a series of problems. Perhaps the starkest statistic is that in 2008 15.4 percent of the US population was uninsured (US Census Bureau, 2010), with 18.9 percent of non-elderly adults lacking protection from either market or government sources (Kaiser Family Foundation, 2010, p. 1). In addition, many millions of others are underinsured, leaving them vulnerable to potentially significant medical expenses. About three-quarters of people filing for bankruptcy and citing medical costs as a primary cause report that they had some insurance (Thorne and Warren, 2008, p. 66).

In the UK, issues about access revolve around whether and when specific treatments will be available rather than about who will pay. The historical dilemma for the NHS has been about how to ration the care that it provides – and underlying that is the question of how much the government is prepared to fund. Mostly the NHS has rationed in a 'covert' manner that attempts to deflect explicit blame away from the government (Delamothe, 2008b, p. 1344). Historically the medical profession was a participant in the blame avoidance game in a relationship described by Klein as 'the double bed' (Klein, 2006). Reflecting the mutual dependence of the state and the medical profession after the establishment of the NHS, GPs took on the role of gatekeeper to more specialized services, enabling the NHS to stay within its allocated budget. In return the state stood relatively to the side in terms of potential intervention in the medical profession. This rationing does not go unnoticed but much of it is not interpreted as rationing and political leaders avoid the term altogether. The visible, and somewhat quantifiable, face of that rationing has been waiting lists, which explains 'the totemic importance' attached by 'government and the electorate, not to mention foreign observers of the NHS' to those waiting lists (Delamothe, 2008b, p. 1344).

Lack of insurance in the US and delays in getting treatment in the UK are the very immediate signs to patients of the problems with health care delivery. For the respective governments there is another pressing, and in the US unremitting, issue: rising health care costs. Health spending has followed an upward trajectory in both countries, but that has been much more accelerated in the US than in the UK. In the latter, health spending as a percentage of gross domestic product (GDP) rose from 3.9 percent in 1960 through 7.0 percent in 2000 and was 8.7 percent in 2008. In the US the numbers were 5.2 percent in 1960, 13.4 percent in 2000 and 16.0 percent in 2008 (OECD, 2010). The underlying explanation for this phenomenon is that the UK government imposes a ceiling on NHS spending while the US government imposes no such restrictions on global health spending, even in the programs that it funds. Indeed, government's tight control of the purse strings in the UK resulted in the country having the lowest spending on health care as a percentage of GDP of the western European nations at the end of the twentieth century. Hence, in 2000, when other nations were already looking to contain health expenditures, Prime Minister Tony Blair pledged to increase UK spending on health care to bring the country up to average EU levels. At that point France spent 10.1 percent of GDP on health care while for Germany the figure was 10.3 percent (OECD, 2010). Conversely, the US was an outlier at the other end of the spectrum, spending a significantly higher percentage of GDP on health than any other OECD nation. It is unsurprising that the US spends more than other countries on health since there is a correlation between a nation's wealth and its health care spending, but the overspend is significantly disproportionate (McKinsey Global Institute, 2008, p. 10). There are various explanations for this, but higher costs are a central part of the equation (Oberlander and White, 2009).

One consequence is that many Americans do not have a means of paying for their health care needs, yet simultaneously health care spending has increasingly squeezed both the US government and the corporate sector. Direct health care expenditure by government has taken up an increasing slice of both federal and state government spending over the last 30 years. Government spending on the Medicare program is all federally funded. In 1970 Medicare took up only 3.5 percent of the federal budget. That figure rose to 5.8 percent by 1980 and then 8.6 percent in 1990. By 2000 Medicare consumed 12.1 percent of the federal budget (Moon, 2006, p. 38). In fact the initial rules governing payments under Medicare, a publicly funded program, illustrate well the power of providers in the US system. In enacting the legislation the Johnson administration and supporters in Congress overcame significant opposition from the medical profession, but they also conceded much ground to those providers (Jacobs, 2005, p. 46). The 1965 law allowed providers to charge what they deemed appropriate and in the immediate years after implementation, hospital and physician fees rose 'markedly' (Marmor, 2000, p. 84). Changes were made to reimbursement methods in the early 1980s when there was a shift from retrospective payments on the basis of the charges that hospitals and doctors demanded, to prospective payments whereby fees would be paid according to an amount settled in advance for each procedure. This was a significant extension of the administrative role of government (Oberlander, 2003, pp. 120–6), but while it limited payments per procedure it did not limit the number of procedures and so did not constitute a global cap on aggregate Medicare spending.

Federal and state governments fund Medicaid jointly with incentives to the states to spend on the program in order to receive more federal largesse. Given the means-tested nature of Medicaid eligibility, it is a program that sees increased demand in economic downturns. Clearly this helps contain the numbers of uninsured, but it means that increased demand for services comes at those points in time when government revenues decline. This is particularly problematic for state governments trying to balance their budgets (see the Kaiser Commission on Medicaid and the Uninsured, 2010, for an assessment of Medicaid's finances during the economic crisis).

Overall, the situation of the Medicare and Medicaid programs reveal much about the chaos afflicting American health care arrangements. Reflecting that the constituencies who receive benefits from the programs are likely to be the highest health risks in the population (the elderly and the poor) the costs associated with them rise, apparently inexorably. Hence, the Congressional Budget Office (CBO)'s projections for the next ten years issued in January 2010 (before the passage of the ACA) stated: 'The biggest single threat to budgetary stability is the growth of federal spending on health care – pushed up both by increases in the number of beneficiaries of Medicare and Medicaid (because of the aging of the population) and by growth in spending per beneficiary that outstrips growth in per capita GDP' (CBO, 2010a, p. 21).

Further to the strain on government finances, health care costs also hurt many American businesses. For example, William Clay Ford, then chair of the Ford Motor Co., reflected in 2004: 'During the four-year period through 2003, [Ford's] health insurance premiums increased by 11.4 percent, compared to 2.2 percent for overall inflation. This is a pace we cannot sustain' (quoted in Morris, 2006). The options open to businesses looking to reduce their costs are to pass more of the cost for insurance on to employees or to stop offering insurance altogether. Any such steps then exacerbate the problem of uninsurance.

Overall, the different problems outlined above reflect both the alternative trajectories that health care policy has taken in the two countries and also the underlying issue that organizing a comprehensive health care system is inevitably hugely problematic. The flaws in the US system seem more profound because high spending has not led to universal care, but in the UK a historic legacy of low spending left gaps in care that were not easy to fill even as spending increased through the 2000s. And finding remedies for the problems has become increasingly problematic as changing demographics, particularly population aging, and improved medical technologies add to the strain on services. New treatments can be very expensive with an uncertain success rate. Making decisions about whether to provide funding for these new treatments is especially awkward in the UK where the need to maintain the cap on aggregate spending means that different treatments may be in competition with each other. This landscape is further complicated by the rise of 'consumerism' as a range of organized groups campaign on behalf of victims of particular illnesses. In the UK context this has exposed more of the previously hidden techniques of rationing to the light of day (Harrison and McDonald, 2008, pp. 115–18).

As policy-makers have struggled to find solutions to the problems of health care the political terrain has become more polarized. In the US, debates have followed established ideological lines as Democrats seek to expand coverage to more of the uninsured and Republicans rebuke their opponents for trying to 'socialize' American medicine. Whatever the half-truths that often arise during this debate, it is an argument of substance reflecting deep division. In the UK the ground in the health care fight is more muddied. The NHS remains highly popular (Delamothe, 2008c, p. 1469) and mainstream politicians continue to champion its principles, but since the 1980s the NHS has increasingly become a political football.

'Obamacare': the socialization of American medicine?

At the signing ceremony for the ACA, President Obama reflected that finally the US recognized 'the core principle that everybody should have some basic security when it comes to their health care'. In contrast, House Republican Leader John Boehner lamented: 'This is a somber day for the American people' (quotes in Stolberg and Pear, 2010). The ACA is in fact scheduled to rearrange many aspects of existing health care organization over the next decade, making it difficult to judge the law's likely long-term institutional significance. But while assessments about the ACA's impact can only be provisional it is possible to ask to what extent it seems likely to shift the nature of the US health care state, lessen the number of uninsured and restrain the cost burden of health care to the US economy.

In terms of reducing the number of uninsured, two measures contained in the ACA stand out. First, from 2014, a major expansion of Medicaid is projected to result in coverage for 16 million extra Americans by 2019 (CBO, 2010b) as everyone with an income of less than 133 percent of the federal poverty level will become eligible for the program. Second, again from 2014, state authorities will establish health insurance exchanges that will act as regulated insurance markets for people lacking employer or public insurance. The exchanges will offer a variety of private insurance plans with federal government providing 'premium credits' to help pay the premiums and subsidies to help with out-of-pocket expenses (*Washington Post*, 2010, pp. 75–82). This help will be available, on a sliding scale, to people with income up to 400 percent of the federal poverty level. Insurers will be restricted in how much they can vary premiums so the cost is not prohibitive for people with pre-existing medical problems (Marmor and Oberlander, 2010). The CBO predicts that in 2019, 24 million people will get their health insurance through these exchanges (CBO, 2010b).

Most working-aged Americans employed by mid-size and large employers will continue to receive their insurance as a benefit of employment, but even here the ACA makes potentially important changes. Insurers will not be able to refuse to cover people with pre-existing illnesses and will not be able to impose annual or lifetime caps on their payments for individuals. Furthermore, children are allowed to remain covered by a parent's insurance until age 26. For employers the ACA introduced extra incentives to cover their workforce. Larger firms will face penalties if they do not offer insurance while smaller businesses will be helped to insure workers through the use of temporary subsidies. This will mean, if not explicitly then at least in effect, that employers with over 50 workers will face a mandate to cover some of the costs of insuring their employees (Simon, 2010, pp. 7–8).

A further highly controversial measure, designed to ensure that people take insurance rather than gamble on their health, is to impose fines on people who willingly forego buying insurance. This individual mandate sparked a rush of constitutional challenges, and in December 2010 federal judge Henry Hudson became the first to rule the mandate was unconstitutional in a case in Virginia (Mazzone, 2010). Yet the mandate is an important aspect of the law for insurance companies. Since insurers have been compelled to insure people who constitute a high risk, that needs to be balanced by insuring – and receiving premiums from – people who have a low risk of needing medical care. Hence for insurers the individual mandate will act to mitigate the problem of adverse selection.

As well as improving access for the uninsured the ACA set out to 'bend the cost curve'. This meant that during the legislative process the CBO's scoring of the fiscal impact of reform proposals was critical. In the end the CBO predicted that the net impact on the federal budget of all the aspects of the ACA would be a saving of $143 billion between 2010 and 2019 (CBO, 2010b). That is, the accumulated extra spending involved in the plans described above would be more than offset by savings generated in the Medicare and Medicaid programs and extra revenues such as fees on branded drug manufacturers and insurers and additional hospital insurance tax (CBO, 2010c). The savings are mostly to come from changes to Medicare through cuts to the annual updates of Medicare's fee-for-service payments and reductions in monies paid to Medicare Advantage.[1] Furthermore, an Independent Payment Advisory

Board is to be established. This will make recommendations to Congress for limiting Medicare spending. Congress will consider these recommendations under special rules that mean it cannot simply overrule the suggested savings without proposing alternatives.

Opponents disputed the efficacy of the supposed savings maintaining that the CBO was forced to take unrealistic assumptions about future trends and congressional behavior written into the ACA at face value (Nix, 2010). And it does remain to be seen what will happen when 'irresistible force meets immovable object'. From 1999 to 2008 Medicare grew at a rate that was 2.8 percent per year higher than the annual growth in the rate of GDP. The question is whether it really is politically feasible to stop that growth rate, potentially incurring the wrath of seniors, or to find extra revenues to continue funding that growth (Newhouse, 2010, pp. 6–7).

The ACA is also designed to restrain costs for business and individuals. According to Health and Human Service Secretary Kathleen Sebelius speaking on the *Meet the Press*: 'Every cost cutting idea that every health economist has brought to the table is in this bill' (Politics Daily, 2010). Much emphasis was placed on reducing unnecessary use of medical care. For example, one measure in the bill, which angered labor unions that had negotiated for generous insurance packages for workers, is the so-called 'Cadillac' excise tax on insurance plans that cost over $10,200 for an individual or $27,500 for family coverage that will come into force in 2018. The idea behind this tax is that it will encourage businesses and individuals to look for alternative plans that involve more cost sharing, and hence more cost consciousness (Jacobs and Skocpol, 2010, pp. 140–1). Elsewhere in the bill it is assumed that emphasis on modernizing medical care delivery will bring efficiency and that increasing competition and transparency in the insurance industry will restrain costs. Also it is predicted that the establishment of so-called accountable care organizations that will bring together primary and secondary care doctors as well as hospitals to look after a group of patients will further slow health care inflation (Cutler et al., 2010).

Through these measures the CBO predicts that 32 million extra Americans will be insured by 2019, meaning that 92 percent of the non-elderly population, or 95 percent if unauthorized immigrants are excluded, would be insured (CBO, 2010b). This would still leave the US, alone among industrialized democracies, as having a significant proportion of its population lacking health coverage. Nevertheless, assuming that the ACA is not significantly diluted by reform, its regulations mean that insurance will become affordable for many low-income Americans.

Moreover, people with health problems will not live in fear of losing that insurance.

It is more questionable whether the ACA will deal effectively with the apparently inexorably rising costs in the US health care system. Fundamentally the ACA does not tackle the problems inherent in the supply state – that is, that the hand dealt to producers and providers is stronger than the hand held by consumers (patients) and payers (government and insurance companies). Analysts Ted Marmor and Jonathon Oberlander agree that the ACA contains many ideas advanced by health economists, but conclude that this 'shows that American health policy researchers pay scant attention to international experience'. That is, other countries spend less than the US 'largely by adopting budgetary targets for health expenditures and by tightly regulating what the governments and insurers pay hospitals, doctors, and other medical care providers. Outside of Medicare, the current reform contains no such measures' (Marmor and Oberlander, 2010). This absence of constraining measures on health care providers reflects the decision made by the Obama administration to compromise to get some legislation passed. In particular the decision to attempt to co-opt some of those stakeholders who had opposed previous efforts at comprehensive reform meant that their interests had to be accommodated (Oberlander, 2010).

The Americanization of the British National Health Service?

This subtitle, without the question mark, was the title of an article by the health policy analyst David Mechanic (1995) that explored the impact of changes made by the Thatcher and Major governments to the NHS. Particularly controversial was the decision to divide purchasing agents and providers (Secretary of State for Health, 1989). Purchasers, then in the guise of District Health Authorities, were empowered to spend their budget buying from a provider of their choice. The providers of hospital care were to become autonomous NHS Trusts that would compete to win contracts from purchasers. In addition, GPs could become purchasing agents by adopting the status of GP Fundholders. If they did this they could spend their allocated budget directly buying services for their patients. These plans provoked claims that the NHS was under attack. The British Medical Association (BMA) voted in favor of non-cooperation. Robin Cook, then the Labour Shadow Secretary for Health, maintained that the government was promoting 'market medicine as it is practised across the Atlantic' (quoted in Klein, 2006, p. 153). The idea of an Americanizing influence was given some substance as American analyst

Alain Enthoven had advised the government in the mid 1980s that more emphasis on money following patients would generate greater efficiency in the NHS (Ham, 1994). Yet in implementation the reforms had a muted effect (Klein, 2006, pp. 146–52). The exact nature of the market being created was unclear (Dolowitz et al., 1996) and in the end, the state did not sacrifice that much command while other changes emphasized managerial supervision of the medical profession, meaning that in some ways the state had extended its methods of control. Indeed the Secretary of State who oversaw the legislative changes, Kenneth Clarke, maintained that the purpose all along had been to give 'managers additional tools to challenge doctors' (Greener, 2009, p. 149).

In opposition the Labour Party had promised to undo the reforms but by 2000 the Labour government had adopted a not too dissimilar agenda. The *NHS Plan* issued in July 2000 called for 'sustained increases in funding' but also for 'far reaching changes across the NHS' (Secretary of State for Health, 2000, p. 10). This message was reinforced in a further White Paper in 2002, *Delivering the NHS Plan,* which declared that the '1948 model is simply inadequate for today's needs' (Secretary of State for Health, 2002, p. 3). So, after eliminating GP Fundholding, the government set up Primary Care Trusts (PCTs), which would be able 'to purchase care from the most appropriate provider – be they public, private or voluntary' (ibid., p. 4). This was intended to 'expand choice and promote diversity in supply' (ibid., p. 5). In addition, patients would no longer be 'handed down treatment' but would be given a choice of 'where and when' to be treated (ibid., p. 7).

Thus the Labour government went further towards establishing a health care marketplace than the Tories had previously done by inviting private and not-for-profit providers to compete for contracts in what was termed the 'mixed economy of care' (Greener, 2009, p. 221; Pollock, 2005, p. 200). Furthermore, the government was keen to increase the extent to which money flowed to successful facilities signalling a 'retreat from a command-and-control style of management' (Klein, 2006, p. 232). Related reforms included giving patients a choice of secondary care provider. There were also elements of decentralization. For example, the best-performing hospitals were allowed to set up as Foundation Trusts, giving themselves a greater degree of autonomy. The Department of Health described Trusts as being 'at the cutting edge of the Government's commitment to devolution and decentralization in public services, and are at the heart of a patient led NHS' (Department of Health, 2005, p. 2).

Together the changes enacted during the 1990s and 2000s did end the 1948 command and control model of governance of health care providers in the UK, but it is not clear that the real impacts of the reforms were as significant in practise as was potential in theory. For example, most patients chose their secondary care provider for reasons of geographical convenience rather than according to league tables, thus limiting the impact of patient choice on incentives for providers. A King's Fund study found that 'While the threat of patients choosing a different hospital led some providers to focus more on reputation, there was little evidence of direct competition for patients' custom and choice has not so far acted as a lever to improve quality' (Dixon et al., 2010). Moreover, for all the rhetoric about devolving decision-making the government proved reluctant to let too much power ebb towards providers. For example, the Foundation Trusts remained 'subject to NHS standards, performance ratings and systems of inspection' (Department of Health, 2005, p. 2). The tensions this produced were exemplified by the enduring dilemma about how to balance central and local control. There was some devolution of budgets to frontline health workers but also greater centralization through the use of targets and the creation of the National Institute for Clinical Excellence (NICE) that helped decide the financial as well as medical viability of new drugs (Glendenning, 2003, p. 209).

As it was, by the time of the 2010 general election Labour boasted about the increased expenditure on the NHS and pointed to reduced waiting times as evidence that the extra money invested had been put to good effect. And public satisfaction with the NHS was significantly higher than it had been in 1997 (Cole, 2009), though ironically Labour's lead over the Conservatives as the best party on the issue of health care had declined from a 32 point advantage in April 1997 to just 9 points in March 2010 (Ipsos Mori, 2010). In this context the future of the NHS was not a high-profile campaign issue. Conservatives protested that too much money had been spent on managers and maintained that the NHS needed a period of stability with resources concentrated on frontline staff not health bureaucrats. That stance was reinforced during the 2010 campaign when the Tories promised to ring-fence NHS spending even as they spoke of the need for deep public spending reductions.

Thus neither the Conservatives nor the Liberal Democrats, the constituent parties to the coalition, had suggested major reform of the NHS during their election campaigns and the coalition agreement made no mention of this either. Yet, by the summer Secretary of State Lansley had unveiled plans for reform of the NHS in England that an array of health care experts described as genuinely radical. The NHS Confederation referred to the 'biggest shake-up of the NHS in its history' (NHS Confederation 2011, p. 2).[2] A King's Fund analysis noted that the plans were 'much more ambitious than previous reforms' (Dixon and Ham, 2010, p. 1). An underlying sentiment was the idea that the government's plans represented the 'biggest shift of power and responsibility in the NHS's 62-year history' (Timmins, 2011).

The introduction to the Coalition government's White Paper on the NHS reaffirms the commitment to uphold 'the values and principles of the NHS', going on to define these as a 'comprehensive service, available to all, free at the point of use and based on clinical need, not the ability to pay' (Secretary of State for Health, 2010, p. 3). Accordingly the NHS would remain a state-funded system with access based on social equity. In this context, why then did the White Paper provoke remarks about a radical transformation?

Perhaps the feature of the government's plans that drew the most immediate attention was the decision to abolish PCTs, which were responsible for buying health care services for patients. Instead the bulk of control for commissioning care would be passed to GPs. Also abolished would be the ten existing strategic health authorities in England. GPs would group together in consortia in order to carry out and coordinate their commissioning duties. A newly created NHS Commissioning Board would oversee their work. That Board would have some responsibility for purchasing rarer or higher-tech medical equipment that it might not be appropriate for each GP consortium to purchase separately. The rationale for giving GPs this power is that, as primary care providers, they are best aware of how to distribute resources on behalf of their patients. In addition the change would lead to a reduction in the number of managers in the NHS. For GPs the flip-side of the extra power they will have over their budgets is that they will possibly become the frontline in the terms of rationing care.

Another key aspect of the reform plans concerns hospitals. The White Paper states: 'Autonomy in commissioning will be matched by autonomy for providers' (Secretary of State for Health, 2010, p. 35). Accordingly all NHS Trusts will become self-governing Foundation Trusts. These will remain in the public sector, but will be in competition with providers from the private and voluntary sectors. 'Our aim is to free up provision of healthcare, so that in most sectors of care, any willing provider can provide services, giving patients greater choice and ensuring effective competition stimulates innovation and improvements, and increases productivity within a social market' (ibid., p. 37). An economic regulator, Monitor, will oversee this market, setting prices and promoting competition.

Overall, on paper at least, these proposals look to justify the commentaries emphasizing their radical nature. Much will of course depend on how these new structures work in practise. The implications of the plans are that some market dynamics will be at work. For example, one possible repercussion of the increased autonomy for providers is that they, including public sector Foundation Trusts, will be allowed to fail. Isolated cases of such failure might be tolerable, but it seems unlikely that the government would allow this to happen on a regular basis. Interestingly, the White Paper talks of reducing the power of the government to 'micro-manage and intervene' in the day-to-day affairs of the NHS (Secretary of State, 2010, p. 33). It will be difficult, however, for government to stay out of the fray should a spate of NHS scare stories surface. Devolving power does not necessarily translate into devolving political responsibility.

In the spring of 2011 the government acknowledged the mounting criticism of its plans, including from Liberal Democrat voices within the Coalition, by announcing a pause in the legislative process. In June 2011 the government revealed its revisions to the original proposals. This was widely reported as a significant climb-down by the government (BBC 2011), but the changes were more a slowing and partial diluting of the reform process than a fundamental course correction. Perhaps most importantly, the role of Monitor was adjusted so as to promote collaboration as well as competition and other health professionals were to join GPs in commissioning arrangements.

Conclusion

Overall, therefore, in both the US and UK ambitious reform agendas have been advanced in the health policy arena. The ensuing arguments reflect that the stakes are high for all involved in both political and substantive policy terms. On the other hand, it is not all change. Thinking back to the typologies discussed earlier in the chapter, the ACA makes more of a difference if looking at the OECD's (1987) typology than Moran's (2000) model. The expansion of Medicaid and the subsidies to people buying insurance through the insurance exchanges means that government will be, either directly or indirectly, helping to pay for the care of a greater number of people. Simply put, a significant reduction in the number of uninsured will move the US towards a system of universal care. This should not be overstated since access and treatment levels will be far from equal, but as David Leonhardt (2010) writes, the redistributive aspects of the ACA make it the most significant measure tackling inequality in the US in a generation. But the measures to control costs look less certain and clearly established. It is interesting that the Obama administration has been more vocal in its criticism of the primary payers in the system, that is the insurance industry, rather than doctors, hospitals or even pharmaceutical companies (see, for example, Sebelius, 2011). Insurers make for a more convenient political fall-guy than doctors and hospitals, but while insurers may raise premiums higher than necessary, it is the provision of health care that really drives costs. And in this context it is not fully evident that the measures in the ACA about the regulation of providers are decisive enough to guarantee that cost increases will be slowed in the long term. Most obviously, in comparison with the NHS, whatever the plans to control public sector spending, there is no global cap and providers are not dependent on contracts with government. Thus if, for example, there are meaningful cuts to payments to providers for Medicare treatments, then these providers may simply absent themselves from treating Medicare beneficiaries as many already have stopped doing Medicaid work because of the lower reimbursement rates paid by government for treating Medicaid patients (Newhouse, 2010, p. 8). In short, the ACA might have further diminished the extent to which US health care acts a true market, but it has far from 'socialized' American medicine.

With regard to the UK it is tempting to ask why the Coalition government embarked on such an ambitious reform program at a time when the NHS was recording high satisfaction levels. Why fix something that was not obviously broken? When explaining the rationale for the plan the prime minister emphasized the need to improve health care outcomes in an era of fiscal pressures: 'the NHS faces enormous financial pressures in the years ahead – driven by factors ranging from ageing and obesity, through to the cost of new drugs and technologies. Sticking with the status quo and hoping extra money will meet the challenges is not an option. If we want to deliver better results for patients, we need modernisation' (Cameron, 2011). Understanding the potential significance of the reform plans in this instance is best done by employing Moran's typology rather than the OECD's. The latter, with its emphasis on patterns of funding and access, would downplay the Coalition government's proposals. Yet the changes to the status of GPs and hospitals, and the further opening up of the NHS budget to private providers, means that the NHS has decisively left the 1948 settlement behind. In December 2010, Nigel Edwards, then the acting chief executive of the NHS Confederation, reflected that rather than the 'centrally planned and managed' organization of 1948 the NHS would resemble 'a regulated industry' (Edwards, 2010). Nevertheless, given the commitment to continued government funding and equality of access it is a rhetorical step too far to talk of the Americanization of the NHS.

What is clear is that health care politics is unlikely to wane in its intensity. For one thing, the problem of providing comprehensive care at an acceptable cost is not going to go away. Moreover, health care consumes a huge chunk of economic activity and brings into play fundamental values about individual responsibility and social solidarity. As such, political figures can hardly leave it alone.

Notes

1. Medicare Advantage (MA) is a scheme whereby private managed care plans compete for business against traditional fee for service Medicare. Yet, rather than this competition lowering costs it transpired that MA cost 'an average of $1,000 more per beneficiary per year than it costs to treat the same beneficiaries through traditional Medicare' (Angeles and Park, 2009, p. 1).
2. The NHS Confederation is an independent body made up of the various organizations in the NHS as well as other independent health care providers.

References

Angeles, January, and Edwin Park (2009) *Curbing Medicare Advantage Overpayments Could Benefit Millions of Low-Income and Minority Americans* (Washington, DC: Center for Budget and Policy Priorities).

Barr, Nicholas (2004) *Economics of the Welfare State* (Oxford: Oxford University Press).

BBC (2011) 'Cameron backs wholesale changes to NHS plans', 14 June, www.bbc.co.uk/news/uk-politics-13757380.

Blumenthal, David, and James Morone (2010) *The Heart of Power: Health and Politics in the Oval Office* (Berkeley: University of California Press).

Cameron, David (2011) 'PM Article on the Health and Social Care Bill', 27 January, www.number10.gov.uk.

CBO (2010a) *The Budget and Economic Outlook: Fiscal Years 2010 to 2020* (Washington, DC: Congress of the United States).

CBO (2010b) 'H.R. 4872, Reconciliation Act of 2010', 18 March 2010.

Cole, Andrew (2009) 'More Spending on NHS has Led to Highest Satisfaction Rates in 25 Years', *British Medical Journal*, 338, 7 February , 315.

Cutler, David, Karen Davis and Kristof Stremikis (2010) *The Impact of Health Reform on Health System Spending*, The Commonwealth Fund and the Center for American Progress.

Delamothe, Tony (2008a) 'A Centrally Funded Service, Free at the Point of Delivery', *British Medical Journal*, 336, 21 June, 1410–12.

Delamothe, Tony (2008b) 'A Comprehensive Service', *British Medical Journal*, 336, 14 June, 1344–5.

Delamothe, Tony (2008c) 'How the NHS Measures Up', *British Medical Journal*, 336, 28 June, 1469–71.

Department of Health (2005) *A Short Guide to NHS Foundation Trusts* (London: Department of Health Publications).

Dixon, Anna, Ruth Robertson, John Appleby, Peter Burge, Nancy Devlin and Helen Magee (2010) *Patient Choice: How Patients Choose and How Providers Respond* (London: The Kings Fund).

Dolowitz, David, David Marsh, Fiona O'Neill and David Richards (1996) 'Thatcherism and the Three "R"s: Radicalism, Realism and Rhetoric in the Third Term of the Thatcher Government', *Parliamentary Affairs*, 455–70.

Edwards, Nigel (2010) 'Is Whitehall Ready to Let Go of the NHS?', *Guardian*, 15 December.

Esping-Andersen, Gosta (1990) *The Three Worlds of Welfare Capitalism* (Cambridge: Polity Press).

Glendenning, Caroline (2003) 'Health Policies', in Nick Ellison and Chris Pierson (eds), *Developments in Social Policy 2* (Basingstoke: Palgrave Macmillan), pp. 194–210.

Greener, Ian (2009) *Healthcare in the UK: Understanding Continuity and Change* (Bristol: Policy Press).

Ham, Christopher (1994) *Management and Competition in the New NHS* (Oxford: Radcliffe Medical).

Harrison, Stephen, and Ruth McDonald (2008) *The Politics of Health Care in Britain* (London: Sage).

Howard, Christopher (2007) *The Welfare State Nobody Knows: Debunking Myths About US Social Policy* (Princeton: Princeton University Press).

Ipsos Mori (2010) 'Best Party on Key Issues: Health Care', www.ipsos-mori.com.

Jacobs, Lawrence (1995) 'Politics of America's Supply State: Health Reform and Technology', *Health Affairs*, 14(2), 143–57.

Jacobs, Lawrence (2005) 'Health Disparities in the Land of Equality', in James Morone and Lawrence Jacobs (eds), *Healthy Wealthy and Fair: Health Care and the Good Soci*ety (New York: Oxford University Press), pp. 37–63.

Kaiser Commission on Medicaid and the Uninsured (2010) *Medicaid's Continuing Crunch in a Recession: A Mid-Year Update for State FY 2010 and a Preview for FY 2011* (Washington, DC: Kaiser Family Foundation).

Kaiser Family Foundation (2010) *Health Insurance Coverage of the Total Population, States* (Washington, DC: Kaiser Family Foundation).

Klein, Rudolf (2006) *The New Politics of the NHS: From Creation to Reinvention* (Oxford: Radcliffe Publishing).

Leonhardt, David (2010) 'In Health Bill, Obama Attacks Wealth Inequality', *New York Times*, 23 March.

Marmor, Theodore R. (2000) *The Politics of Medicare,* 2nd edn (New York: Aldine de Gruyter).

Marmor, Theodore R., and Jonathan Oberlander (2010) 'The Health Bill Explained at Last', *New York Review of Books*, 19 August, electronic edition, www.nybooks.com/issues/2010/aug/19/.

Mazzone, Jason (2010) 'Can Congress Force You to be Healthy?' *New York Times*, 16 December.

Mechanic, David (1995) 'The Americanization of the British National Health Service', *Health Affairs*, Summer, 51–67.

McKinsey Global Institute (2008) *Accounting For the Cost of US Health Care: A New Look at Why Americans Spend More*, McKinsey and Company.

Moon, Marilyn (2006) *Medicare: A Policy Primer* (Washington, DC: Urban Institute Press).

Moran, Michael (1999) *Governing the Health Care State: A Comparative Study of the United Kingdom, the United States and Germany* (Manchester: Manchester University Press).

Moran, Michael (2000) 'Understanding the Welfare State: The Case of Health Care', *British Journal of Politics and International Relations*, 2(2), 135–69.

Morris, Charles (2006) *Apart at the Seams: The Collapse of Private Pension and Health Care Protection* (New York: Century Foundation Press).

Newhouse, Joseph (2010) 'Assessing Health Reform's Impact on Four Key Groups of Americans', *Health Affairs*, 29(9), 1714–24.

Nix, Kathryn (2010) 'Top 10 Disasters of Obamacare', Heritage Foundation Web Memo, 30 March, www.heritage.org.

NHS Confederation (2011) *Liberating the NHS: What Might Happen?* (London: NHS Confederation).

Oberlander, Jonathan (2003) *The Political Life of Medicare* (Chicago: University of Chicago Press).

Oberlander, Jonathan (2010) 'Long Time Coming: Why Health Reform Finally Passed', *Health Affairs*, 29(6), 1112–16.

Oberlander, Jonathan, and Joseph White (2009) 'Public Attitudes Towards Health Care Spending Aren't The Problem; Prices Are', *Health Affairs*, 28(5), 1285–93.

OECD (1987) *Financing and Delivering Health Care: A Comparative Analysis of OECD Countries*. (Paris: OECD).

OECD (2010) Directorate for Employment, Labor and Social Affairs, *OECD Health Data for 2010* (Paris: OECD).

Politics Daily (2010) 'HHS Secretary Kathleen Sebelius on NBC's Meet the Press', 7 March, www.politicsdaily.com.

Pollock, Allyson (2005) *NHS plc: The Privatisation of Our Health Service* (London: Verso).

Ramesh, Randeep, and Rachel Williams (2010) 'NHS Trusts Aim for Private Profits', *Guardian*, 2 August.

Saldin, Robert (2010) 'Healthcare Reform: A Prescription for the 2010 Republican Landslide?', *Forum*, 8(4), Article 10.

Sebelius, Kathleen (2011) 'Everyone Prospers Under Health Law', *Politico*, 14 March, www.politico.com.

Secretary of State for Health (1989) *Working for Patients* (London: HMSO).

Secretary of State for Health (2000) *The NHS Plan* (London: HMSO).

Secretary of State for Health (2002) *Delivering the NHS Plan* (London: HMSO).

Secretary of State for Health (2010) *Equity and Excellence: Liberating the NHS* (London: HMSO).

Simon, Kosali (2010) *Implications of Health Care Reform for Employers* (Washington, DC: Center for American Progress).

Stolberg, Sheryl Gay, and Robert Pear (2010) 'Obama Signs Health Care Overhaul Bill, with a Flourish', *New York Times*, 23 March, p. A1.

Thorne, Deborah, and Elizabeth Warren (2008) 'Get Sick, Go Broke', in Jacob Hacker (ed.), *Health at Risk: America's Ailing Health System and How to Heal It* (New York: Columbia University Press), pp. 66–87.

Timmins, Nicholas (2011) 'Pros and Cons of a Delicate Operation', *Financial Times*, 20 January, www.ft.com.

US Census Bureau (2010) 'People without Health Insurance Coverage by Selected characteristics, 2007, Current Population Survey, 2008 and 2009 Annual Social and economic Supplements'.

Washington Post (2010) *Landmark: the Inside Story of America's New Health-Care Law and What It Means for Us All* (New York: Public Affairs).

12
From 9/11 to 2011: The 'War on Terror' and the Onward March of Executive Power?

John E. Owens and Mark Shephard

Over a decade ago, 9/11 became the iconic event in US and UK politics. The atrocities in New York and Washington represented not only a new type of terrorist phenomenon but also one that signaled new aggressive assertions of executive power by the Bush administration and the Blair government at the expense of Congress and Parliament, and new dangers to the rule of law and protection of civil liberties (Owens, 2010; Shephard, 2010). Both President Bush and Prime Minister Tony Blair accepted the imprimatura of a global 'war on terror' (Owens and Dumbrell, 2008, p. 2). In the United States, the Bush administration worked with Congress to formulate and implement revised legal definitions of terrorism; new search, arrest and surveillance powers; and to legislate huge increases in federal spending on the military, law enforcement, surveillance, database management, border control, capital control, and intelligence capacities. Claiming 'inherent' and 'plenary' powers, Bush administration officials also effectively authorized and organized state kidnapping of alleged terrorists both in the US and abroad ('extraordinary rendition'), interned suspects in military facilities in the US and abroad without legal redress, and sanctioned abuse and torture of detainees by US personnel, private contractors and foreign governments. Although Congress undertook a considerable amount of oversight of the so-called 'war on terror', the effects on policy were marginal, whether under Democratic or Republican congressional majorities. In Britain, Tony Blair 'quickly established himself as the most visible and prominent international supporter of Bush's "war on terror"' (Dumbrell, 2008, p. 236). Taking advantage of

Britain's strongly majoritarian governmental structure, Blair's government invented new executive powers and on an incremental basis enhanced the power of the British executive in response to 9/11 and the 7/7 bombings in London, and frequently sought to shade his government from public and parliamentary scrutiny. Typically, British MPs were inactive and ineffective overseers of the Blair government, as security needs trumped demands for effective parliamentary oversight and influence.

Ten years on from 9/11 and notwithstanding the killing of the alleged perpetrator of these and other atrocities in May 2011, the threat from terrorism, emanating primarily from jihadists, continues. We ask, to what extent has the momentum towards greater executive power and discretion ushered in by US and British counterterrorism efforts been maintained by the Obama administration and the Cameron government and/or checked by Congress and Parliament? Did the policy thrust of the US 'war on terror' change significantly with Barack Obama's election? With the return to Democratic unified government, did Congress become less acquiescent and more challenging on 'war on terror'-related issues? Or did the Democrat-controlled House and Senate essentially follow Obama's lead in changing the tone of the US 'war on terror' without changing the policies or the balance of executive–legislative relations? For the UK, did the election of a Conservative–Liberal Democrat Coalition government maintain or reduce executive discretion in respect of counterterrorism policy, and did parliamentary control and checks over the government's administration of policy strengthen significantly?

Obama, Congress and the 'ongoing struggle'

In his 2008 election campaign, President-elect Obama promised to 'turn the page' on the policies of the Bush Administration and inaugurate a new era of moral and civic renewal. As a senator, Obama had criticized the expansive nature of Congress' 2001 and 2003 'use of force' resolutions and the Bush administration's assertion of 'inherent' and 'plenary power'. In answers to the *Boston Globe*'s questionnaire, he rejected 'the view that the President may do whatever he deems necessary to protect national security' and disavowed 'extreme and implausible claims of presidential authority' (Savage, 2007). In office, Obama rejected the 'war on terror' nomenclature in favor of the 'enduring struggle against terrorism and extremism' or the 'ongoing struggle' (Obama, 2009a), and nominated as head of the Office of Legal Counsel and Solicitor General prominent constitutional lawyers fiercely critical of the Bush administration's expansive view of executive power. Within two days of his inauguration, moreover, the new president signed executive orders revoking the Bush administration's severe limits on public access to presidential records, closing Guantánamo (albeit with some caveats), ending military tribunals, and prohibiting the Central Intelligence Agency (CIA) from maintaining its so-called 'black sites' overseas. Bush's Executive Order (EO) 13440 (2007) and every executive directive, order, and regulation relating to the detention or interrogation of individuals issued by any executive branch lawyer after 9/11 was also revoked and primary authority over detention policies was transferred to the Justice Department. The new president also signaled a much less aggressive and more respectful approach to Congress. During Senate confirmation hearings, Obama's nominees for Attorney General and CIA Director, Eric Holder and Leon Panetta, repeatedly stressed their wishes to work with Congress to write new detention and other anti-terror legislation and keep legislators better informed of their activities. Echoing Obama's election pledge, Holder categorically rejected the view that the president possessed 'inherent' power to override congressional statutes: '[N] o one is above the law', he insisted. 'The president has the constitutional obligation to make sure that the laws are faithfully executed' (US Senate Judiciary Committee, 2009, pp. 23, 30).

Before Obama took office, former Vice President Cheney averred that the new president would 'appreciate' the expansions of executive power achieved during the Bush administration and 'not likely … cede that authority back to the Congress' (quoted in Bolton, 2008, p. A1). Despite eschewing Bush's 'inherent' powers doctrine and proposing 'conversations' with Congress on new legislation, many of Obama's actions have not confounded Cheney's prediction. Indeed, the revisions to US torture and interrogation policy instigated by Obama were implemented unilaterally by executive order, without congressional statute or approval, thereby allowing Obama or a successor to overturn the new policies by another executive order written by the same president or one of his successors. Obama also did not abandon all claims to exert other unilateral powers and, indeed, when he subsequently did so he typically invoked the same foundational legislation as Bush, chiefly the 2001 use of force resolution, which Congress made no effort to repeal or amend. Thus, Attorney General Holder justified the killing of Osama bin Laden 'as an act of national self-defense' consistent with Congress' 2001 use of force resolution that authorized the president 'to use all necessary and appropriate force' against those involved in the 9/11 attacks (Williams, 2011; see also Rollins, 2011).

While Obama promised to close Guantánamo and renounced the Bush administration's 'enemy combatant' label for designating terrorist suspects, it soon became clear that he would pursue policies that were similar to those of the Bush administration. When suspected terrorists held in detention sought *habeas corpus* relief pursuant to the 2008 *Boumediene* decision,[1] Obama's Justice Department filed legal memoranda in the US District Court of the District of Columbia holding to the Bush administration's position that the president had the unilateral authority (based on the 2001 use of force resolution) to detain terrorist suspects indefinitely without criminal charges or *habeas corpus* rights, even when they were detained outside a traditional 'battlefield' (Center for Constitutional Rights, 2009). The new administration would use the same law-of-war principles as its predecessor in a further 200 cases (Glaberson, 2009) pending an administration task force's comprehensive review of detention policy.

It was not long before liberals in Congress controlled by his own party objected to Obama's continuation of Bush administration detention policy. They proposed new detainment legislation that became the subject of House and Senate hearings held in June and July 2009. At the same time, however – and much more significant politically – a growing groundswell of public and congressional opposition developed toward Obama's proposals to close Guantánamo, create a new system of preventive detention and transfer 50 or so of the more than 200 terrorist suspects remaining at Guantánamo to the US for trial.[2] Five months into the new administration, this groundswell produced a 90–6 Senate vote in favor of an amendment to a fiscal year (FY) 2009 supplemental appropriations bill that specifically prohibited the administration from using any monies to fund the transfer, release, or incarceration of any Guantánamo detainees in the US. The House took similar action in July 2009. When Attorney General Eric Holder proposed prosecution of the alleged 9/11 perpetrators in a New York court, the public backlash intensified so that in December 2010 Obama was forced to sign a defense authorization bill that included strict new limits on transferring of Guantánamo detainees for trial in the civil courts, the purchase or construction of any facility within the US to house them, and on their transfer to third countries without the Defense Secretary confirming the safety of doing so.

Despite Obama committing himself to working with Congress to 'develop an appropriate legal regime so that our efforts are consistent with our values and our Constitution' (Obama, 2009c), no new legislation was requested by the administration and Congress failed to take any autonomous action. Meanwhile, the administration continued to petition the courts to deny *habeas corpus* rights to terrorist detainees and to move suspects around the world beyond the reach of the US Constitution in order to enforce indefinite detention. Effectively, both the Obama administration and Congress absolved responsibility for enacting new preventive detention legislation – with the consequence that unilateral discretion over detainees remained with the administration without judicial oversight. Faced by suits filed by individual detainees, the courts could only rule on a case-by-case basis, with the result that law and policy became contradictory and incoherent. De facto, detainee policy rested with the judicial discretion of the US District Court in Washington, DC, to whom Congress had delegated responsibility for ruling on detainee cases. Judge Thomas F. Hogan of the Court complained in late 2009 that his fellow judges hearing detainee cases were essentially in the business of creating 'different rules and procedures ... different rules of evidence ... [and] substantive law' (quoted in Denniston, 2009). Even civil liberties groups were content with this ad hoc approach (Finn 2009a, p. A1), fearing legislation even more detrimental to the rule of law. Indeed, requesting new legislation from Congress was politically fraught, for it would require legislators to repeal or at least amend the 2001 congressional use of force resolution in order to confine the president's discretion, which most legislators would not want. Such was public, media and congressional hostility to detainees being tried in civil courts that such a course also risked congressional enactment of an indefinite detention law that would not be limited by wartime conditions and, therefore, have serious implications for civil liberties in peacetime.

An immediate consequence of legislative inaction was that 20 terrorist suspects, whom the courts had ordered to be released from Guantánamo after eight years' detention, were subsequently obliged to remain at the facility because of the congressional prohibition on them entering the US and the inability of the administration to find them suitable homes in other countries. Finally, in March 2011, the combination of congressional and public opposition and Obama's unwillingness to expend further political capital in the run-up to his re-election bid reconciled him to the reality of the legislative impasse, the defeat of his policy, and exclusive reliance on unilateral presidential action. He signed a new executive order resuming the Bush administration's trials by military commissions and maintaining indefinite detention for the remaining detainees at Guantánamo. 'Congress has been AWOL', complained South Carolina Republican Senator Lindsey Graham, 'We've done a lot of demagoguing, but we haven't provided any solutions' (Starks and Stern, 2011, p. 622).

Not only did Obama maintain the Bush administration's policy of indefinite detainment unmitigated by congressional statute, his Justice Department invoked the same 'state secrets' doctrine in order to shut down court suits to Bush administration detentions involving allegations of extraordinary rendition, torture and suppressing evidence. Obama promised to support new state secrets legislation proposed by leading liberal Democrats, which sought to require a federal judge to examine disputed evidence in such trials rather than dismiss a case outright based solely on the government's assertion that disclosure would endanger national security. The administration resiled from that position and opted for new Justice Department rules for invoking the state secrets privilege. Again, however, as with detainee policy, discretion would rest with the executive rather than a court interpreting a congressional statute so that Obama or one of his successors could reverse the rules. Moreover, Holder's new rules did not include the most significant part of the proposed congressional legislation, which would require a formal court review to determine whether a court case would result in 'significant harm' to national security if it proceeded. Indeed, even as Holder published the new guidelines, within weeks of Obama's inauguration the Justice Department went to court to dismiss lawsuits relating to President Bush's extraordinary rendition program on the same basis as the Bush administration, that they threatened US national security (Schwartz, 2009, p. A1).

Still, the new administration did not confine its invocation of state secrets to extraordinary rendition. Obama also followed Bush in using warrantless wiretapping by the National Security Agency (NSA) to intercept American citizens' communications and then invoking state secrets to dismiss suits against this illegal activity. In April 2009, the *New York Times* disclosed that the NSA had exceeded the leeway provided by the 2008 Foreign Intelligence Surveillance Act (FISA) Amendments by continuing warrantless wiretaps, even though a few months earlier the Justice Department had informed House and Senate Intelligence and Judiciary Committees of these illegal activities and given assurances that they had been 'reined in'. Skeptical Congress members doubted that the 'overcollection of data' was inadvertent, but doubted whether their committees had sufficient technical expertise to conduct effective oversight in this highly sensitive policy area (Risen and Lichtblau, 2009, p. A1). The federal courts were less equivocal. First, administration officials, including the director of the NSA, refused to cooperate 'because', a federal judge wrote in *al-Haramain Islamic Foundation Inc.* v. *Bush* (May 2009), 'they assert, plaintiffs' attorneys do not "need to know" the information that the [Northern District of California] court has determined they do need to know' (Johnson, 2009, p. A1). In other words, the Obama administration adopted the same hubristic view as its predecessor: the court had no right whatsoever to rule on the legality of the program because plaintiffs could not prove they were subjected to the secret eavesdropping (and thus lacked standing to sue) and in any event the NSA program was such a vital 'state secret' that courts were barred from adjudicating its legality. Ten months later, the same court completely rejected those arguments. Dismissing what it called the government's 'impressive display of argumentative acrobatics', the court not only confirmed the illegality of the NSA's surveillance program but also castigated the Obama administration for attempting to place itself above the law. The state secrets doctrine amounted to 'unfettered executive-branch discretion' that had 'obvious potential for governmental abuse and overreaching'. The FISA law passed by the Congress in 2008 trumps the administration's state secrets claim (Savage and Risen, 2010, p. A1).

On torture and interrogation policy, the Obama administration also insisted on administration discretion untrammeled by new congressional legislation. During nomination hearings before the Senate, Obama's nominee for CIA Director asserted the agency's need for discretion and refused to rule out using torture or extraordinary rendition; he would, however, keep the Congress better apprised of the CIA's activities (Mazzetti, 2009, p. A1) and be governed by more restrictive rules than his predecessors, consistent with Obama's January 2009 executive orders. Although leading Congress members proposed new anti-torture legislation and various committee hearings were convened following disclosure of documents providing evidence of 'unauthorized, improvised, inhumane, and undocumented' interrogation methods by (often untrained) CIA officers and contractors on detainees (Finn et al., 2009, p. A1), Congress refused to write any new legislation that either brought past crimes and practices to book or refined existing statutory policy to reflect new strictures contained in Obama's executive orders. As with detainee policy, Congress' refusal to act meant that Obama or his successors could undo policy he had made by executive order. Moreover, notwithstanding Obama signing an executive order permitting interrogation methods included in the US Army Field Manual on interrogation, when Congress included new provisions in its FY2010 intelligence authorization legislation requiring videotaping of CIA interrogations in Iraq and requiring information on covert intelligent activity to be given to the entire House and Senate Intelligence Committees, Obama threatened a veto on the grounds that Congress was seeking to intrude on the president's national security prerogatives. Ultimately, the legislation required disclosure of covert activities but with the caveat that the president need not oblige Congress if he asserts in writing that doing so would harm US national security (Mulero and Starks, 2010, p. 2295).

Finally, President Obama significantly escalated and intensified the military campaign against the Taliban in Afghanistan and Pakistan – as Bush would likely have done – and strongly committed his administration to international efforts against al Qaeda and other terrorist networks. A month after taking office, the president announced that US combat troops in the Afghanistan/Pakistan theater would increase to 68,000 and unambiguously committed the US to preventing the return of a Taliban government and to enhancing Afghanistan's 'military, governance and economic capacity'. Obama also continued the Bush administration's policy of extrajudicial targeting and killing of al Qaeda leaders, culminating in US Navy SEALs' killing of Osama bin Laden in May 2011. Following the Senate Select Committee on Intelligence's disclosure in 1975 that the CIA had been involved in several murders or attempted murders of foreign leaders, in 1976, President Gerald Ford signed an executive order banning political assassinations abroad. Every succeeding president until George W. Bush renewed that order, although it did not prevent the Clinton administration from targeting bin Laden in Afghanistan. Obama too did not renew the prohibition and followed Bush in targeting al Qaeda leaders, often by unmanned drones. Notwithstanding acting as judge, jury and executioner, the president proudly announced to a jubilant nation, 'justice has been done' at least according to his interpretation of US law.[3]

As US casualties rose and opinion polls showed declining support for US military involvement in Afghanistan, the Democratic Congress put down markers requiring the president to submit a report assessing the extent to which the Afghan and Pakistani governments were 'demonstrating the necessary commitment, capability, conduct and unity of purpose to warrant the continuation [of administration policy]' (US Congress, House of Representatives, Committee on Appropriations, 2009, p. 68). Months later, Congress insisted on integrating funding for the wars in Iraq and Afghanistan into the annual defense appropriations bill for the first time since 2001 and cut the administration's Afghanistan Security Forces Fund request. Even so, three months after receiving a warning from the US theater commander in September 2009 of a 'serious and deteriorating' situation in Afghanistan and Pakistan and a request for a significant increase in US troops, Obama deployed an additional 30,000 US troops and was forced to delay troop withdrawal until 2014. Despite the US public increasingly disapproving Obama's handling of the war, despite total war costs exceeding those for the post-2003 Iraq war and occupation, and despite public support for the president's congressional party declining, as in previous wars, fear of the consequences of a precipitous withdrawal of US troops persuaded Congress to continue its support (Fisher, 2000; Peterson, 1994, p. 217). With public support for the military campaign in Afghanistan remaining weak, however, the killing of bin Laden apparently provided the president with the necessary catalyst to announce in June 2011 that 'we have put al Qaeda on a path to defeat', the 'tide of war is receding', and 33,000 US troops would be withdrawn by September 2012.

Although Obama has adopted a less presidentialist style, a more respectful tone in his dealings with the Congress, and a greater willingness to engage in conversations with Congress (Owens, 2011), his administration has pursued almost identical (albeit more nuanced) 'war on terror' policies, and used more or less all the powers demanded and exercised by the Bush administration. That is, although the tone of presidentialism has softened, its substance has continued – and not without a little pedantry.[4] Undoubtedly, Congress has challenged and in some cases checked the Obama administration but such challenges and checks have been rare, and specifically on the closure of Guantánamo, Congress effectively resisted taking the discretion *away from* the president. In short, ten years after 9/11, the contours of counterterrorism policy and the balance of power between Congress and the president remain those set by the Bush administration. Owens (2008) suggested that the combination of George W. Bush's presidentialism, the 9/11 atrocities and the administration's so-called 'war on terror' may have provided the 'flip-over dynamics' in the evolution of the US's constitutional order towards the further consolidation of executive government. That analysis further suggested that even if a Democrat won the presidency, the transformation would endure – as long as the permanent 'war' itself endured. Ackerman (1999, pp. 2334–45) suggested a ten-year test. From the perspective of 2011, it seems the flip-over has endured.

Cameron, Coalition government, and counterterrorism policy

Post-9/11, Parliament has created new powers for the executive that increased the British government's power vis-à-vis Parliament. While this has had important consequences for executive–legislative relations, the power gain incurred significant costs. Most evident was the protracted demise of Tony Blair's political capital over Iraq; despite the prime minister's concessions to Parliament, such as granting the parliamentary liaison committee greater access to the prime minister and giving MPs the right to vote on war with Iraq, he overcommitted. As over US extraordinary rendition practices, Parliament's police patrol oversight of Britain's involvement in Iraq was exposed as weak. Nevertheless, MPs sometimes raised parliamentary fire alarms, most notably against 90-day detention of terrorist suspects without charge under Section 41 of the 2000 Terrorism Act. Indeed, the parliamentary revolt that resulted contributed to Blair's decision to resign his premiership and led his successor to concede the need for greater balance between Parliament and the government, albeit in language that granted the government sufficient latitude to perpetuate the executive's de facto anti-terrorism powers.[5]

At first glance, it appears that much changed under the Conservative–Liberal Democrat Coalition, which formed the new government after the 2010 general election. The government allowed, for example, detention without charge to lapse from 28 to 14 days, scrapped the ID card scheme, and removed control orders. These shifts in policy, however, did not represent major rollbacks of Britain's counterterrorism state, nor were they the products of greater or more effective legislative scrutiny per se. Inasmuch as they occurred, they were the products of political compromise within the coalition and events conspiring to undo the best-laid plans.

In their 2010 election manifesto, the Conservatives sought to counter the perception that Labour followed US foreign policy too closely and promised adherence to 'own values' and 'moral authority' (Conservatives, 2010b), which paradoxically suggested a Bush-like sense of *déjà vu*. This approach by the Coalition government's dominant party contrasted starkly with Liberal Democrat promises of a more measured and world-integrative approach to foreign policy. As, however, the new government sought to address counterterrorism issues, it was the Liberal Democrats – as the junior partners – who faced the steepest learning curve and who were steered more towards Conservative goals of state protection over civil liberties.

That said, the new Conservative–Liberal Democrat Coalition government promised to 'reverse the substantial erosion of civil liberties following Labour's election loss in 2010, and roll back state intrusion' (Conservative Party, 2010a, p. 6). The formal post-election agreement that the two parties reached included repealing unnecessary anti-terror and criminal legislation, scrapping ID cards, extending freedom of information, restoring rights to non-violent protest, reviewing libel laws to protect freedom of speech, and ending storage of internet and email records without good reason. The Conservatives were keen 'to restore trust' and 'improve the workings of Government' (Conservative Party, 2010b) and to this end promised to introduce a National Security Council (within the cabinet), review and consolidate counterterrorism and security laws, and conduct a review of the government strategy aimed at preventing vulnerable people from becoming terrorists (Conservatives, 2010b). Leaving aside the obvious difficulty of 'spotting emerging risks and dealing with them before they become crises' (Cameron and Clegg, 2010) in a constantly changing world (for example, the multiple civilian uprisings in the Middle East and North Africa), the new government's first priority – and the largest single challenge to national security – was addressing what it believed to be the unsustainability of UK central government's finances and the consequent need to make efficiency savings in all budgets, including those for national security. Thus, when the need for humanitarian military intervention in Libya suddenly arose, for example, criticism was heaped on the government's Strategic Defence and Security Review (SDSR) from all sides (Moon, 2011, col. 756; Leigh, 2011, col. 772; Jenkin, 2011, col. 793).

The new government was also somewhat naive in promising speedy delivery on its promises, given its coalitional character and the need therefore for intra-coalition discussions and consultation with relevant interest groups. For instance, the scrapping of the 'intrusive' £4.5 billion ID card scheme and National Identity Register was supposed to be achieved within the first 100 days of the government. In the event, Parliament took longer than anticipated to enact the legislation; the bill was not cleared until December 2010. That said, ID cards and the National Identity Register were scrapped (as were plans to introduce fingerprinting in passports), providing evidence of the new government's rolling back of the counterterror state and a significant achievement for the Conservative–Liberal Democratic Coalition. If Labour had been re-elected in 2010, this policy change would likely not have occurred.

Still, the new government's embracing of civil liberties has been selective. Following a large demonstration in London against the government's spending cuts, Home Secretary Theresa May (Conservative) told the Commons in late March that her government would also consider amending Section 44 of the 2000 Terrorism Act (ruled as illegal by the European Court of Human Rights in January 2010) with a view to using 'pre-emptive banning orders' against protesters and banning protesters from covering their face with masks or balaclavas.[6] May also refused to rule out dawn raids and snatch-squads against protesters (May, 2011b: col. 27). By March 2011, moreover, the government had announced any plans to stop the police from filming protesters (in contravention of Section 8 of the Human Rights Act) or from uploading images to Crimint, a general database for criminal intelligence (Lewis and Vallée, 2009). Notwithstanding the Coalition Agreement's promise to 'end the storage of internet and email records without good reason', other proposals contradicted this promise, including acquiring and storing internet and email records, which was buried in the government's SDSR, a new streamlined National Crime Agency and Border Police Command to replace the National Policing Improvement Agency, and the creation of a European Union-wide network of travel databases to record the movements and personal details of millions of air passengers within Europe, which would supplement existing requirements travel between Europe and the US.

Indeed, clear tensions developed between the two coalition parties supporting Cameron's government on a number of 'war on terror'-related issues involving the balance between civil liberties and protection of the public. Evidence of such tensions were manifest in the substantial increase in backbench rebellions in Parliament, which have become the norm rather than the exception, with rebels from the coalition parties expressing doubts over temporary continuation of control orders, detention without trial proposals, and the war in Afghanistan (Cowley and Stuart, 2010, p. 4).[7]

In their 2010 election manifesto, the Liberal Democrats were explicit in wanting to scrap control orders (Liberal Democrats, 2010b, p. 94). Ultimately, both parties agreed to review counterterrorism and security powers, including reducing detention without trial from 28 to 14 days (by permitting the de facto January 2011 reversion to 14 days) and making control orders 'less intrusive and more focused' (UK Home Office, 2011, p. 6). As headlines, both measures looked like significant departures from the previous Labour government's policy. With Labour opposition support (Cooper, 2011, col. 311), however, the Cameron government opted to err for public protection over civil liberties concerns, for example, by proposing draft emergency legislation to allow reversion of detention without trial to 28 days 'in response to multiple coordinated attacks and/ or during multiple large and simultaneous investigations' (UK Home Office, 2011, p. 14, para. 29). Replacement of the control order system also amounted more to window dressing than to substantive reform. The government's 'approach that scrapped control orders and introduced more precisely focused and targeted restrictions, supported by increased covert investigative resources, would mitigate risk while increasing civil liberties' (ibid., p. 39, para. 20), raised more questions than answers. How is increasing covert investigative resources compatible with increasing civil liberties? What are focused and targeted restrictions? Professing to end the creeping threat to British civil liberties, Home Secretary May generated considerable mirth on opposition benches as she sought to differentiate between her new ostensibly higher test of 'reasonable belief' in order to prompt a control order and the previous government's reliance on 'reasonable suspicion', and between an 'overnight residence requirement' and 'curfews' (May, 2011a, col. 308). Meanwhile, in his report on existing control order legislation, the independent reviewer of terrorist legislation, Lord Carlile (Liberal Democrat), concluded that the existing system 'continued to function reasonably well' (Carlile, 2011, p. 1), and criticized the hitherto 'poorly informed debate', which had resulted from the exclusion of the then opposition (Liberals and Conservatives) from decision-making (ibid., para. 47, p. 21). In order to avoid future 'regrettable' opposition commitments to uninformed positions (ibid., para. 45, p. 20), Carlile recommended discussions on whether the Coalition government's replacement Terrorism Prevention and Investigation Measures (T-Pims), should include two vetted members of the opposition.

Ongoing controversy over the European Court of Human Rights' rulings against the deportation of terror suspects and other issues provided a further source of tension for the Coalition government. Under the 1998 Human Rights Act, the UK cannot deport terror suspects if they are likely to be subjected to torture or degrading human treatment. As part of the review of counterterrorism and security legislation, the Coalition government wanted to explore options that would extend the UK's ability to deport foreign nationals. Bowing to Conservative backbench pressure, Cameron also floated the idea of a British Bill of Rights to replace the European legislation 'because it is about time we ensured that decisions are made in this Parliament rather than in the courts' (Cameron, 2011, col. 955).

Like President Obama, Prime Minister Cameron also committed the Coalition government to military and political efforts against the Taliban in Afghanistan and Pakistan, which he dubbed a 'necessary war'. In July 2010, however, Cameron announced that the UK would withdraw the 10,000 British troops from Afghanistan by 2015, following a transition period to Afghan control between 2011 and 2014, subject to conditions on the ground. MPs from different parties heavily criticized the announcement, questioning the desirability of pre-announcing to the enemy a withdrawal timetable (albeit a conditional one); thenceforth, Parliament and the public would likely judge Cameron's performance on Afghanistan by his success in adhering to that deadline. Given

Afghanistan's political history and the views of many of those on the ground, that date looked ambitious. One reason Cameron may have made his announcement was to reassure the UK public that the mission had an end in sight. Polls still showed a majority of Brits (57 percent) opposed to military operations involving British soldiers (Angus Reid/ Public Opinion, 2010b) and the public underestimating the extent of British fatalities in the conflict (365 by mid May 2011). Clearly, Cameron's government was on the back foot and so under pressure to be seen to be delivering. Evidence of such pressure emerged when Major General Gordon Messenger, strategic communications officer to the Chief of the Defence Staff, told the House of Commons Defence Committee in October 2010 that only recently had resources matched the scale of the challenge in Afghanistan, which neatly coincided with Conservative MPs' view that the Labour Government had under resourced British troops (UK Parliament, House of Commons Defence Committee, 2010). Three months later – and much more seriously – the Conservative-chaired Foreign Affairs Committee raised doubts about the way the prime minister has developed and communicated the Coalition government's strategy for withdrawing British forces. They focused in particular on the announcement of a withdrawal date, which they argued 'may embolden the insurgency or encourage a more general perception among the West's enemies that its foreign policy commitments are wholly at the mercy of domestic public opinion'. The committee's highly critical report urged ministers to accelerate attempts to negotiate a 'political settlement' with the Taliban and questioned the degree to which actions in Afghanistan actually pertained to the core objective, and whether wider objectives were even attainable (UK Parliament, House of Commons Foreign Affairs Committee, 2011, pp. 74–5). The committee also heard echoes of Blair's 'sofa government' style: Cameron had decided on the 2015 deadline without formally discussing the issue with the cabinet's National Security Council, which is supposed to oversee Afghan policy (ibid., p. 68). Yet, while Parliament has voiced criticism of these government decisions, as in the US, MPs have paid little attention to the actual conduct of the war, particularly British involvement in extra-judicial attacks by armed drones on so-called 'high value targets', and the collateral damage to innocent Afghan civilians (Cole, 2011, p. 20).

Looking to the future of Britain's 'war on terror', particularly in light of the possible implementation of the Coalition government's constitutional proposals, the kind of inter-party tensions evident within the current government may become a common feature, making rolling back the British state and returning power to Parliament and the people less likely (Bognador, 2011a). While the public overwhelmingly rejected the introduction of the alternative vote electoral system – which would have made Coalition governments more likely – new proposals introduced in May 2011 to require the House of Lords to be wholly elected would, if implemented, undoubtedly give the chamber added, if not equal, legitimacy to the Commons and necessitate the kind of inter-cameral bargaining and compromise that is conducted in the US, with negative consequences for political accountability and responsibility. Similarly, proposals in the 2011 Parliamentary Voting System and Constituencies Act to reducing membership of the Commons from 650 to 600 without reducing the number of ministerial posts (which constitute the payroll vote) will mean fewer backbenchers available to scrutinize the government. Provisions in the Fixed-term Parliaments Bill to remove the prime minister's power to call an election could also reduce government responsiveness to Parliament between elections.

The US and Britain: counterterrorism, executive–legislative relations, and conditionality

It is clear from the previous analysis that the accretion of executive power in relation to the so-called 'war on terror' under the Bush administration and the Blair government has been maintained and, in certain cases, accelerated under their successors, particularly in regard to the military campaigns in Afghanistan and Pakistan, despite some softening of tone under the Obama administration and some changes – and some window dressing – by the new Coalition government under Cameron. Why has this been so?

First, the threat of terrorist attacks remains and the respective governments' perceptions of that threat remain high, as it does among the public. Yet, in a democratic society, there can be no simple equation between crises/external shocks as catalyst and increased executive power as product. Much depends also on the actual nature of the crisis/external shock and the ability of executives to define such events/conditions as requiring executive power accretions. Given adequate and appropriate leadership skills and temperament (Langston, 2007; Pfiffner, 2008, pp. 223–48; Tucker, 2009, pp. xxv–xxvi); enhanced politicization and centralization of executive institutions (Bennister, 2008; Moe, 1985; Norton, 2003, 2007); personalized, plebiscitary government and party systems (Foley, 2000; Lowi, 1986, pp. xi–xii, 180; Poguntke and Webb, 2005; Rimmerman, 1993; Rudalevige, 2005), and the need for swift and decisive action at a time of national danger, a president or prime minister will be best positioned to take the policy initiative clothing him/herself in symbolic authority and applying appropriate security rhetoric and public appeals.

Notwithstanding their more restrained tones, both the Obama and Cameron administrations have remained committed to strong executive action to counter the terrorist threat. Although the actual risk to life remains far less than the perception (Mueller, 2005, 2006), broad public and legislative support has reinforced those commitments even when such actions touched on civil liberties. Framing issues in terms of fighting terrorism can increase support for specific laws, measures, policies and executive leaders (Haider-Markel et al., 2006), which engenders increased support by legislators through a 'rally round the flag effect'. Poll results for both the US and the UK show strong public support for and acceptance of counterterrorism measures (DSTL, 2010; Pew Research Center, 2010), including government control orders (Kellner, 2011) and use of intelligence obtained through torture (Agiesta 2009; Radford, 2010). When, however, a terrorist attack occurs or is foiled, public pressure mounts for stronger measures at the expense of civil liberties, particularly among those most concerned about being a terrorist victim (Merolla and Zechmeister, 2009; Davis, 2007).

A priori, the balance of executive–legislative relations across different political systems *may* react uniformly to crises and external shocks. Yet, Bush and Blair were more successful in strengthening executive power further than were John Howard in Australia and Jean Chrétien, Paul Martin, and Stephen Harper in Canada because their capacity to do so was constrained by parliamentary politics (Larkin and Uhr, 2010; Molloy, 2010). Indeed, these constraints are more important than formal constitutional impediments or the respective number of veto points those systems produce. This chapter has shown that the overall balance of executive–legislative relations in respect to the 'war on terror' in the US and the UK has remained stable, and in favor of the executive, although both Congress and Parliament did occasionally check the executive – in the US, by strengthening congressional oversight of the NSA and the intelligence community, by integrating funding for the wars in Iraq and Afghanistan insisting on new limits on the USA PATRIOT Act; and in the UK by abandoning the previous Labour government's plans to introduce ID cards and a National Identity Register, and by reducing the length of detention without charge. In the case of the Obama administration, however, the most significant congressional check – over the proposed closing of Guantánamo – had the effect of *maintaining* rather than weakening executive discretion and keeping the detainees in judicial limbo. In both systems, moreover, significant attempts to curtail executive power and strengthen civil liberty concerns failed, notably over state secrets and torture in the US and over new control orders in the UK. Ultimately, as with Bush and Blair, public safety and strong executive power trumped strengthening civil liberties and weakening executive discretion.

Notes

1. By a five-to-four vote, the US Supreme Court held that the Congress had unconstitutionally stripped the federal courts of jurisdiction over cases filed on behalf of the Guantánamo detainees without providing for any acceptable substitute procedure. The Court insisted that detainees were permitted to file *habeas corpus* suits to challenge their continued detention.
2. Fifty percent of those surveyed in June 2009 said they disapproved of closing the facility, according to a *Washington Post–ABC News* poll, up significantly from a Pew poll in February.
3. Whether Obama's targeting al Qaeda leaders for extrajudicial execution in this and other instances violated international law is another matter. Article 23b of The Hague Convention, adopted by the US and other nations in 1907, prohibits 'assassination, proscription, or outlawry of an enemy, or putting a price upon an enemy's head, as well as offering a reward for an enemy "dead or alive".'
4. Thus, while eschewing Bush's 'war on terror' label, the Obama administration's *National Security Strategy* document commits the US to 'fighting a war [*sic*] against a far-reaching network of hatred and violence' and boldly asserts that '[w]e are at war [*sic*] with a specific network, al-Qaeda, and its terrorist affiliates' (US White House, 2010, pp. 4, 20).
5. Flinders and Kelso's more optimistic assessment of Parliament's capacity for fire alarm influence (2011), which stresses particularly the gap between expectations and institutional capacity for influence, ignores the possibility that a government may lose a parliamentary battle at time *t* but succeed at time *t+1*, as the Labour government found when it sought to extend detention of terrorist suspects without charge to 28 days (Shephard, 2010). Parliament's capacity for influence is also much more limited on defence and security issues than on other issues (ibid.).
6. Section 44 gives the police and the Home Secretary power to define any area in the UK for any period of time wherein they may stop and search any vehicle or person, and seize 'articles of a kind which could be used in connection with terrorism' without 'reasonable suspicion' that an offence has been committed.
7. The coalition includes 306 Conservative and 57 Liberal Democrat MPs, which provides the Cameron government with a majority of 38. However, its effective majority is 40, which is almost double the 21-seat majority enjoyed by the Conservative government elected in the 1992 general election.

References

Ackerman, Bruce (1999) 'Revolution on a Human Scale', *Yale Law Journal*, 108: 2279–349.

Agiesta, Jennifer (2009) 'Torture: The Memos and Partisan Reaction', *Washington Post*, 26 April, voices.washingtonpost.com, accessed 20 October 2010.

Angus Reid/Public Opinion (2010a) 'Three-in-Four Britons Foresee a Terrorist Attack in the Next Year. Three-in-five Americans Believe a Terrorist Attack is Likely to Happen in their Country – Only 38 per cent of Canadians Concur', 11 November, www.angus-reid.com, accessed 20 March 2011.

Angus Reid/Public Opinion (2010b) 'Most Britons Continue to Regret Sending Soldiers to Afghanistan', 21 December, www.angus-reid.com, accessed 3 April 2011.

Bennister, Mark (2008) 'Blair and Howard: Predominant Prime Ministers Compared', *Parliamentary Affairs*, 61(2): 334–55.

Bogdanor, Vernon (2011) *The Coalition and the Constitution*, Video of lecture, Canterbury, University of Kent, 2 March, www.kent.ac.uk/politics/, accessed 31 March 2011.

Bolton, Alexander (2008) 'Cheney Says Obama should be Grateful to Bush', *The Hill*, 15 December, p. A1.

Cameron, David (2010a) 'PM Article in *Wall Street Journal*: UK-US Relations', 20 July, www.number10.gov.uk, accessed 28 March 2011.

Cameron, David (2011) Speech. House of Commons. *Hansard. Debates*, 16 February, col. 955.

Cameron, David, and Nick Clegg (2010) 'Foreword', in *United Kingdom. Government, 'A Strong Britain in an Age of Uncertainty: The National Security Strategy'*, CM 7953, October.

Carlile, Lord (2011) *Sixth Report of the Independent Reviewer Pursuant of Section 14(3) of the Prevention of Terrorism Act 2005*, 3 February, www.homeoffice.gov.uk, accessed 28 March 2011.

Center for Constitutional Rights (2009) 'Obama Administration Offers Essentially Same Definition of Enemy Combatant Without Using the Term' (New York: Center for Constitutional Rights).

Cole, Chris (2011) 'We Mustn't Ignore the Fact that British Drones Kill Too. We Claim Moral Superiority Over the US on Drone Deaths, yet a Wall of Silence Surrounds Our Own Record', *Guardian*, 13 May, p. 20.

Conservative Party (2010a) 'Conservative-Liberal Democrat Coalition Negotiations: Agreements Reached 11 May 2010', www.conservatives.com, accessed 24 August 2010.

Conservative Party (2010b) 'Where We Stand/National Security', www.conservatives.com, accessed 24 August 2010.

Cooper, Yvette (2011) Speech. House of Commons. *Hansard. Debates*, 26 January, col. 311.

Cowley, Philip, and Mark Stuart (2010) 'A Coalition with Wobbly Wings: Backbench Dissent since May 2010', 8 November, p. 4, www.revolts.co.uk, accessed 31 March 2011.

Davis, Darren W. (2007) *Negative Liberty: Public Opinion and the Terrorist Attacks on America* (New York: Russell Sage Foundation).

Defence Science and Technology Laboratory (DSTL), Office of Security and Counter Terrorism (OSCT), Ministry of Defence (2010) 'What Perceptions do the UK Public have Concerning the Impact of Counter-terrorism Legislation Implemented since 2000?' Occasional Paper 88 (London: Home Office), March.

Denniston, Lyle (2009) 'Commentary: Did Boumediene Leave Too Much Undone? A Key Judge's Lament over Detention', 22 December, www.scotusblog.com, accessed 25 August 2010.

Dumbrell, John W. (2008) 'Working With Allies. US-UK Relations, the Iraq Invasion, and the Future of the "Special Relationship"', in John E. Owens and John W. Dumbrell (eds), *America's 'War on Terror': New Dimensions in US Government and National Security* (Lanham, MD and Plymouth: Lexington Books), pp. 233–52.

Finn, Peter (2009a) 'Administration Won't Seek New Detention System', *Washington Post*, 24 September, p. A1.

Finn, Peter, Joby Warrick and Julie Tate (2009) 'CIA Releases its Instructions for Breaking a Detainee's Will', *Washington Post*, 25 August, p. A1.

Fisher, Louis (2000) *Congressional Abdication on War and Spending* (College Station, TX: Texas A&M Press).

Flinders, Matthew, and Alexandra Kelso (2011) 'Mind the Gap: Political Analysis, Public Expectations and the Parliamentary Decline Thesis', *British Journal of Politics and International Relations*, 13, 249–68.

Foley, Michael (2000) *The British Presidency: Tony Blair and the Politics of Public Leadership*, 2nd edn (Manchester: Manchester University Press).

Glaberson, William (2009) 'U.S. Won't Label Terror Suspects as "Combatants"', *New York Times*, 13 March, p. A1.

Haider-Markel, Donald P., Mark R. Joslyn and Mohammad Tarek Al-Baghal (2006) 'Can we Frame the Terrorist Threat? Issue Frames, the Perception of Threat, and Opinions on Counterterrorism Policies', *Terrorism and Political Violence*, 18(4), 545–59.

Jenkin, Bernard (2011) Speech. House of Commons. *Hansard. Debates*. 21 March, col. 793.

Johnson, Carrie (2009) 'Showdown Looming On "State Secrets". Judge Threatens to Penalize U.S. in Wiretap Case', *Washington Post*, 26 May, p. A1.

Kellner, Peter (2011) 'Curtailing Civil Liberties?' *YouGov*, 10 January, today.yougov. co.uk, accessed 20 March 2011.

Langston, Thomas (2007) '"The Decider's" Path to War in Iraq and the Importance of Personality', in George C. Edwards and Desmond S. King (eds), *The Polarized Presidency of George W. Bush* (Oxford and New York: Oxford University Press).

Leigh, Edward (2011) Speech. House of Commons. *Hansard. Debates*. 21 March, col. 772.

Lewis, Paul, and Marc Vallée (2009) 'Revealed: Police Databank on Thousands of Protesters. Films and Details of Campaigners and Journalists may Breach Human Rights Act', *Guardian*, 6 March, www.guardian.co.uk, accessed 28 March 2011.

Liberal Democrats (2010a) 'Defence and International Affairs', 23 April, iowlibdems. org.uk, accessed 29 March 2011.

Liberal Democrats (2010b) *Change that Works for You: Building a Fairer Britain*, May, network.libdems.org.uk, accessed 28 March 2011.

Lowi, Theodore J. (1985) *The Personal President: Power. Invested Promise Unfulfilled* (Ithaca, NY: Cornell University Press).

Mazzetti, Mark (2009) 'Panetta Open to Tougher Methods in Some CIA Interrogations', *New York Times*, 5 February, p. A1.

May, Theresa (2011a) Speech. House of Commons. *Hansard. Debates*, 26 January, col. 308.

May, Theresa (2011b) Speech. House of Commons. *Hansard. Debates*, 28 March, col. 27.

Merolla, Jennifer L., and Elizabeth J. Zechmeister (2009) *Democracy at Risk: How Terrorist Tthreats Affect the Public* (Chicago: University of Chicago Press).

Moe, Terry M. (1985) 'The Politicized Presidency', in John E. Chubb and Paul E. Peterson (eds), *The New Direction in American Politics* (Washington, DC: Brookings Institution), pp. 235–71.

Moon, Madeline (2011) Speech. House of Commons. *Hansard. Debates*, 21 March, col. 756.

Mueller, John (2005) 'Simplicity and Spook: Terrorism and the Dynamics of Threat Exaggeration', *International Studies Perspectives*, 6, 208–34.

Mueller, John (2006) 'Is there Still a Terrorist Threat? The Myth of the Omnipresent Enemy', *Foreign Affairs*, September/October.

Mulero, Eugene, and Tim Starks (2010) 'Long-Delayed Intelligence Authorization Bill Clears', *CQ Weekly*, October 4, 2295.

Norton, Philip (2003) 'Governing Alone', *Parliamentary Affairs*, 56(4), 543–59.

Norton, Philip (2007) 'Tony Blair and the Constitution', *British Politics*, 2(2), 269–81.

Obama, Barack (2009a) Interview with *Al Arabiya* news channel, www.alarabiya. net, accessed 28 January 2009.

Obama, Barack (2009b) 'Press Availability with Prime Minister Rudd of Australia', www.whitehouse.gov, accessed 28 March 2009.

Obama, Barack (2009c) 'Remarks by the President on National Security', www. whitehouse.gov, accessed 21 May 2009.

Owens, John E. (2008) 'Presidential *Aggrandizement* and Congressional Acquiescence in the "War on Terror": A New Constitutional Equilibrium?', in John E. Owens and John W. Dumbrell (eds), *America's 'War on Terror': New Dimensions in US Government and National Security* (Lanham, MD and Plymouth: Lexington Books).

Owens, John E. (2010) 'Congressional Acquiescence to Presidentialism in the US "War on Terror": From Bush to Obama', in John E. Owens and Riccardo Pelizzo (eds), *The 'War on Terror' and the Growth of Executive Power?* (New York: Routledge).

Owens, John E. (2011) 'A "Post-Partisan" President in a Partisan Context', in James A. Thurber (ed.), *Obama in Office. The First Two Years* (Boulder, CO: Paradigm Books).

Owens, John E., and John W. Dumbrell (2008) 'America's "War on Terror": New Dimensions in US Government and National Security', in John E. Owens and John W. Dumbrell (eds.) *America's 'War on Terror': New Dimensions in US Government and National Security* (Lanham, MD and Plymouth: Lexington Books), pp. 1–24.

Peterson, Paul (1994) 'The President's Dominance in Foreign Policy Making', *Political Science Quarterly*, 109(2), 215–34.

Pew Research Center (2010) 'Continued Positive Marks for Government Anti-Terror Efforts. But Many Say U.S. Has Been Lucky in Avoiding Attack', 22 October (Washington, DC: Pew Research Center for the People and the Press), people-press.org, accessed 22 March 2011.

Pfiffner, James P. (2008) *The Modern Presidency*, 5th edn (Belmont, CA: Thomson/ Wadsworth).

Poguntke, Thomas, and Paul Webb (2005) *The Presidentialization of Politics: A Comparative Study of Modern Democracies* (Oxford and New York: Oxford University Press).

Radford, Ploy (2011) 'Tough on Terror', *YouGov*, 2 December, today.yougov.co.uk, accessed 20 March 2011.

Rimmerman, Craig A. (1993) *Presidency by Plebiscite: Reagan-Bush Era in Institutional Perspective* (Boulder, CO and Oxford: Westview Press).

Risen, James, and Eric Lichtblau (2009) 'E-Mail Surveillance Renews Concerns in Congress', *New York Times*, 17 June, p. A1.

Rollins, John (2011) 'Osama bin Laden's Death: Implications and Considerations', *CRS Report for Congress Report R41809* (Washington, DC: Congressional Research Service).

Rossiter, Clinton L. (1948) *Constitutional Dictatorship. Crisis Government in the Modern Democracies* (Princeton: Princeton University Press).

Rudalevige, Andrew (2005) *The New Imperial Presidency. Renewing Presidential Power After Watergate* (Ann Arbor: University of Michigan Press).

Savage, Charlie (2007) 'Barack Obama's Q&A', *Boston Globe*, 20 December, www.boston.com/news, accessed 17 December 2008.

Savage, Charlie, and James Risen (2007) 'Federal Judge Finds N.S.A. Wiretaps Were Illegal', *New York Times*, 31 March, p. A1.

Schwartz, John (2009) 'Obama Backs Off a Reversal on Secrets', *New York Times*, 9 February, p. A1.

Shephard, Mark (2010) 'Parliamentary Scrutiny and Oversight of the British "War on Terror": Surrendering Power to Parliament or *Plus ça change*?', in John E. Owens and Riccardo Pelizzo (eds), *The 'War on Terror' and the Growth of Executive Power?* (London and New York: Routledge).

Starks, Tim, and Seth Stern (2011) 'Government Lacks Plan for How to Deal with Terrorist Enemies', *CQ Weekly*, 21 March 2, 622–9.

Tucker, Spencer C. (2009) *U.S. Leadership in Wartime: Clashes, Controversy, and Compromise*, Vol. 1 (Santa Barbara, CA: ABC-CLIO).

UK Home Office (2010) 'A Strong Britain in an Age of Uncertainty: The National Security Strategy', CM 7953, October, www.official-documents.gov.uk, accessed 28 March 2011.

UK Home Office (2011) 'Review of Counter-Terrorism and Security Powers', CM 8004, January, www.homeoffice.gov.uk, accessed 28 March 2011.

UK Parliament, House of Commons Defence Committee (2010) *Oral Evidence*, 26 October, HC554-i.

UK Parliament, House of Commons Foreign Affairs Committee (2011) *Report*, February, HC514.

US Congress, House of Representatives, Committee on Appropriations (2009) Report 111-105. 111th Congress, First Session. *Making Supplemental Appropriations for the Fiscal Year Ending September 30, 2009, and for Other Purposes*, 12 May.

US Congress, Senate, Committee on the Judiciary (2009) Hearings. *Executive Nomination of Eric H. Holder Jr., to be Attorney General of the United States*, 111th Congress, First Session, 15 January.

US White House (2010) *National Security Strategy* (Washington, DC), May.

Williams, Pete (2011) 'Bin Laden Killing was Legally Justified, Holder says. "It was a Kill or Capture Mission … He Made No Attempts to Surrender"', *NBC News*, 4 May, www.msnbc.msn.com, accessed 17 May 2011.

13
The 'War on Terror' in Court: A Comparative Analysis of Judicial Empowerment

Richard J. Maiman

Introduction

The global phenomenon of 'judicial empowerment' (Hirschl, 2004) has been the subject of increasing scholarly attention over the last decade (Woods and Hilbink, 2009). The UK is one of the many nations whose courts have recently undergone significant expansions of their legal powers. Although judges in the UK still lack the ultimate authority exercised by their counterparts in the US and elsewhere – to declare laws and executive acts unconstitutional – there is no mistaking their increasing prominence in debates on major issues of public policy. But prominence is not necessarily the same thing as power. In practice, judicial authority does not always live up to the expectations that accompany its creation. Some newly empowered judiciaries have exercised their authority quite aggressively, while others have used their tools only sparingly, if at all. Still others have met with such political resistance that their efforts have amounted to very little (Ginsburg and Moustafa, 2008).

This chapter examines how the augmentation of judicial power in Britain has played out in practice. This is done by comparing some recent rulings of the UK's highest court with those of the US Supreme Court. Since a definitive picture is well beyond the scope of this article, my analysis is limited to a single subject area: cases involving challenges to the exercise of government authority in connection with the so-called 'war on terror'. Specifically, I focus on eight of the leading cases decided by the US Supreme Court and the Appellate Committee of the House of

Lords, respectively, in the aftermath of 9/11.[1] Because these eight cases constituted only a small fraction of all the judgments handed down by the two courts in this time period, it is possible that similar analyses of decisions on other issues could lead to conclusions different from those reached here. But I would argue that these particular cases are especially useful for exploring the issue of judicial empowerment since they pose perhaps the severest test of judicial authority – whether, and to what extent, judges are willing to check the capacity of the political branches to protect national security in a time of crisis.

The four US Supreme Court cases discussed here – *Hamdi* v. *Rumsfeld* (2004), *Rasul* v. *Bush* (2004), *Hamdan* v. *Rumsfeld* (2006) and *Boumediene* v. *Bush* (2008)[2] – all were brought by or on behalf of prisoners held at Guantánamo Bay, challenging aspects of their treatment by the US government; the Court's decisions collectively addressed the questions of whether and how the detainees could challenge the legality of their detention, and in what forums and with what procedures such prisoners could be tried for violating the laws of war. The four House of Lords judgments all concerned the rules applicable to the government's treatment of foreign nationals suspected but not convicted of terrorist activity, and in particular, the amount of coercion the government could use to control such persons' activities and the kinds of evidence that could be used in court proceedings against them. These cases are *A (FC) and others (FC)* v. *Secretary of State for the Home Department* (2004); a second case by the same name decided in 2005; a set of four related cases from 2007 (counted here as a single case because they dealt with similar issues, though with somewhat different outcomes): *Secretary of State for the Home Department* v. *JJ and Ors.; Secretary of State for the Home Department* v. *E and Anor;* and *Secretary of State for the Home Department* v. *MB/ Secretary of State for the Home Department* v. *AF* ; and a 2009 case, *Secretary of State for the Home Department* v. *AF and Anor.*[3] Despite the many specific factual and legal differences between the US and UK cases – variation of the kind that is unavoidable in cross-national studies – they are similar enough in their essential subject to allow for valid side-by-side comparisons.

Judicial empowerment in the US and the UK

The US Supreme Court is the prototype of an empowered judiciary. For more than two centuries, the Court's authority to overrule executive and legislative actions has been an established – though often controversial – fact of American political life. That story has been exhaustively documented and debated and need not be revisited here. Suffice it to say that while scholars disagree sharply in their normative assessments of the Court's overall record of judicial review – whether it has strengthened or undermined American democracy, and whether it has enhanced or diminished the institutional legitimacy of the Court itself – there is simply no question that among the judiciaries of the world, the US Supreme Court has had the longest and most extensive history of active involvement in public policy-making. Thus, it is an appropriate reference point to use in assessing the degree to which any particular national court can be described as empowered.[4]

Judges played an influential policy-making role in Britain for several centuries through the development and application of the common law. Starting in the early Victorian era, however, and continuing through the first half of the twentieth century, judicial policy-making in the UK became notably circumscribed as the principle of parliamentary sovereignty took hold in constitutional thinking – except in the sense that the judges' ostentatious deference to the administrative state had the effect of reinforcing and legitimizing the status quo. This ostensibly non-political stance was promoted by successive Lord Chancellors and Lord Chief Justices as a means of protecting the judiciary's prestige, if not necessarily its independence. One measure of this project's success is the frequency with which leading judges were called on to chair blue-ribbon panels and public inquiries into highly politicized issues because they themselves were widely perceived as being politically unbiased (Stevens, 2002).[5]

The judges' lengthy self-exile from the political arena came to an end in the 1970s with a sharp increase in the use of judicial review, which in the British context refers to a judicial determination of whether a public official has acted in accordance with statutory standards. Behind the expanded use of judicial review was the proliferation of complex social and economic legislation, enacted under both Labour and Conservative governments, which typically involved substantial delegation of authority to government ministers. In exercising judicial review, British judges were taking on an important, if not always highly visible, political role. It was not, however, an entirely *new* role. Rather, it was a case of judges once again acknowledging, 'as they had always done except in their period of amnesia, that part of their duty was to require public authorities to respect certain basic rules of fairness in exercising power over the citizen' (Wade, 2000, p. 63).

But the growth of judicial review was merely a prologue to the most significant stimulus to judicial empowerment in the UK, the passage of the Human Rights Act (HRA) 1998 during the first Blair Government. By 'domesticating' the civil and political rights codified in the European Convention on Human Rights (ECHR), the HRA held all public authorities in the UK – including Parliament itself – accountable to convention restrictions that now would be justiciable in British courts. Judges were given the authority (in fact, the duty) to examine statutes and official actions that were challenged on ECHR grounds. If they concluded that such laws or conduct could not be found in conformance with the convention, they were obliged to issue 'declarations of incompatibility' calling the government's attention to the discrepancy. While declarations of incompatibility are not, in theory, the same as findings of unconstitutionality, in practice they have carried virtually the same force. Of the approximately two dozen declarations of incompatibility issued by UK courts to date, none has been either ignored or defied by the government. The HRA thus has come to be seen by many in Britain as the functional equivalent of an entrenched bill of rights, despite the continued absence of a written constitution or a custom-built 'British bill of rights' (Bevir and Maiman, 2009).

In Britain, then, the 'war on terror' coincided almost exactly with unrelated political-legal developments that already had begun to transform the role of the judiciary. The major questions in the post-9/11 period were whether and how Britain's judges would use their powers – those associated with judicial review as well as their new HRA-based authority – to participate meaningfully alongside the government and Parliament in determining the substance of anti-terrorism law and policy. How did the Law Lords respond to this challenge? And how did their responses compare to those of their counterparts on the US Supreme Court?

The 'war on terror' decisions

When these judgments are looked at collectively, it is clear that the arguments advanced by the US and the UK governments in defense of their anti-terrorism policies received remarkably little judicial support. Although the cases were by no means all total government defeats, not one of them could be described as an unqualified victory. The US Supreme Court rejected the Bush administration's claim that the President could deny Guantánamo inmates the right to challenge their detention before neutral third parties (*Hamdi* and *Rasul*); held that the President could not establish a system of military commissions to conduct war crimes trials without congressional authorization (*Hamdan*); and found that legislation denying Guantánamo inmates access to federal habeas corpus proceedings fell short of constitutional requirements and, moreover, that the procedures established by that law were not an adequate substitute for conventional habeas corpus review (*Boumediene*). Virtually the only victory the Court gave to the Bush administration was its holding in *Hamdi* that the Authorization for the Use of Military Force (AUMF) resolution passed by Congress in September 2001 gave the President sufficient authority to order that battlefield captives be detained indefinitely at Guantánamo Bay. However, in *Hamdi* the Court also declined even to consider the administration's preferred position: that the President had the constitutional power to issue such an order even without congressional action.

Meanwhile, the Law Lords denied the government the authority to hold non-British nationals suspected of terrorist activities indefinitely (*A/2004*); rejected the government's claimed power to use evidence in an immigration tribunal possibly procured through torture by a foreign state but without British complicity (*A/2005*); ruled that the Home Secretary could not issue control orders against terror suspects requiring home curfews of 18 hours a day (*JJ*) – while upholding curfews of 12 and 14 hours, respectively (*E* and *MB*); decided that the appointment of security-vetted special advocates in control order proceedings involving secret evidence was not an adequate protection of suspects' right to a fair trial *(AF/2007)*; and held that the Home Secretary could not rely on secret evidence in applying for control orders against terror suspects (*AF/2009*).

Table 13.1 summarizes the collective outcomes of these eight decisions in terms of their restrictions on government actions: five executive orders, actions, or proposals were held to either violate or lack the support of law, a provision of an act of Congress was found unconstitutional, and a section of a parliamentary statute was declared incompatible with the European Convention. In terms of their responses to the claims of the other branches of their respective governments, there is little to distinguish one set of judgments from the other. However, to look more closely at the nuances of the decisions, the following sections will focus, in turn, on what the courts had to say about executive, legislative, and judicial authority.

Table 13.1   Summary of US Supreme Court and UK House of Lords judgments restricting government actions, 2004–09

	US Supreme Court	*UK House of Lords*
Executive action	Denied President authority to prohibit detainees from accessing review of legality of detention (*Hamdi, Rasul*).	Denied Home Secretary authority to rely on third-party torture evidence in court (*A/2005*).
	Denied President unilateral authority to establish military tribunals (*Hamdan*).	Denied Home Secretary authority to impose curfew orders with 18-hour home curfews (*JJ*).
		Held that the use of special advocates in control order hearings was not sufficient protection of fair trial right (*AF/2007*).
		Denied Home Secretary authority to use secret evidence in applications for control orders (*AF/2009*).
Legislative action	Declared habeas corpus – stripping provisions of the Military Commissions Act unconstitutional for failing to meet suspension requirements of Article 1, Section 9 (*Boumediene*).	Declared indefinite detention provision of Anti-Terrorism Act 2001 incompatible with Articles 5 and 14 of European Convention (*A/2004*).

Executive authority

One of the most conspicuous features of anti-terrorism policies in both the US and the UK (and elsewhere) was the development and use of greatly expanded executive powers. Following 9/11, President Bush's legal and political advisers aggressively advanced the 'unitary executive' doctrine in defense of untrammeled presidential authority with respect to all Article 2 functions; meanwhile, the steady accumulation of prime ministerial prerogatives and the accompanying decline of both cabinet and parliamentary independence over several decades left Blair with considerable scope for exercising unilateral authority. Finding their existing powers less than adequate, however, both leaders sought and received legislative approval for new executive authority, which in the US included statutory instruments such as the AUMF and the US Patriot Act, and in the UK, a series of comprehensive anti-terror laws.

In both countries, these measures soon drew legal challenges from civil liberties organizations. The first two of these cases – *Hamdi* and

Rasul – reached the US Supreme Court in 2004, brought not by, but on behalf of, the named appellants. At issue were the legality of the Guantánamo Bay detentions themselves and whether the administration could bar its prisoners (which it classified as 'unlawful combatants') from initiating federal habeas corpus proceedings. In *Hamdi*, a case involving the only known US citizen held at Guantánamo, the court employed a broad reading of the AUMF to uphold the President's blanket detention order but rejected the administration's argument that it could deny detainees access to neutral third party review of the legality of their detention. Justice Sandra Day O'Connor's majority opinion struggled to find a middle ground between locking the Guantánamo inmates out of federal court, on the one hand, and throwing the courtroom doors wide open, on the other. Trying to be sensitive both to military exigencies and to individual rights, O'Connor avoided specific reference to habeas corpus proceedings, holding that 'a citizen-detainee seeking to challenge his classification as an enemy combatant must receive notice of the factual basis for his classification, and a fair opportunity to rebut the Government's factual assertions before a *neutral decisionmaker*' (emphasis added). But in the companion case of *Rasul*, brought on behalf of a non-citizen detainee, Justice John Paul Stevens' majority opinion showed none of O'Connor's deference to the administration. Eschewing the vague middle ground of *Hamdi*, Stevens bluntly concluded that US law 'confers on the District Court jurisdiction to hear petitioners' *habeas corpus* challenges to the legality of their detention at the Guantánamo Bay Naval Base'. Though the Bush administration could rightly claim that its basic detention policy had been vindicated, it was left with the unwelcome task of developing a process of neutral third-party review of some 800 individual cases.

Two years later, Stevens' majority opinion in *Hamdan* again gave the administration rather rough treatment. Declining to read the AUMF even more expansively than in *Hamdi*, Stevens found no legal basis for the President's executive order establishing military commissions to try a number of Guantánamo detainees for war crimes. Nor did Stevens accept the President's argument that the constitution permitted him to act unilaterally even without such authority. While 'emphasizing that Hamdan does not challenge, and we do not today address, the Government's power to detain him for the duration of active hostilities', Stevens concluded that 'in undertaking to try Hamdan and subject him to criminal punishment, the Executive is bound to comply with the Rule of Law that prevails in this jurisdiction'. The President's military commission plan fatally lacked the imprimatur of Congress. Stevens' opinion was laced with an unmistakable tone of impatience and frustration with the Bush administration. It may have reflected his frustration at the administration's decision (which was not at issue in the *Hamdan* case) to respond to the letter of O'Connor's *Hamdi* opinion while ignoring Stevens' *Rasul* holding altogether, by implementing its own system of military-staffed 'combatant status review tribunals' (CSRTs) as an alternative to conventional federal court habeas corpus review. Clearly the administration's strategy was to continue using unilateral authority until it was explicitly ordered not to.

The question in the first 'war on terror' case heard by the House of Lords, *A/2004*, was whether a provision of the 2001 Anti-Terrorism Act authorizing the indefinite detention of foreign nationals suspected of terror-related activities who could not be legally deported, violated Articles 5 (liberty and security of the person) and 14 (freedom from discrimination) of the ECHR. This in turn raised the question of whether the government's formal derogation from Article 5 was consistent with the two conditions set for derogation by ECHR Article 15. The first requirement is that a 'war or other public emergency [is] threatening the life of the nation'. Writing for eight of the nine law lords hearing the case, Lord Justice Bingham concluded that 'great weight should be given to the judgment of the Home Secretary, his colleagues and Parliament on this question, because they were called on to exercise a pre-eminently political judgment'. Bingham's deferential language seemed to echo O'Connor's effort in *Hamdi* to acknowledge the pressures on a beleaguered government to respond effectively to a military threat of unknown proportions. However, his conciliatory tone disappeared as soon as he addressed the second Article 15 derogation requirement: that a signatory 'may take measures derogating from its obligations under this Convention [only] to the extent strictly required by the exigencies of the situation' – the test of proportionality. On this second question, the court reserved a much larger role for itself because under the jurisprudence of the European Court of Human Rights the proportionality question – unlike the public emergency question – was *not* considered a matter of ministerial discretion. As Bingham put it,

[T]he greater the legal content of any issue, the greater the potential role of the court, because under our constitution and subject to the sovereign power of Parliament it is the function of the courts and not of political bodies to resolve legal questions. (*A/2004*)

Bingham then proceeded to dismantle the argument that the indefinite detention measure was indeed 'required by the exigencies of the situation' and concluded by rebuking the government for using

> an immigration measure to address a security problem [which] had the inevitable result of failing adequately to address that problem (by allowing non-UK suspected terrorists to leave the country with impunity and leaving British suspected terrorists at large) while imposing the severe penalty of indefinite detention on persons who, even if reasonably suspected of having links with Al-Qaeda, may harbour no hostile intentions towards the United Kingdom.

If Bingham's exasperation with the government was clear in *A/2004*, the Law Lords' treatment of the government was more measured and respectful – closer to O'Connor's approach than to Stevens' – in two subsequent decisions involving the admissibility of evidence – even though the government still lost both cases. In *A/2005*, the court decided unanimously that evidence obtained through torture by another nation is inadmissible in a British court proceeding. However, the court then adopted, by a margin of five to two, an admissibility test favorable to the government, requiring the court to establish 'by means of such diligent enquiries into the sources that it is practicable to carry out and on a balance of probabilities that the information relied on by the Secretary of State *was* obtained under torture'. The two dissenters (Lord Bingham and Lady Hale), objected that such a standard would undermine the effect of the ban by placing the burden of proof of torture on the claimant. Their preferred alternative was that challenged evidence be considered inadmissible whenever the court 'is unable to conclude that there is not a real risk that the evidence has been obtained by torture'.

The Law Lords' judgment in *Secretary of State for Home Affairs* v. *AF*, the 2009 case dealing with the admissibility of secret evidence in court, points to another, perhaps ironic, element of judicial empowerment – that the rule of law can sometimes saddle judges with responsibility for decisions with which they personally disagree. While the court unanimously supported a complete prohibition against the use in court proceedings of any evidence not disclosed to the defendants, several members made clear their own lack of enthusiasm for this result. They strongly preferred the position urged by the government, the continued use of a more flexible 'fairness' standard to determine admissibility. The court had adopted this test in deciding an earlier version of the same case two years earlier. In the meantime, however, that case had gone to

Strasbourg on appeal, resulting in a ruling that ECHR Article 6 prohibited the use of undisclosed evidence, a sweeping precedent which the House of Lords now considered itself obliged – however reluctantly – to follow.

In the set of 2007 cases, the Law Lords delivered a mixed verdict on a variety of challenges to the government's control order regime. In *JJ*, Lord Bingham, applying principles established by the European Court of Human Rights, found that a control order involving an 18-hour home curfew (which had already been reduced to 16 hours by the Home Secretary) was incompatible with ECHR Article 5. It was a close call, however, with two of the five judges contending that such treatment did not constitute a deprivation of liberty because it did not amount to actual imprisonment. Indeed, in *JJ*'s two companion cases, *E* and *MB*, the Law Lords decided unanimously that control orders requiring 12 and 14 hours of home confinement, respectively, did *not* violate the convention. Regarding the use of undisclosed evidence, their lordships held that the 'special advocates' appointed by the government to help defend the suspects were not in themselves sufficient to safeguard the suspects' right to a fair trial; however, rather than explicitly prohibiting the use of such evidence, they left it to the lower court to decide in each case whether fairness had been achieved. Thus, while the government could claim that the court had 'upheld the control orders regime and judged that no existing control orders need to be weakened' (Dyer, 2007), critics of the system contended that it had been dealt a serious blow. If nothing else, the decisions made it clear that there were still serious questions about the government's control order policy that only judges could answer.

Legislative authority

Another aspect of judicial empowerment is the extent to which judges are willing to scrutinize legislative actions to determine whether they adhere to extrinsic standards. In the US, of course, those limits are set by the text of the Constitution itself, which is subject to judicial interpretation. Britain had no such standard against which its judges could measure domestic legislation until the Human Rights Act 1998 gave them the authority to determine whether parliamentary acts conformed to ECHR requirements.

In one of the US cases under consideration – *Boumediene* v. *Bush* (2008) – the Supreme Court used its ultimate power, that of nullifying a provision of federal law. In Section 7 (a) of the Military Commissions Act (MCA) of 2006, Congress had explicitly removed the federal courts' jurisdiction over all habeas corpus petitions filed by Guantánamo prisoners, including petitions already pending at the time the law was passed. This provision, sponsored by the Bush administration, was intended to remove the ambiguity that the Supreme Court had previously found in the jurisdiction-stripping language in the Detainee Treatment Act of 2005 (in *Hamdan*). In his majority opinion in *Boumediene*, Justice Anthony Kennedy accepted that while Congress clearly intended the ban on habeas corpus to apply to all past, present, and future detainee cases, the law did not comply with the constitutional requirement that Congress 'shall not' suspend the writ of habeas corpus 'unless when in cases of rebellion or invasion the public safety may require it' (Article 1 Section 9]). The MCA, Kennedy wrote, 'does not purport to be a formal suspension of the writ; and the Government, in its submissions to us, has not argued that it is. Petitioners, therefore, are entitled to the privilege of *habeas corpus* to challenge the legality of their detention'.

The UK cases also included one in which the Law Lords exercised their own 'ultimate weapon,' the declaration of incompatibility with the ECHR. In the *A/2004* case (already discussed in the previous section in connection with executive authority), the House – after finding that the indefinite detention provision of the 2001 Anti-Terrorism Act could not be considered a proportional response to the demands of the declared public emergency – took the logical next step by issuing:

> a declaration under section 4 of the Human Rights Act 1998 that section 23 of the Anti-Terrorism, Crime and Security Act 2001 is incompatible with articles 5 and 14 of the European Convention insofar as it is disproportionate and permits detention of suspected international terrorists in a way that discriminates on the ground of nationality or immigration status.

While this was not the first such declaration to be issued since the HRA came into force in 2000, it was undoubtedly the most dramatic, striking at the heart of the first major anti-terrorism initiative enacted under the Blair government. Thus it became the most significant test of the government's commitment to its own Human Rights Act. Would the government accept the court's decision? If so, what steps might it take to find a legally acceptable way of handling non-UK terror suspects whom it could neither deport nor put on trial? Early in 2005, a few months after the *A/2004* decision, the Home Secretary introduced new legislation repealing the 'incompatible' section of its 2001 anti-terrorism law, replacing it with language authorizing the issuance of 'control orders' placing restrictions, requirements, and prohibitions on the activities of persons suspected of involvement in terror-related activities. This legislation, designated the Prevention of Terrorism Act 2005, would become the subject of the control orders cases discussed in the previous section.

Judicial authority

The most basic indicator of an empowered judiciary is simply whether it has the self-confidence to decide cases that question the legitimacy of executive and legislative actions. No court can be said to be truly empowered unless it demonstrates the capacity to push back against political action that in the judges' view has exceeded legal limits. This does not mean that whenever judges defer to the executive they show a lack of empowerment, since statutory or constitutional provisions often will provide unambiguous support for executive and legislative authority. However judges might decide such a case on its merits – even if they finally uphold the arguments of the executive or legislature about the extent of its powers – one would expect an empowered judiciary to defend its own authority whenever they perceive that it has been questioned or challenged. Empowered judges would be particularly determined to dispel any doubt that their assigned task of preserving the rule of law in the process of governance is as legitimate as those of the other branches. Perhaps the most famous statement of such a claim is Chief Justice John Marshall's assertion in *Marbury* v. *Madison*[6] that '[i]t is emphatically the province and duty of the judicial department to say what the law is'. Since *Marbury*, Supreme Court justices have periodically quoted Marshall's dictum, reminding the other branches and the public of the court's essential place in the constitutional order.[7]

Only a few court cases, in fact, involve direct challenges to judicial authority; on the contrary, most cases, by their very existence, implicitly acknowledge and accept the court's legitimacy as a decision-maker. However, among the cases examined here there were several in which at least some of the judges apparently felt that their authority had been called into question and needed to be reinforced. For example, the Bush administration's argument in *Hamdi*, that federal courts could not use habeas corpus proceedings to question the President's unilateral authority over the Guantánamo detainees, seemed to imply that by agreeing to hear the case on its merits the court already was trespassing on presidential turf. Justice O'Connor's majority opinion emphatically rejected that position, making it clear that we necessarily reject the Government's assertion that separation of powers principles mandate a heavily circumscribed role for the courts in such circumstances. Indeed, the position that the courts must forgo any examination of the individual case and focus exclusively on the legality of the broader detention scheme cannot be mandated by any reasonable view of separation of powers, as this approach serves only to *condense* power into a single branch of government. We have long since made clear that a state of war is not a blank check for the President when it comes to the rights of the Nation's citizens.

In *Hamdan*, Justice Stevens explicitly invoked the language of *Marbury* to dispose of the government's argument that since the Constitution had no extra-territorial application, the court had no authority over proceedings at Guantánamo Bay:

> The Constitution grants Congress and the President the power to acquire, dispose of and govern territory, not the power to decide when and where its terms apply. To hold that the political branches may switch the Constitution on or off at will would lead to a regime in which they, not this Court, say 'what the law is.'

And finally, discussing the importance of the writ of habeas corpus in *Boumediene,* Justice Kennedy forcefully defended the role of the judiciary in such cases. While acknowledging that '[t]he law must accord the Executive substantial authority to apprehend and detain those who pose a real danger to our security', Kennedy went on to assert that

> [s]ecurity subsists, too, in fidelity to freedom's first principles. Chief among these are freedom from arbitrary and unlawful restraint and the personal liberty that is secured by adherence to the separation of powers. It is from these principles that the judicial authority to consider petitions for *habeas corpus* relief derives. Our opinion does not undermine the Executive's powers as Commander in Chief. On the contrary, the exercise of those powers is vindicated, not eroded, when confirmed by the Judicial Branch. Within the Constitution's separation-of-powers structure, few exercises of judicial power are as legitimate or as necessary as the responsibility to hear challenges to the authority of the Executive to imprison a person.

The House of Lords used similarly forceful language to defend its prerogatives against perceived threats or challenges. As we have already seen, Lord Justice Bingham was willing to defer in *A/2004* to the executive's judgment that a national emergency existed (the threshold requirement for derogating from the convention article prohibiting indefinite detention without trial), but he firmly rejected the government's assertion that his court was not entitled to apply a second test – that of proportionality – to determine whether the action was lawful. Bingham wrote:

> the courts are not effectively precluded by any doctrine of deference from scrutinising the issues raised … I do not in particular accept the distinction which [the Attorney General] drew between democratic institutions and the courts. It is of course true that the judges in this country are not elected and are not answerable to Parliament. It is also of course true … that Parliament, the executive and the courts have different functions. But the function of independent judges charged to interpret and apply the law is universally recognised as a cardinal feature of the modern democratic state, a cornerstone of the rule of law itself.

An implied challenge to judicial authority was an underlying issue in *JJ*, one of the 2007 control order cases, prompting Lord Bingham to emphasize that, contrary to the government's suggestion, the Home Secretary had no power to issue control orders that violated ECHR Article 5. If a judge found that a control order issued by the Home Secretary did breach Article 5, that order was null and void, and the judge was obliged to quash it, not simply (as the government contended) to order that the minister correct the defect. As is often the case, the judicial prerogative was framed here as a matter not of power but of statutory duty. However, there is no mistaking the court's clear purpose, which was to underscore *judicial* supremacy in this area of policy. Baroness Hale stated the position starkly in her concurrence: '[O]nly a court may deprive people of their liberty. The Home Secretary has no power to make such an order.'

Conclusion

This brief comparison of leading 'war on terror' cases by the highest courts in the US and the UK has found a shared determination by the courts to hold officials of their governments to legal limits. Though space does not permit a more detailed analysis of the cases, including concurring and dissenting opinions, it is important not to leave the impression that either court was monolithic in its views. Justice Stevens and Lord Bingham were the strongest voices on their respective courts against executive overreach, but they did not always speak for all their colleagues. Justice Clarence Thomas made it clear that he would have given the Bush administration everything it wanted in these cases – and possibly more. Among the Law Lords, Lord Carswell was notably sympathetic to many of the government's arguments, and Lord Hoffmann more selectively so. Still, looked at in their entirety, these judgments are unmistakably the work of highly empowered judges, confident of their own institutional authority and committed to using it to hold the other departments of government accountable to appropriate statutory and constitutional rules.

Given the long history of judicial empowerment in the US, it is not so surprising that the Supreme Court was so willing and able to check and balance the power of the political branches. But keeping in mind how recently the Law Lords had acquired some of their powers, it is perhaps more remarkable that their decisions displayed as much independence as they did. In this section I offer a partial explanation for the rapid pace of judicial empowerment in the UK. It borrows from a framework developed by Charles Epp (1998) to account for the occurrence of 'rights revolutions' around the world. Epp emphasized the importance of a 'support structure for legal mobilization' (ibid., p. 131) consisting of advocacy organizations equipped with adequate funding for litigation, and a rights-oriented legal profession. Similarly, to function effectively, judges must have the support of legal advocates – both individuals and organizations – who support an empowered judiciary either as an end in itself or as a means of helping them achieve their own policy goals. Such an infrastructure undoubtedly exists in the US, where litigation has long been seen as 'an integral part of the dialogue by which constitutional standards are shaped and reshaped under changing conditions' (Feldman, 1992, p. 56). In the late nineteenth century, the 'Supreme Court bar' was dominated by corporate lawyers, who worked with considerable success to persuade the court to overturn federal and state regulations on constitutional grounds. For much of the twentieth century, it was mostly organizations on the political left who used the courts to litigate on behalf of their causes.[8] That balance has shifted in the last several decades, however, as activists on the political right have stopped complaining about 'judicial activism' and begun using it to their advantage (Maiman, 2004). Since the Reagan era, they have been working through political channels to build a more conservative federal judiciary, and then litigating aggressively in favor of such issues as government accommodation of religion, and corporate campaign spending, and against affirmative action and gun control (Southworth, 2008).[9] Meanwhile, the ranks of left-leaning litigation groups have also continued to grow. Apart from their impacts on specific policies, the litigation activities these groups collectively provide gives crucial support for an empowered judiciary. By seeking – indeed, demanding – judicial decisions on major issues of public policy, litigation organizations reinforce the legitimacy of courts as policy-makers, even when – as is sometimes the case – such rulings overturn longstanding precedents.

Compared to that of the US, Britain's litigation infrastructure is still in nascent form; reflecting its origins in the UK's recent 'rights revolution', it continues to be dominated by rights-oriented advocacy organizations. Writing in the mid 1990s, Epp identified the organization once known as the National Council for Civil Liberties (NCCL) and since 1989 as Liberty, as one of the 'main components' of Britain's rights infrastructure. This observation echoed that of Carol Harlow and Richard Rawlings (1992), who in chronicling earlier pressure group litigation activities described Liberty as the organization that 'has more claim than most to be the founder of modern English pressure through law' (ibid., p. 292). In the years preceding the Human Rights Act, when alleged ECHR infringements by the UK could be redressed only through litigation at the European Court of Human Rights in Strasbourg, Liberty compiled an impressive record of victories against the British government. In the 1980s and 1990s, the organization campaigned for incorporation of the European Convention into domestic law, and lobbied for adoption of the HRA after Labour's election in 1997. As Epp has observed, the codification of rights usually 'provides popular movements with a potential tool for tying judicial power to their purposes' (1998, p. 201); since the HRA came into force in 2000, most of Liberty's domestic and Strasbourg litigation has been arguing for expansive interpretations of convention provisions. The organization also has devoted itself to defending the Human Rights Act against its critics.

A second pillar of the UK's 'judicial empowerment infrastructure' is the organization called JUSTICE. Founded in 1957 as a non-partisan law reform group, JUSTICE made a name for itself in the 1980s and 1990s by winning a series of high-profile cases on behalf of victims of miscarriages of justice. After persuading the government to establish its own criminal justice watchdog agency, JUSTICE made the decision to cease all direct sponsorship of cases and focus its litigation program exclusively on third-party interventions. The organization concluded that it could have more influence on the direction of the law if it were able to participate in cases without the burden of defending a particular client's case. One of the longest-standing backers of a written bill of rights for Britain, JUSTICE lobbied hard for passage of the HRA and over the past decade has been an active intervener in HRA cases (and others), While JUSTICE's agenda is somewhat broader than Liberty's, encompassing law reform issues which are outside of Liberty's sphere, its highest policy priority today is human rights. While their positions are often not identical, JUSTICE and Liberty have a particularly close working relationship and, for the sake of efficiency, frequently sign on to each other's interventions. Both organizations also litigate jointly with other rights advocacy groups like the Child Poverty Action Group, the Joint Council for the Welfare of Immigrants, Amnesty International, Interights, and the Children's Legal Centre, when their policy agendas intersect.

It should come as no surprise, then, that both Liberty and JUSTICE were involved in all of the 'war on terror' litigation discussed here. Liberty was an intervener in *A/2004, A/2005* (as part of a coalition of 14 organizations), and *E*. JUSTICE intervened in *JJ, MB*, and *A/2009* (jointly with three other groups), and also made an intervention in a European Court of Human Rights appeal, *A and Others* v. *The United Kingdom* (App. No. 3455/05), arising from the control order cases.[10]

The political effectiveness of individual advocacy organizations can be measured in various ways – for example, by the frequency with which they appear as direct litigants or interveners, or have their contributions cited in opinions, or see their positions prevail in court rulings. The *collective* contribution that such groups make to judicial empowerment comes from the alliance of interests between judges who are attempting – often in the face of political resistance – to carry out their responsibilities, and litigators whose political goals depend on judicial authority being effectively exercised. Signs of this symbiotic relationship are readily observable – inside the courtroom, of course, but outside as well. In 2009, a luncheon in Washington, DC, marking the retirement of Nadine Strossen as the president of the American Civil Liberties Union (ACLU), was attended by no less than three sitting Supreme Court justices, including one – Antonin Scalia – who rarely agrees with the ACLU but is on record as respecting its substantive contributions to the Court's decision-making. Later that same year, the now-retired Lord Bingham, speaking in London at Liberty's 75th anniversary event, paid fulsome tribute to the organization's 'principled' role in protecting rights and liberties. He also took the occasion to issue a strong defense of the Human Rights Act, describing as 'a travesty of the truth' the charge that judges were acting 'undemocratically' when they enforced European Convention rights. Shortly before Bingham's death the following year, Liberty's director, Shami Chakrabarti, contributing to a newspaper series titled 'My Legal Hero', returned the judge's compliment and affirmed the mutuality of their interests:

Through decisions on the internment of foreign terror suspects in Belmarsh prison and on the admissibility of evidence obtained through torture, Lord Bingham formed a badly needed bulwark against the excesses of the 'war on terror' and methodically dissected and discredited successive affronts to the British system of due process. (Chakrabarti, 2010)

Increasingly, judges in the UK are being criticized, as they have been for years in the US, for allegedly contributing to a democratic deficit by being too responsive to the demands of 'unrepresentative' pressure groups.[11] No doubt these criticisms will eventually begin to abate, just as they have in the US, as a more diverse collection of organizations learn to use litigation to help advance their policy goals. Over time, this will further strengthen the already impressive state of judicial empowerment in the UK.

Notes

1. Since October 2009 the UK's highest court has been known as the Supreme Court. This is one of several statutory changes intended to underscore the court's independence – including a more transparent process of judicial appointment, exclusion of future Supreme Court appointees from the House of Lords, and relocation of the Court to its own building, separate from the Houses of Parliament. Since the decisions discussed here all predate the name change, this chapter uses the court's older title, the Appellate Committee of the House of Lords, along with its more familiar informal names: the House of Lords, the House, and the Law Lords.
2. *Hamdi* v. *Rumsfeld* 542 US 507 (2004); *Rasul* v. *Bush* 542 US 466 (2004); *Hamdan* v. *Rumsfeld* 548 US 557 (2008); *Boumediene* v. *Bush* 553 US 723 (2008).
3. *A and Ors.* v. *Secretary of State for the Home Department* [2004] UKHL 56; *A and Ors.* v. *Secretary of State for the Home Department* [2005] UKHL 71; *Secretary of State for the Home Department* v. *JJ. and Ors.* [2007] UKHL 45; *Secretary of State for the Home Department* v. *MB/Secretary of State for the Home Department* v. *AF* [2007] UKHL 46; *Secretary of State for the Home Department* v. *E and Anor.* [2007] UKHL 47; *Secretary of State for the Home Department* v. *AF and Anor.* [2009] UKHL 28.
4. It should be noted, however, that on questions related to national security, the Supreme Court has often demonstrated less independence than in other areas, giving considerable deference to the executive and legislative branches – particularly when those branches have acted in concert. A number of the Court's least enduring decisions – for example, *Ex Parte Quirin* 317 US 1 (1942), *Korematsu* v. *United States* 323 US 214 (1944), and *Dennis* v. *United States* 341 US 494 (1951) – were made under the pressure of perceived threats to national security, reflecting the Supreme Court's zeal to grant the President and Congress broad powers during times of crisis.

5. Although this practice continues, the judges who take on such tasks today cannot expect the same reflexive deference from press and public that they once received (Morrison, 2004).
6. *Marbury* v. *Madison* 5 US 137 (1803).
7. For example, in *United States* v. *Nixon* 418 US 683 (1974), after Chief Justice Warren Burger rejected the President's reading of 'the Constitution as providing an absolute privilege of confidentiality for all Presidential communications', he pointedly added: 'Many decisions of this Court ... have unequivocally reaffirmed the holding of *Marbury* v. *Madison* that "[i]t is emphatically the province and duty of the judicial department to say what the law is."'
8. The organizations that had the greatest presence and policy impact in court during this period are the National Association for the Advancement of Colored People (NAACP) and the American Civil Liberties Union (ACLU), both of which specialize in constitutional litigation. More recently, litigation based on environmental protection laws has been used by a variety of environmental groups.
9. A number of these groups are now involved in litigation aimed at persuading federal courts, and ultimately the Supreme Court, to find the Obama administration's health care reform law unconstitutional.
10. These interventions were not all equally successful. JUSTICE's intervention at Strasbourg, arguing that the use of 'special advocates' in control order proceedings involving secret evidence did not reduce its unfairness, probably helped influence the European Court of Human Rights to adopt the sweeping precedent that the House of Lords subsequently felt obliged to follow in *AF*. On the other hand, the argument that Liberty made in its *E* intervention – that all non-derogating control orders are incompatible with Article 6 – was rejected by the Law Lords.
11. A recent British think tank report made the same criticism of the Strasbourg court: 'it is admitted within the Council of Europe itself that the court is too easily subject to the influence of non-governmental organizations and lobbies, which sometimes sponsor cases for political reasons' (Pinto-Duschinsky, 2011, p. 46).

References

Bevir, M., and R. Maiman (2009) 'Judicial Reform and Human Rights', in T. Casey (ed.), *The Blair Legacy: Politics, Policy, Government, and Foreign Affairs* (New York: Palgrave Macmillan).
Chakrabarti, S. (2010) 'My Legal Hero: Lord Bingham of Cornhill', *Guardian*, 18 August.
Dyer, C. (2007) 'Lords Back Terror Law Orders on Suspects, but Give Them New Rights', *Guardian*, 1 November.
Epp, C.R. (1998) *The Rights Revolution: Lawyers, Activists, and Supreme Courts in Comparative Perspective* (Chicago: University of Chicago Press).
Feldman, D. (1992) 'Public Interest Litigation and Constitutional Theory in Comparative Perspective', *Modern Law Review*, 52, 44–72.
Ginsburg, T., and T. Moustafa (2008) *Rule by Law: The Politics of Courts in Authoritarian Regimes* (New York: Cambridge University Press).

Harlow, C., and R. Rawlings (1992) *Pressure Through Law* (London: Routledge).

Hirschl, R. (2004) *Towards Justocracy: The Origins and Consequences of the New Constitutionalism* (Cambridge, MA: Harvard University Press).

Maiman, R.J. (2004) '"We've Had to Raise Our Game": Liberty's Litigation Strategy Under the Human Rights Act 1998', in S. Halliday and P. Schmidt (eds), *Human Rights Brought Home: Socio-Legal Perspectives on Human Rights in the National Context* (Portland, OR, and Oxford: Hart Publishing).

Morrison, D. (2004) 'My Report on Lord Hutton', *Guardian*, 3 February.

Pinto-Duschinsky, M. (2011) *Bringing Rights Back Home: Making Human Rights Compatible with Parliamentary Democracy in the UK* (London: The Policy Exchange).

Southworth, A. (2008) *Lawyers of the Right: Professionalizing the Conservative Coalition* (Chicago: University of Chicago Press).

Stevens, R. (2002) *The English Judges: Their Role in the Changing Constitution* (Oxford: Hart Publishing).

Wade, H.W.R. (1980) *Constitutional Fundamentals* (London: Stevens & Sons).

Woods, P.J., and L. Hilbank (2009) 'Comparative Sources of Judicial Empowerment: Ideas and Interests', *Political Research Quarterly*, 62, pp. 745–52.

14
Conclusion: Anglo-American Politics in the Age of Austerity

Terrence Casey

Critical junctures in the political and economic development of nations are not always self-evident to those living through them. In late 2008, however, it was obvious that momentous events were upon us. The financial system came crashing down and the world teetered on the brink of depression. The collapse of the grand banking houses of Wall Street seemed to bury in their rubble the free market model that had governed the US and UK for the previous 30 years. This was a crisis of Anglo-Saxon capitalism (Gamble, 2009a, p. 7). The logical expectation was that the political economies of both states would branch off onto a different path, even if the new route was not obvious. And yet, as chronicled in this volume, so much of what has occurred since then belies this prediction. In terms of public policy, economic governance, and political trends, there has been far more consistency than change. Lack of regulation in the financial sector was blamed by many for causing the crisis, yet changes in financial regulation have been relatively unobtrusive. Politics has been shaken up with the rise of the Tea Party movement in the US and the advent of a Conservative-Liberal Democrat Coalition government in the UK, yet this highlights that the trends have broken more toward the right, even if not definitively so. The flip side is that left-wing parties, with a brilliant opportunity to make a case for the progressive agenda, have remained on the back foot, unable to articulate an alternative approach. This is not to say that our perceptions of the economic world are unchanged. Perhaps only the most dedicated (classical) liberal still retains an undiluted faith in the ability of financial markets to self-correct. Even so, there has not been a wholesale popular rejection of the neoliberal economic framework. So where are we now? What follows is a tentative attempt to map the contours of British and American society, economy, and politics in the aftermath of the crash.

Living in an austere age

The first legacy of the crash is the diminished economic prospects of millions of citizens, producing social impacts that are both wide and deep. US gross domestic product (GDP) has returned to pre-crash levels, but Britain's will not do so until at least 2013, and that is assuming that estimates of moderately revived growth are accurate.[1] The same is true in terms of average income. British per capita GDP dropped by 5 percent from 2008 to 2009 and only regained about half of that by 2010. The US saw a 3 percent decline, but has returned to 2008 levels.[2] Core inflation remains fairly low in the US; Britain is experiencing greater inflationary pressures. As of mid 2011 the recovery, such as it is, has been rather anemic in both economies.

Millions lost their jobs during the recession and many have yet to find new work. Headline unemployment rates, however, underestimate the suffering. According to the US Bureau of Labor Statistics (BLS), the basic rate of unemployment was 9.4 percent in the first quarter of 2011. An alternative measure[3] that includes marginally and underemployed workers puts the figure at 16.5 percent. The UK has fared slightly better, as unemployment peaked at just over 8 percent, below the 11 percent reached in the 1990–92 recession. Both the US and UK have also seen a fall in the overall employment rate. Just over 68 percent of Britons are in the labor force, down from 73 percent at the peak of the cycle (Campos et al., 2011, p. 7). The equivalent figures for the US dropped from 67 percent in 2001 to 64 percent in 2011.[4] The US has also experienced a sharp increase in the percentage of long-term unemployed (defined as greater than 27 weeks by the BLS), a trend most evident among young workers. Structural unemployment has long been a concern for the British economy, although its affects have generally been regionally concentrated. Underlying labor markets faults have been exposed by the crash. Even with recovery, US labor markets are increasingly polarized, with job opportunities for higher and lower skilled occupations, but declining opportunities in the middle, particularly for blue collar production workers (Autor, 2010). Those who lost jobs in the recession may see a permanent decline in their income, even after they find work again. Mervyn King, Governor of the Bank of England, went so far as to suggest that living standards may never recover from the crisis (*Independent* (Online), 2 March 2011).

The crisis began with the collapse of the US housing market, so US homeowners felt the pain even if still employed. House prices peaked at 200 percent of their 2000 value in late 2007 then collapsed, losing more than a quarter of that value through 2009. The market has stabilized since at similar levels to 2003.[5] With plummeting house values and rising interest rates, many who had taken out high adjustable-rate subprime mortgages saw their monthly payment skyrocket, sending them into default. While painful for those involved,[6] even at the height of the crisis only a very small percentage of houses went into foreclosure in the US. Even fewer did so in the UK and far fewer than during the housing bust of the early 1990s (Campos et al., p. 45).[7] The surge of foreclosed homes nevertheless produced a glut of housing stock, keeping prices depressed. Even those still paying their mortgages saw the value of their major economic asset decline or flatline. Houses were no longer the 'piggy bank' from which people could draw via home equity loans to finance their expenses. Nor was this the only drain on wealth, as stock prices and retirement plans also shrank. From 2007 to 2009, the majority of American families (63 percent) experienced losses in wealth with a median percentage change of –18 percent (Bricker et al., 2011, p. 8). For the wider middle class, the crash represented a serious deterioration in their wealth. The macro-economic impact has been decreased net consumption and increased savings, at least in the US, creating a continued drag on growth.

All of this comes on top of longer-term concerns about rising income inequality and declining social mobility. The oft-cited work of Thomas Piketty and Emmanuel Saez (2004) argues that real median wages have stagnated in the US since the late 1970s, while the share of income garnered by those at the upper end of the scale has increased precipitously. Greater inequality can be ameliorated by social mobility, but some evidence suggests that this has declined in the US in recent decades (Bradbury and Katz, 2009). Britain only ranks just ahead of America on this front (*The Economist* (Online), 7 April 2011). For progressive critics this is the inevitable result of a breakdown of the social bargain established in the post-war era. Whereas government policy used to redistribute the fruits of growth, now it all goes to those lucky few at the top (Reich, 2010; Hacker and Pierson, 2010). Whether inequality has truly risen over the last three decades is contested (see especially Reynolds, 2007) and turns on questions of data selection and interpretation that cannot be adjudicated here. It does not appear that the recession has worsened the situation in the UK, at least (ONS, 2010). Nor is there a direct correspondence between standards of living and income distribution; median US household GDP increased 18 percent from 1980 to 2008, after all (US Census Bureau, www.census.gov).

Whatever the proper empirics on income, there is a sense of economic insecurity that has crept particularly into the American economic consciousness, developing from the 'financialization' of economic life. Individuals used to have some distance between themselves and global finance. With the liberalization of financial markets and the democratization of credit, financial activity penetrated into an ever widening range of economic and social activities. Particularly in the United States, the shift from defined benefit to defined contribution pension schemes, which now constitute around 70 percent of all American pensions (*The Economist*, 9 April 2011), serves to expand the pool of funds to institutional investors and connect personal financial security directly to market movements. Jacob Hacker describes this as 'the great risk shift', wherein individuals are increasingly burdened with the risks inherent in transforming from a system of social insurance to one of personal financial responsibility (Hacker, 2006). Britain, with its more generous welfare state and National Health Service, has also experienced this trend, but to a lesser extent.

Has the crisis produced a general desire to change this, to reject the 'risk shift' and to reinvigorate state-sponsored social protections? The British and American electorates as a whole are certainly hesitant to countenance significant cuts in core welfare programs, be it Medicare, Social Security, or the National Health Service. At the same time there is no groundswell for returning to the social bargain of the past. For a start, many of the trends that created this situation long predate the neoliberal era and are so deeply embedded in both societies that they would be difficult to dislodge. Defined contribution pensions, for example, means that millions of average Americans, not just the denizens of Wall Street, have an interest in keeping financial markets flexible so as to maximize returns. Americans have not rejected the idea of financial intermediaries playing a significant role in their lives. What they are opposed to is poorly managed financial intermediation, particularly if it ends in a government bailout. Americans seem also to have reverted to their default suspicions of activist government, at least now that the worst of the crisis has passed. The British for their part have grown more economically conservative than they were a generation ago and seem to have accepted (in broad terms) that state spending must be reduced in order to revive growth. The acceptance of the utility and efficacy of the free market among the general public was undoubtedly shaken by the financial crisis, yet the evidence to date suggests that it is still intact.

Finally, there is the question of homeownership, the main conduit between most individuals and the financial system. The crisis began because too many people bought too many houses that they could not afford with rather slipshod mortgages. Much of the reason this situation developed is that politicians of all stripes see widespread homeownership as a desirable goal of public policy. It is part of what we are as nations, an indicator of achieving the American Dream, central to the conception of the United States and Britain as democratic capitalist countries. Plus, even though house price inflation precipitated the crisis, politicians have an incentive to see house prices rise again in order to kickstart the economy (Hay, 2009). Governments are thus faced with a paradox: they need stable housing markets, yet economic growth requires rising house prices, which can lead to destabilizing bubbles. This helps to explain, for example, the hesitance of the Obama administration to commit to a plan for winding down Fannie Mae and Freddie Mac. It remains to be seen how well London and Washington manage this paradox in the next decade.

Where does this all leave American and British society? Obviously much depends on the future course of the economy, and nothing would solve these problems quicker than a good run of above average GDP growth. Given the impasse over the US federal budget and the lingering sovereign debt crisis in the euro zone, a second serious downturn is possible, although policy-makers are more attuned to the dangers now. With the weight of public and private debt, the more probable outcome is an extended period of sluggish growth. To foretell what this might mean for our societies, one need only look to Japan, where a 'Lost Decade' (initiated by the bursting of a property bubble, no less) metastasized into 'Lost Decades', with no end in sight. The Japanese post-war 'economic miracle' was built upon legions of dedicated 'salarymen' working relentlessly for major corporations in exchange for lifetime employment. Years of economic stagnation have corroded this system, with many Japanese companies downsizing their permanent workforce and replacing them with temporary or part-time workers. Younger workers bear the brunt of these changes. After years of diligent work in school and university, they face a world of bleak employment prospects. In 2010, one in five Japanese university graduates failed to find full-time employment (CBC News (Online), 8 October 2010). Without permanent employment, possibilities for marriage and family dwindle as well. Japan is now experiencing its second 'Lost Generation' whose economic and social prospects are worse than their parents. The parallels with Japanese experience are certainly imperfect. They face the challenge of an aging and shrinking population, as well as the innate conservatism of many Japanese institutions. That 'lost' has become such a ubiquitous adjective in describing the Japan, however, is a worrying portent of what could happen to our societies should long-term stagnation set in.

The debt challenge

The post-crash economies in both states are faced with two great challenges; the first being the debt crisis, which is actually the concurrent problems of public and private (mainly consumer) debt. The trick is to resolve the public debt problem without exacerbating private debt. Politics in both nations are now intensely focused on deficit reduction, with the coalition focusing on substantially cutting the deficit within the terms of this parliament with the hope that this will increase market confidence, spending, and investment. Success, if it happens, is still some years off ,while the pain of budget cuts is hitting hard and fast. The Lib Dems are fully on board for now,[8] but the details may yet strain the coalition. In the US, under current budgetary guidelines the public debt will be reaching 100 percent of GDP by the end of the decade. While both major parties express a desire to reduce the deficit, an ideological gulf remains, with Democrats insisting on raising taxes (although only on 'the rich') and Republicans demanding greater spending cuts (while assuring voters that entitlement programs will be protected). In summer 2011 the Republicans drew a line in the sand, demanding that raising the debt ceiling must be connected to serious deficit reduction. At the time of this writing, negotiations are ongoing.

The details of competing debt reduction plans need not concern us here. The key point is that fiscal necessity is pushing both Washington and London to look much more seriously at reducing the size of the state (even if not stated so bluntly) than at any point since the 1980s. What is immediately striking is that the debate is not whether government spending needs to be reduced, it is about the relative distribution between spending cuts versus tax increases. Budget-cutters so far seem to have the edge. In Britain, where the opposition Labour Party can do little more than verbally oppose these cuts, Cameron's government has staked its re-election prospects on the success of this strategy. With divided government in Washington, the situation is more muddled, although the ratios of difference have narrowed and moved more toward the Republican side, provoking disenchantment among liberals with Obama. There is an enormous distance between cuts proposed and cuts made, and the path is strewn with political landmines. Still, the debate is pushing in what is thought of as a more conservative direction. Assuming that trends continue, we may see the ironic result that the global financial crisis, billed by so many as the end of neoliberalism, will serve to realize one of the original yet unfulfilled promises of neoliberalism – to reduce the size of the state.

When it comes to private debt, there is some divergence between the US and UK. The last ten years saw a sharp rise in consumer debt, peaking in 2007 at 183 percent of disposable income in the UK and 138 percent in the US.[9] Both numbers have fallen since, but the UK Office of Budget Responsibility (OBR) projected in early 2011 that household debt would again rise to 173 percent of disposable income by 2015. At the same time the financial obligations ratio (the ratio of debt payments to disposable income) compiled by the US Federal Reserve fell from its peak of 18.8 percent in the second quarter of 2007 to 16.6 percent at the end of 2010, similar to where it was in the early 1990s. The Fed shows that while non-revolving consumer credit, especially student loans, demand is rising; demand for revolving credit, such as credit cards, is falling (Bloomberg (Online), 7 April 2011). UK consumer debt, having dropped off after the crisis, is heading back up while the downward trend in the US has not yet bottomed out. Nevertheless, growth requires consumption and excessive debt burdens get in the way. Reducing the levels of debt (public and private) in the economic system is a prerequisite for renewed growth. The open question is, if household debt continues to rise, will consumption be stifled as consumers focus their money on debt servicing rather than new consumption?

A new growth model?

The second great challenge, intimately related to the first, is how to revive growth. From the early 1980s, the neoliberal economic model reigned supreme, emerging from its Anglo-American heartlands to colonize much of the globe. The financial crisis produced obituaries that were swift and unequivocal: 'the Anglo-liberal growth model is irretrievably and irreversibly compromised' (Hay, 2010a, pp. 25–6.); 'neoliberalism has self-destructed' (Mykhnenko and Birch, 2010, p. 255); 'The current crisis, and the responses to it, seem to have delivered a death blow to neo-liberalism' (Fine, 2009, p. 1). The death of the king, of course, usually signals the coronation of a new monarch. As noted in Chapters 3 and 7 above, however, alternative modes of economic governance are noteworthy in their absence. It should also be remembered that, 'After the trauma of Black Wednesday and the exit of the pound from the exchange rate mechanism (ERM) in 1992, the British economy grew steadily and uninterruptedly for the next 16 years, the longest sustained period of growth in modern history' (Gamble, 2009b, p. 450). The US record was similar, albeit with a brief downturn in the early 2000. The free market may have crashed spectacularly in 2008, but it had delivered the goods for many years prior, complicating arguments for replacing it. Neoliberalism's detractors dismiss the boom, though. In effect, the entire neoliberal era is treated as a bubble, with growth exaggerated by the inflated values of artificially created financial assets rather than real economic gains. With flat wages, consumption was maintained through rising personal indebtedness, while the rentier class collected the bulk of the gains for themselves. For critics, neoliberalism was nothing more than a gilded house of cards.

Comparative perspective is useful in assessing this claim. Particularly for the British economy, the Keynesian era was also one of absolute gain but relative decline. With the switch to neoliberalism, both economies saw improved relative performance on output and employment. British per capita GDP over the last 50 years is marked by a distinct U-curve compared to Germany and France: declining throughout the Keynesian years and reviving after 1980.[10] Even on productivity, Britain's traditional weakness, although it still lags behind, the gap narrowed in the 1990s and 2000s.[11] Starting from a dominant position, America saw other major industrialized powers, particularly Germany and Japan, catching up on income and productivity for the first three decades after the Second World War. Those trends stabilized in the 1980s, reversing course (albeit well below the post-war supremacy) from the 1990s onward. As the most recent recession was a global affair, the downturn in the Anglo-Saxon economies were matched by recessions elsewhere, even if not of always equal magnitude. It is thus not yet clear if the current downturn is indicative of a change in trends in relative performance.

The crash of 2008 certainly wiped out some of the economic gains made to that point, but it did not negate all that came before it. To this end one must distinguish between the drivers of growth in different periods. Policies in the 1980s are best characterized as 'shock therapy' (Fine, 2009); breaking the market impediments of the Keynesian era. Both the US and UK saw improved growth rates, followed by economic overheating and a recession in the late 1980s and early 1990s. Growth in the 1990s rested on a salubrious combination of expanding developing markets, the costs advantages of increasingly globalized production, and the productivity boost delivered by a new wave of information technology. The last decade, however, saw diminishing returns to both globalization and technology. Combined with a recession, the disruption of 9/11, and the challenges of two wars, there was great potential for an extended slowdown. In this environment policy-makers chose the easy option of boosting output via loose credit and fiscal stimulus, even if not explicitly recognized at the time. Americans saw taxes cut, domestic spending increased, and a house price boom due to low interest rates. The UK followed suit, albeit without the tax cuts and with proportionally much higher spending increases. Low unemployment in the latter New Labour years was brought about by a vast increase in public sector jobs (Froud et al., 2011). Overall, growth in the decade was fueled by debt, both public and private. To simplify the point, the 1980s were a period of neoliberal transition, the 1990s an era of 'good growth', and the 2000s a decade where policy-makers relied on a quick, easy, but ultimately unsustainable growth formula. From this perspective, rather than seeing the crash as the inevitable outcome of the model, the crisis resulted from financial excesses exacerbated by ill-considered public policy. It was a crisis within neoliberalism rather than a crisis of neoliberalism.

This is hardly an uncontested argument. Colin Crouch (2009) describes neoliberalism as a system of 'privatized Keynesianism'. Capitalism suffers from a paradox: profitability requires labor flexibility, rendering workers less secure and confident consumers, and undermining profitability. The post-war Keynesian model smoothed the business cycle and protected vulnerable workers through the extension of the welfare state. State spending in democratic systems ratcheted ever upward, however, creating inflationary pressures and undermining growth. In Crouch's depiction, Thatcher and Reagan did not really alter the economic model; they merely shifted the locus of growth financing.

> two things came together to rescue the neo-liberal mode from the instability that otherwise would have been its fate: the growth of credit markets for poor and middle income people, and the derivatives and futures markets among the very wealthy. This combination produced a model of privatized Keynesianism … Instead of governments taking on debt to stimulate the economy, individuals did so. (Crouch, 2009, p. 390)

Colin Hay echoes this idea in his portrayal of an 'Anglo-liberal growth model', adding that private debt-driven consumption required governments to keep property values rising (Hay, 2009, 2010). Rising private debt is thus transformed from an unfortunate outcome of misguided policies into a central tenet of the neoliberal model. If the Achilles' heel of Keynesianism was a politically-motivated 'spending ratchet', the weakness of neoliberalism is a market-motivated 'debt ratchet'.

Neoliberalism's sins thus transmute from omission to commission, with governments intentionally encouraging the growth of private debt to stimulate growth. The problem for this argument, for one, is that it extrapolates the trends of 2000s to the entire neoliberal era. The key causes of the crisis – the housing bubble, fed by subprime mortgages and spread through securitization – were not occurring (or only just beginning) in the 1980s and 1990s. Nor does 'privatized Keynesianism' take seriously that financial liberalization could have developed along any alternate and more economically stable path. Take a simple counterfactual: What if the US Federal Reserve had raised interest rates much earlier? Permissive monetary policy was a prerequisite for the crisis. More effective macro-economic management could have averted, or at least ameliorated, the inflation of asset prices *ceteris paribus*. The Crouch and Hay argument is more exact as a description of events than as a theoretical construct. In fairness, though, this only handles part of their critique. Yes, sound macro-economic management might have avoided instability, but would it have come at the cost of reduced growth? If the contours of financial liberalization remain largely intact, can the Anglo-Saxon economies return to vibrant and sustainable growth?

The question is whether the neoliberal model needs repair or replacement (Gamble, 2010, p. 13). One fix that has received new life, particularly from politicians on the right who are loath to critique the free market, is the need to rebalance the economy. Economic 'imbalance' has numerous meanings, relating to trade balances, fiscal deficits, excessive public spending, regional disparities, or sectoral issues, depending on the source (Froud et al., 2011, pp. 9–10). The latter is the most frequently cited and relevant here. We are said to have become overly reliant on the profits of financial intermediation to drive growth while manufacturing erodes – too much 'trading paper' and not enough 'making things'. Germany, with its stable manufacturing and export base, is held as the exemplar of advanced country economic management in a globalized world. Politically this is an appealing moderate, reformist approach, yet it is likely a non-starter. Fundamentally this requires policies to divert investment out of the financial sector and into manufacturing. Governments on both sides of the Atlantic have attempted to revive declining manufacturing areas for decades with little success. Deindustrialization stems more from larger technological developments and shifts in the global political economy. Swimming against these tides is no more likely to work now than in the past. Nor will diverting funds from the financial sector – where both

Wall Street and the City have an international comparative advantage – guarantee a concomitant increase in manufacturing activity. More to the point, for good or ill, the financial sector contributes substantially to economies of both states, especially in the UK. Despite the turmoil of recent years, it is once again a growing sector. It would be difficult to reduce the role of finance without harming the macro-economy in the short term. In a period when politicians' fates hang on a precarious recovery, this seems a terrific gamble.

Another path is to craft specific regulations that will prevent financial market excesses. Part I explored causes and responses to the crisis, which included a combination of new institutions and regulations, such as the new US Consumer Finance Protection Bureau, and establishing means of 'macro-prudential' surveillance. Will these be enough to prevent a future meltdown? Analysis of that question is a book unto itself and as these changes are still being finalized and implemented, their full impact has yet to be revealed. The larger question is whether they were properly focused and get to the heart of the potential for economic revival with a neoliberal political economy. The fundamental rationale for liberalizing financial markets is to more effectively funnel capital into productive investment, increasing economic output. The major argument against unregulated financial markets is that it creates incentives for highly leveraged, speculative activity that enhances financial firms' profits without adding to the 'real economy'. Will the financial sector, undisciplined by a reformed regulatory framework, avoid again being drawn into another speculative bubble and guide capital into productive investment? Or are the incentives faced by the 'electronic herd' so great that they cannot help but get drawn in by the huge payoffs promised by increasing leverage and speculation? Can relatively unregulated financial markets in this sense be 'socially efficient' (or are the new regulations enough to make them so)? Can these systems both return to the long-term trend rate of growth while avoiding financial destabilization? These are the most important questions in considering the future of the Anglo-American political economies. They are also, unfortunately, incredibly difficult to answer. The answers rely, after all, on developing non-subjective distinctions between 'speculative investment' and 'productive investment', for example. Is Facebook a productive investment? Are profits made from trading derivatives socially useless speculation if they have the result of increasing the value of many individuals' retirement accounts?

Finance plays a basic role in modern economies. To use an anatomical analogy, it is the 'cardiovascular system' pumping needed capital to the rest of the body economic. After years of unhealthy living (leveraged speculation), it suffered a massive coronary in 2008. The question is whether the patient has learned the lesson. Will those markets, working within the constraints of post-crash regulations, serve as effective intermediaries for guiding productive investment, or will they plunge into another bout of speculative excess? At the moment the answer to this question is disquietingly indeterminate.

For those who see venal financiers as the chief culprits responsible for our current woes, this is an unsatisfactory answer. Previous crises ushered in periods of ideological polarization and contestation, producing new political-economic orders. But ideological polarization requires that there be ideological poles. The most stunning intellectual development since 2008 is that those looking for alternative economic models to counter the free market model have been met with deafening silence. Certainly there has been a renewed interest in Keynesianism, yet the nostalgia for Keynes comes more as a form of triage, a way to prevent further decline, than a foundation for future prosperity. The crisis also presents an opening for advocates of green development, which has a certain intellectual appeal, but not much of an electoral appeal in the US or the UK.[12] The promise of environmental sustainability without any trade-off in material standards of living remains elusive. Previous crises of capitalism all had counter-movements waiting in the wings for some years, poised with argument and organization. For the intellectual hegemony of neoliberalism to be dislodged, a counter-hegemonic framework must first be developed that speaks directly to our current problems, appeals to the electorate, and offers some reasonable prospect of reviving economic performance. None has yet to emerge, at least none that has resonance outside of university faculty lounges. We are thus most likely to see the development of a new phase of neoliberalism, not its elimination (Gamble, 2009b, p. 461). The open question is whether this neo-neoliberalism will, after some years of retrenchment, return Britain and America to prosperity.

The new politics of the old politics

The two previous major economic crises of the last 100 years – the Great Depression and the stagflation of the 1970s – represented fundamental turning points in the political development of both nations. One would have expected a seismic event on the scale of the 2008 crash to shift the political ground more than a bit. There have certainly been unique political turns, some even quite surprising. Nevertheless, based on events so far, there has not been the sort of shift in political order in either nation as experienced in the past.

Events since 2008 have certainly been shaped by the crash. The crisis secured Barack Obama's landslide election and created the political conditions for him to pursue an aggressive legislative agenda in the first half of his term. Despite three consecutive victories under Tony Blair, New Labour never quite lived up to people's expectations. The lackluster leadership of Gordon Brown could not stand up to the political strains of a financial collapse that happened under his watch. Disappointment with Labour produced a sizeable swing to the Conservatives, but even David Cameron's 'detoxified' Tory brand was insufficient to secure an overall majority, leading to a Coalition government. In the United States the backlash against an explosion of government spending and deficits produced the Tea Party movement, its political impact transmitted through the Republican Party, resulting in major gains in the 2010 midterm elections. The political legacy of the crash to date is, in sum, that the United States initially saw a shift to the left and support for more activist policies. However, the fruits of these efforts (the stimulus package, 'Obamacare') produced a conservative countermovement, returning the nation to divided government. Polls (summer 2011) indicate that American voters are not enamored with either Democrats or Republicans. With such volatile swings of the political pendulum, it is hard to predict how this will play out in the 2012 election cycle. In the UK voters rejected an ostensively left-wing government (although one which accepted the free market model), but have yet to completely embrace a more conservative regime. The Cameron government's goal of reducing the deficit (which voters see as necessary) mainly by cutting spending (the specifics of which they often oppose) while reviving the economy (which remains sluggish) leaves them with precarious political prospects.

Anglo-American politics have not been radically reordered in the aftermath of the crash, yet it is not accurate to suggest that politics has settled back into pre-crisis modes. Electorates are restive, volatile. In itself this is nothing new; trends toward party dealignment and electoral volatility have continued steadily since the 1960s. A new sense of angst among voters opens the possibility for deeper transformation. Some suggest that the failure to reform the political and economic system raises the specter of a turn to more extremist political forces, particularly xenophobic, isolationist, anti-statist movements – the Tea Party on steroids, as it were (Reich, 2011, pp. 79–81; Gamble, 2010, p. 13). For all of the bluster of the Tea Party, though, its main issues (opposition to higher taxes and 'big government') are positions comfortably nestled in the Republican camp. The movement shows every indication of following the path of past third-party movements: having its ideas and supporters absorbed into a major political party. The likely vehicles for right-wing radicalism in Britain – the United Kingdom Independence party (UKIP) or the British National Party (BNP) – remain small, marginalized movements that have made no meaningful electoral gains. And while isolationism or protectionism could manifest within the mainstream parties, there simply have not been major figures advocating such an approach to date. One cannot rule out the possibility of so radical a move to the right, but the evidence that such is occurring in Britain and America is relatively minimal.

Some might suggest that the radical economic right dominated the previous era, so one would expect a strong counter from the left. The great unsolved mystery of post-crash politics is: Where is the left? After decades of retreat the state came roaring back to clean up the aftermath of the crash. The moment seemed ripe for a left-wing revival, and the landslide election of Obama seemed to indicate just that. Once the initial luster of the Obama administration wore off, the American public seemed to reply to his call of 'Yes, We Can!' with 'Yes, But We'd Prefer You Didn't!' Having passed his priority health care legislation, and faced with a rising conservative tide, Obama has since retreated to the political center, trying to position himself above the partisan fray. Left-wing Democrats may be disenchanted, but they have nowhere else to go. Under Ed Miliband's leadership the Labour Party has been able to score only a few tactical victories against the Coalition government and has edged ahead in the polls (July 2011). A strategic vision that would encourage voters to return to the fold remains elusive, however.

After the sharp ideological conflicts of the Thatcher-Reagan years, the 1990s and 2000s were periods of relative political tranquility. First with Bill Clinton, then with Tony Blair, the major left-wing parties tied their flag to the mast of the Third Way, which accepted deregulated markets as a means of producing the prosperity needed to fund the welfare state. The 'post-war consensus' was effectively replaced with a 'neoliberal consensus'. The major left-wing parties in the UK and US have yet to find their voice in the aftermath of the crisis mainly because to do so would be to repudiate their own past. Colin Hay reasonably argues that in historic terms we are still in early days; the present political conjuncture may in retrospect look more like 1974 than 1979 (Hay, 2011, p. 3). Profound political changes may yet arise which will only acquire meaning after the fact. Again, this depends on how long the recession drags on. Anglo-American politics may yet spin off in unforeseen directions.

International transformations

Most of this volume examines the crash in terms of domestic politics. It would be remiss, however, to not briefly discuss the international repercussions. Part of the underlying conditions – the deep systemic causes – for the crisis were the imbalances accumulating in the global economy in the years prior, with some countries (especially the US and UK) running huge current account deficits matched by the growing surpluses of others, both advanced (such as Germany and Japan) and developing economies (especially China, but also India, Brazil, and so on), as well as oil-producing states. What was missing was a means of recycling these surpluses without destabilizing the financial system (Gamble, 2009a, p. 119); China's 'savings glut' begat America's 'credit boom'.[13] The trillions of dollars flooding into US markets kept interest rates low. Increased demand for assets from international purchasers also produced a proliferation of supply; that is, the US financial sector produced more exotic assets to sell, which proved to be more toxic in the long run (Cabalerro and Krishnamurthy, 2009). The assumption was that the innovation, efficiency, and flexibility of financial markets would be able to absorb these huge cashflows without engendering systemic dangers. That, of course, proved a false hope. 'In effect, the global imbalances posed stress tests for weaknesses in the United States, British, and other advanced-country financial and political systems – tests those countries did not pass' (Obstfeld and Rogoff, 2009, p. 4).

International imbalances have been underemphasized in many explanations of the crash (including in this volume) because they did not develop as pessimists predicted, with a disorderly unwinding of international accounts: transnational credit drying up, the dollar depreciating rapidly, rising inflation, and a sharp increase in interest rates – a classic balance of payments crisis (Blanchard and Milesi-Ferretti, p. 12). Moreover, the crash harmed the surplus states as well, as export markets dried up with the onset of recession. Still, global imbalances helped to create the conditions in which a crisis could develop. Some natural adjustment has occurred since as decreased US consumer spending served to halve the current account deficit from its nadir in 2006. Even though the financial contagion spread from the US, enormous amounts of capital continue to be funneled back into the US through Treasury bond purchases. Both the then prime minister, Gordon Brown, and President Obama pushed for coordinated stimulus through the G20 and were met with resistance from others, especially Germany's Angela Merkel.[14] The selection of Christine Lagarde to replace the disgraced Dominique

Strauss-Kahn as head of the IMF does not indicate an institution ready to reconstitute its organization or mission to deal with a changed global environment. In short, the international conditions that inflated the bubble have not abated, attempts to coordinate orderly readjustment through the G20 have come to naught, and the basic architecture of the Bretton Woods institutions remains unaltered.

All of this raises a bigger question: Does the global financial crisis represent the end – or perhaps the beginning of the end – of western (and specifically American) global economic and political dominance? Scholars of international politics have long recognized that the late twentieth century saw a shift in power toward East Asia. If the past century was the 'American century', this 'rise of the rest' may harken a 'post-American world' (Zakaria, 2009). The United States entered the twenty-first century as a 'unipolar' power, but failed to maintain that status, responding to 9/11 with two wars that, on best outcome, will fall uncomfortably between victory and defeat, and a financial crisis that brought the economy to its knees. The facts remain that the US economy is four times as large as Japan or China, the dollar is the preferred medium of international exchange and investment, and America remains a technological leader. That being said, 'If the Iraq War and George W. Bush's foreign policy had the effect of delegitimizing America's military-political power in the eyes of the world, the financial crisis has had the effect of delegitimizing America's economic power' (Zakaria, 2009, p. xxi).

Power shifts are to be expected in global politics. Economic power shifted decisively and irretrievably from Britain to the United States after the First World War. Then again, the reality and practice of this did not manifest with policy-makers until after the Second World War. US foreign and economic policy in the 1920s and 1930s was narrowly focused, driven by nationalistic concerns, unwilling to make serious sacrifices for the collective good. The consequences were devastating. China today is in a somewhat analogous position. They have not yet supplanted the United States and their 'inevitable' rise to dominance suffers from a hint of hyperbole.[15] For all of the dynamism of the Chinese economy, it has its own political and economic problems. Rapid development engenders myriad social and environmental disruptions. Corruption is a persistent problem in a Chinese Communist Party whose legitimacy is based on continuous rapid growth. The manufacturing base has yet to fully scale the technological ladder, developing as an assembly platform for products designed elsewhere more than a true creator of products. And despite its spectacular growth, China remains a poor country. Even with that, its power and influence will certainly increase over the next few decades.

The big question for the early twenty-first century is whether China will use its newfound position to help stabilize the international system, or pursue more narrowly nationalistic policies.

China's economic rise was coincident with the era of globalization in the latter quarter of the twentieth century. Globalization and its relationship to the global financial crisis is a complex phenomenon and a thorough discussion is well beyond the scope of this chapter. Globalization has both cheerleaders and detractors, backed by arguments both legitimate and strained. Since globalization is synonymous with liberalized trade and capital flows, it has always had a strong Anglo flavor. Can globalization continue? Andrew Gamble contends that the greatest danger stemming from the crisis is the potential return to protectionism (Gamble, 2009a). Niall Ferguson sees the symbiotic relationship between these two economies – 'Chimerica' as he calls it – as the key to determining the future direction of the global economy. If they fall out, globalization is done for (Ferguson, 2009). Neither side has moved in that direction, but the dangers are evident. America needs to save more and consume less – and stop borrowing money from China to do so. China needs to rely less on exports and promote domestic consumption, reducing the surpluses it has been recycling overseas. Whether leaders in either state have the wisdom or the will to push these systemic needs against domestic pressures is uncertain. Even if so, managing such a transition in an orderly manner is difficult. As the US economy continues to stagnate, the Federal Reserve may feel bound to pursue further quantitative easing. Doing so will exert downward pressure on the dollar. How long will Chinese officials be willing to hold on to tens of trillions of dollars in Treasury bonds if the value of those assets is steadily declining?

Without a doubt, closer integration into global markets has created positive gains, especially for countries like China, while wreaking havoc in others, such as Thailand in 1997 and Argentina in 2001. But for all that, the most recent era of globalization saw hundreds of millions of people lifted out of poverty. To see that process reversed would be perhaps the most unfortunate legacy of the crash.

Final thoughts

At the end of the day, we are left with far more questions than we have confidence of answers. This in itself should not be too surprising. After all, we are only three years out from the crash. Think of someone scanning the horizon in 1932, three years after 'Black Thursday' in 1929, trying to chart the course of events 20 years hence – the incredible depths of the Great Depression, the political extremes that this wrought, the cataclysmic world war, and yet ultimately the stunning revival of the western economies. One would have to have been quite the Nostradamus indeed to have foreseen all of that. The contributors to this volume can thus legitimately plead humility and eschew any claim to be able to project the specific contours of the political economy of the UK and the US in 2021 or even 2031.

As discussed in this volume, the sources of this crisis were many and complex. At root, however, the problem was that too many people – and too many people who should have known better – failed to distinguish between *risk*, which is probable and measurable, and *uncertainty*, random events which strain the strictures of *homo economicus* (Ferguson, 2008, p. 343). Thus when extreme uncertainty entered the system in the fall of 2008, they were ill prepared to deal with it. As Carmen Reinhardt and Kenneth Rogoff (2009) argue in their study of financial crises, the prerequisite for calamity is a sense that 'it cannot happen here'. Financial leaders and policy-makers had convinced themselves that the sophistication and complexity of financial markets following a diversity of strategies rendered a systemic collapse, in all probability, a very low risk. To the shock and horror of all concerned, it was quickly discovered that the system was not at all diversified; financial actors were, in fact, quite synchronized in their behavior (Rajan, 2005, p. 318). And once the major players started to fall, capped by the collapse of Lehman Brothers, everyone else was dragged down with them. At the very least, then, one would hope that the primary legacy of the crash is to demolish the sense that 'it cannot happen here' and that politicians, financiers, and even individual consumers will adjust their behavior accordingly. Then perhaps we can hope it will not happen again.

Notes

1. Data from the International Monetary Fund (IMF), World Economic Outlook Database, April 2011.
2. Data from the IMF, World Economic Outlook Database, April 2011.
3. Officially known as U-6, this includes total unemployed, plus all marginally attached workers, plus total employed part time for economic reasons, as a percent of the civilian labor force plus all marginally attached workers.
4. Data from the US Bureau of Labor Statistics.
5. Based on the 20-city Composite Case-Schiller Housing Index released in April 2011.
6. Ironically, many with subprime mortgages escaped the worst. They had put little money into their homes, so when the value plummeted, they just walked away.

7. High inflation and the Exchange Rate Mechanism prevented interest rates from being lowered in the early 1990s, increasing negative equity and repossessions.
8. After a Q&A session with David Cameron in Nottingham in March 2011, Liberal Democrat leader Nick Clegg was caught on a still live microphone telling the PM, 'If we keep doing this we won't have anything to bloody disagree on in the bloody TV debates.'
9. About three-quarters of this debt is in mortgages. Data from the Organization for Economic Cooperation and Development (OECD).
10. In 1960, UK per capita GDP stood at 108 percent of West German income and 129 percent of France. By 1980 UK per capita GDP had fallen to 87 percent compared to Germany and 91 percent compared to France. The respective figures were 103 percent and 111 percent in 2007. Data from the US Bureau of Labor Statistics.
11. In 1990, the UK's GDP per hour worked was 77 percent of France's, 81 percent of Germany's, and 87 percent of the EU-15 average. In 2010 those figures were 93 percent, 95 percent, and 100 percent, respectively. Data from the Total Economy Database, The Commerce Board/Groningen Growth and Development Centre (www.ggdc.net).
12. The Green Party scored the victory of leader Caroline Lucas in the Brighton Pavilion constituency in the last election. But it was the only seat they won. Nationally they only secured one percent of the vote in the 2010 general election, far fewer than UKIP (3.1 percent) or the BNP (1.9 percent).
13. The US has become the 'consumer of last resort' while China became the new 'workshop of the world'. Chinese surpluses were plowed back into American investments, both Treasury bonds (many purchased by the central bank) and asset backed securities. For China this kept its currency artificially low, enhancing exports, and 'self-insured' against future financial crises, such as that which swept East Asia in 1997.
14. Merkel is hamstrung by domestic politics; German taxpayers do not want to bail out their spendthrift Greek cousins.
15. One should temper the predictions of China's rise with the recollection of all of those who confidently predicted that Japan would rule the twenty-first century just a few decades ago.

References

Autor, David (2010) 'The Polarization of Job Opportunities in the US Labor Market: Implications for Employment and Earnings', 30 April, Center for American Progress.

Blanchard, Olivier, and Gian Maria Milesi-Ferretti (2009) 'Global Imbalances: In Midstream?' IMF Staff Position Note, SPN/09/29, 22 December.

Bradbury, Katherine, and Jane Katz (2009) 'Trends in US Family Income Mobility, 1967–2004', Federal Reserve Bank of Boston Working Paper No. 90-7.

Bricker, Jesse, Brian Bucks, Arthur Kennickell, Traci Mach and Kevin Moore (2011) 'Surveying the Aftermath of the Storm: Changes in Family Finances from 2007 to 2009', Federal Reserve Board, Divisions of Research & Statistics and Monetary Affairs, 2011-17 (Washington, DC: Federal Reserve Board).

Caballero, Ricardo, and Arvind Krishnamurthy (2009) 'Global Imbalances and Financial Fragility,' *American Economic Review*, 99(2), 584–8.

Campos, Celia, Alistair Dent, Robert Fry and Alice Reid (2011) 'Impact of the Recession', *Regional Trends*, 43, 2010-11 (London: ONS).

Crouch, Colin (2009) 'Privatized Keynesianism: An Unacknowledged Policy Regime', *British Journal of Politics and International Relations*, 11(3), 382–99.

Fine, Ben (2009) 'Neo-Liberalism in Retrospect? – It's Financialisation, Stupid'. Paper presented at Developmental Politics in the Neo-Liberal Era and Beyond, 22–24 October, Center for Social Sciences, Seoul National University.

Fround, Julie, Sukhdev Johal, John Law, Adam Leaver and Karel Williams (2011) 'Rebalancing the Economy (or Buyer's Remorse)', Centre for Research on Socio-Cultural Change (CRESC) Working Paper No. 87, Manchester University, January.

Gamble, Andrew (2009a) *The Spectre at the Feast: Capitalist Crisis and the Politics of Recession* (Basingstoke: Palgrave Macmillan).

Gamble, Andrew (2009b) 'British Politics and the Financial Crisis', *British Politics*, 4(4), 450–62.

Gamble, Andrew (2010) 'The Political Consequences of the Crash', *Political Studies Review*, 8(1), 3–14.

Hacker, Jacob (2006) *The Great Risk Shift: The Assault on American Jobs, Families, Health Care, and Retirement and How You Can Fight Back* (New York: Oxford University Press).

Hacker, Jacob, and Paul Pierson (2010) *Winner-Take-All Politics: How Washington Made the Rich Richer and Turned its Back on the Middle Class* (New York: Simon and Schuster).

Hay, Colin (2009) 'Good Inflation, Bad Inflation: The Housing Boom, Economic Growth and the Disaggregation of Inflationary Preferences in the UK and Ireland', *British Journal of Politics and International Relations*, 11(3), 461–78.

Hay, Colin (2010) '"Things can only get worse ...": The Political and Economic Significance of 2010', *British Politics*, 5(4), 391–401.

Hay, Colin (2011) 'Pathology Without Crisis? The Strange Demise of the Neoliberal Growth Model', *Government and Opposition*, 46(1), 1–31.

Mykhnenko, Vlad, and Kean Birch (2010) 'Conclusion: The End of an Economic Order?', in Kean Birch and Vlad Mykhnenko (eds), *The Rise and Fall of Neoliberalism: The Collapse of an Economic Order?* (London: Zed Books).

Obstfeld, Maurice, and Kenneth Rogoff (2009), 'Global Imbalances and the Financial Crisis: Products of Common Causes', Federal Reserve Bank of San Francisco Asia Economic Policy Conference, 18–20 October.

Office of National Statistics (2010) 'Press Release: Income Inequality Remains Stable', 10 June.

Rajan, Raghuram (2005) 'Has Financial Development Made the World Riskier?' Paper presented at 'The Greenspan Era: Lessons for the Future', Symposium sponsored by the Federal Reserve Bank of Kansas City, Jackson Hole, Wyoming, 25–27 April.

Reich, Robert (2010) *Aftershock: The Next Economy and America's Future* (New York: Alfred A. Knopf).

Reinhart, Carmen M., and Kenneth S. Rogoff (2009) *This Time is Different: Eight Centuries of Financial Folly* (Princeton: Princeton University Press).

Zakaria, Fareed (2009) *The Post-American World* (New York: W.W. Norton).

Index